Lecture Notes in Economics and Mathematical Systems

Managing Editors: M. Beckmann and W. Krelle

360

Peter Stalder

Regime Transitions, Spillovers and Buffer Stocks

Analysing the Swiss Economy by Means of a Disequilibrium Model

Springer-Verlag
Berlin Heidelberg New York London Paris
Tokyo Hong Kong Barcelona Budapest

Managing Editors
Prof. Dr. M. Beckmann
Brown University
Providence, RI 02912, USA

Prof. Dr. W. Krelle
Institut für Gesellschafts- und Wirtschaftswissenschaften
der Universität Bonn
Adenauerallee 24–42, D-5300 Bonn, FRG

Author
PD Dr. Peter Stalder
Konjunkturforschungsstelle KOF-ETH an der
Eidgenössischen Technischen Hochschule Zürich
Weinbergstr. 35, CH-8092 Zürich, Switzerland

ISBN 3-540-54056-3 Springer-Verlag Berlin Heidelberg New York
ISBN 0-387-54056-3 Springer-Verlag New York Berlin Heidelberg

Printing and binding: Druckhaus Beltz, Hemsbach/Bergstr.
2142/3140-543210 – Printed on acid-free paper

PREFACE

The macro disequilibrium model for Switzerland presented in this study grew out of a research project which was generously financed by Swiss National Science Foundation. I am indebted to Prof. Hans Würgler and Prof. Heidi Schelbert for encouraging and supporting this work in many ways. The present book is the revised version of a paper that was accepted as a "Habilitationsschrift" by the University of Zürich.

Part of the research leading to this book was done during a stay at Princeton University, where I benefited from a stimulating environment, the gratuitous use of facilities and the helpful advise of Richard E. Quandt.

Earlier disequilibrium studies for Switzerland were discussed in various seminars (Princeton, Université de Montréal, C.O.R.E., 1988 Conference on European Unemployment in Chelwood Gate, 2nd Conference on Disequilibrium Econometrics at INSEE, 1989 European Spring Meeting on Macroeconomics in Paris) and published in the 'European Economic Review' and 'Recherches Economiques de Louvain'. Numerous people - including A.S. Blinder, L. Salvas-Bronsard, J.H. Drèze, S.M. Goldfeld, C. Gourieroux, P. Kooiman, J.P. Lambert, G. Laroque, H.S. Rosen, H.R. Sneessens, J. Waelbroeck and anonymous referees of the two journals - provided constructive comments on these earlier papers. Their suggestions - as well as the critical remarks by a referee of Springer 'Lecture Notes' - are partly reflected in the present book.

It will be obvious to the reader that the specific approach adopted in this investigation owes much to the contributions of Jean-Paul Lambert, Peter Kooiman, Christian Gourieroux, Guy Laroque and Henri R. Sneessens in the field of econometric disequilibirium modelling. These authors let me get valuable insights into their research at early stages by providing me with by then unpublished papers.

I would like to thank all these people and institutions for their help. The views expressed in this paper and any remaining errors are of course my own responsibility.

CONTENTS

		page
1.	INTRODUCTION	1
	1.1 Alternative theories of macroeconomic fluctuations	1
	1.2 Assessment of the controversy - Motivation of the present study	8
	1.3 Scope and limitations of the investigation	16
	1.4 Set-up of the paper	23
2.	THE MICRO MODEL	24
	2.1 Spillovers and transactions	26
	2.2 Discussion of the spillover elasticities	27
	2.3 Regimes	29
	Appendix: Comparision with other spillover-formulations	31
3.	DERIVATION OF THE AGGREGATE MODEL	35
	3.1 Aggregation	35
	3.2 Introduction of error terms	45
	3.3 Adopting an econometrically tractable approximation	47
	3.4 Accuracy of the approximation	49
4.	MODIFIED VERSION: BUFFER ROLE OF INVENTORIES AND UNFILLED ORDERS	56
5.	SPECIFICATION OF THE AGGREGATE ECONOMETRIC EQUATIONS	66
	5.1 Labor supply	67
	5.2 Demand for domestic output	68
	5.3 Notional labor demand, notional goods supply and investment	72
	5.3.1 Preliminaries	72
	5.3.2 Malinvaud's investment model	74
	5.3.3 Adopting a vintage-approach	78
	5.3.4 Scrapping of old equipment	84
6.	STRUCTURE OF THE MODEL, METHOD OF ESTIMATION AND DYNAMIC EXTENSIONS	88
	6.1 Allowing for a trend in labor market mismatch	88
	6.2 Summary of the model	88
	6.3 Method of estimation	91
	6.4 Labor hoarding, partial adjustment and error correction dynamics	93

7. ESTIMATION RESULTS 99
7.1 Empirical versions - Models 1 to 4 99
7.2 Model 1: No buffer stocks, 'static' labor hoarding 101
7.3 Model 2: No buffer stocks, dynamic labor hoarding 107
7.4 Model 3: Allowing for buffer stocks 109
7.5 Model 4: Inclusion of the investment equation 117
7.6 Interpreting Model 4 - Testing a priori parameter restrictions 120
7.7 Intertemporal substitution in labor supply - Comparison with other studies 129

8. TESTING PARAMETER STABILITY 133

9. SIMULATIONS 137
9.1 Fit of the model (static simulation) 137
9.2 Development of the Swiss economy: Regimes and spillovers 140
9.3 The Swiss labor market - A miracle? 146
9.4 Dynamic tracking performance 150
9.5 Simulating short-run and long-run effects of autonomous changes, assessing dynamic stability 156
9.5.1 Short-term impact of a demand shock (Keynesian demand stimulation) 158
9.5.2 Reference simulation for examining long-run effects 160
9.5.3 Checking for dynamic stability 161
9.5.4 Long-run effects of permanent and single-period demand shocks 165
9.5.5 Simulation of a permanent wage (and price) reduction 169

10. SUMMARY AND CONCLUSIONS 176

REFERENCES 186

1. INTRODUCTION

Considerable work has been done in recent years on estimating macroeconomic "rationing" or "disequilibrium" models. Important examples are Sneessens (1983), Artus, Laroque and Michel (1984), Kooiman and Kloek (1985), Sneessens and Drèze (1986), Lambert (1984, 1988) and Laroque (1988), among others. These models are inspired by a branch of economic theory which is associated with the names of Clower, Leijonhufvud, Barro/Grossman, Benassy, Drèze and Malinvaud and has been labelled 'New Keynesian Macroeconomics'. The basic message of this approach is that prices (wages, interest rates) adjust too slowly to clear markets permanently so that some agents (those on the "long" side of a market) get rationed and will revise their trade plans, thus causing spillovers across markets. The various econometric problems of formulating, estimating and testing disequilibrium models are discussed in Gourieroux, Laffont and Monfort (1980,1984), Ito (1980), Quandt (1982,1988), Sneessens (1985) and Laroque and Salanie (1989). The purpose of the present investigation is to develop an econometric two-market disequilibrium model for Switzerland, concentrating on the markets for goods and labor. This introduction attempts to put the disequilibrium approach into theoretical perspective, comparing it with the two main competing paradigms, standard Neo-Keynesian and new-classical models (sections 1.1 and 1.2). The specific features and limitations of the present study are outlined in section 1.3.

1.1 Alternative theories of macroeconomic fluctuations

Ever since the publication of Keynes' **General Theory** there has been an ongoing tension between two opposed views of the functioning of market economies. **Walrasian**-type general equilibrium models consider a complete system of microeconomic markets, assuming that demands and supplies on these markets are made mutually consistent through instantaneous price movements. The set of market clearing prices is established by a mythical 'auctioneer' in a so-called 'tâtonnement'-process. Agents do not face any quantity constraints. They can thus freely choose the optimal levels of output, employment, consumption etc. In such a framework, there is obviously no room for phenomena such as involuntary unemployment, underutilized capacities and the like. The main concern of Walrasian models is to explain the allocation of fully employed (scarce) factors and commodities to alternative uses and the determination of the equilibrium vector of relative prices. Macroeconomic models in the Keynesian tradition, on the other hand, attempt to cope with "real world" problems like unemployment, cyclical fluctuations etc. In order to do so, they deviate from the Walrasian framework in some significant ways: Wage adjustments are sluggish so that the labor market may be out of equilibrium for prolonged periods of time. Adjustments on the goods market take place not primarily through movements in prices or interest rates; it is rather the level of income that brings about an equality between savings and investment in the short run. Consumption demand is a function of realized income instead of being determined by optimizing agents, simultaneously with labor supply, on basis of prices, wages and interest rates.

These two views of the functioning of market economies - Walrasian general equilibrium theory and Keynesian macroeconomics - do indeed not seem to have much in common. The corresponding segmentation of economics into two disjoint subdisciplines has since long been considered an unsatisfactory state of affairs, the more so as the proposition that macroeconomic relationships should have microeconomic foundations is generally accepted among economists. Nevertheless, as far as empirical business cycle analysis, policy evaluation and forecasting are concerned, there was a broad agreement about the appropriateness of the Keynesian framework until the late 1960s. The "understandable demand of the academic profession for theoretical rigor" was dominated by the "indisputable reality of gradual price adjustment" [Gordon (1988)]. The **Keynesian orthodoxy**, as reflected in the pragmatic large-scale econometric models of those days, consisted of an IS-LM core, supplemented with a labor market and - extremely important as to the policy implications of the models - a specification of wage-price dynamics in form of a stable long-run Phillips-curve. By exploiting this tradeoff, "fine tuning" of real output and employment by using either monetary of fiscal policy instruments seemed possible.

The traditional Keynesian paradigm got into severe troubles from the late 1960s on. First, the acceleration of inflation contradicted the optimistic policy conclusions of Keynesian models and endorsed instead the classical proposition - already vigorously advocated by Friedman in his 1967 AEA-presidential address [Friedman (1968)] - that money is neutral in the long run. In the 1970's, adverse supply shocks (most importantly OPEC-I) caused in most Western economies even positive empirical correlations between inflation and unemployment (stagflation), thereby undermining the idea of a stable Phillips-curve tradeoff still further. Apart from these unpleasant facts, the Keynesian paradigm was increasingly challenged on theoretical grounds because of its lack of **microfoundations.** It was shown, most prominently by Lucas and Sargent, that Keynesian econometric models - in order to solve the identification problem - had to rely on arbitrary restrictions which are inconsistent with rational optimizing behavior. In particular, it was the Phillips-curve that got under attack for being 'non-structural'; such a relationship, it was argued, may give a more or less accurate description of an empirical regularity during a certain period of time; but since the estimated slope parameters do not reflect structural characteristics of the economy ('taste and technology') they cannot be regarded as invariant with respect to the 'policy rule' [Lucas (1976), Lucas and Sargent (1978)].

The crisis of the Keynesian orthodoxy has set in motion several new directions of theoretical and empirical research. In what follows, we briefly portray the main developments in order to put the approach of this investigation into perspective:[1]

- New classical macroeconomics (NCM): Taking the Lucas' critique as a starting point, this school emphasizes the importance of deriving macro relationships from the optimizing behavior of individual agents. Based on the elements of (i) **continuous market clearing** (all perceived gains from trade are realized) and (ii) **rational expectations** (expectations are consistent with the model), a modelling approach was proposed which is radically opposed to the Keynesian view and in particular implicates that any predictable policy whatsoever has no effect on the real course of the economy. The rational expectations hypothesis copes - in a very restrictive fashion though - with the problem that economic decisions today depend on a future which, in the absence of a complete set of contingent future markets (the artificial Arrow-Debreu extension of the Walrasian model), is uncertain. This way, the NCM-theorists transform the stable Arrow-Debreu world of general equilibrium into a sequential temporary equilibrium setting while preserving the basic conclusions of the approach. How can models of this type explain real world phenomena like unemployment and economic fluctuations? By introducing a third element, (iii) **imperfect information** of agents about aggregate variables like the average price level and money

---

1. For a more detailed discussion of the competing theories of macro behavior compare, e.g., Fitoussi (1983), Gordon (1981, 1988, 1990), Ramser (1981, 1987), Schelbert (1983), Stalder (1983) and Tobin (1980).

supply. With this assumption, monetary shocks (unanticipated deviations from the policy rule) cause the economy to move along the so-called Lucas supply function. But these movements are voluntary, i.e. they reflect optimal intertemporal decisions of agents given their incomplete information sets. According to this view of the business cycle, there is no serious need nor scope for stabilization policy.[2] As the private economy is inherently stable, the best government can do is to provide a stable environment in order not to create additional information problems.

- Empirical reconstruction of the Keynesian orthodoxy - Neo-Keynesianism: For the proponents of this line of research the empirical failure of Keynesian models in the late 1960s did not mean that the underlying theoretical approach was fundamentally flawed. The wrong predictions were attributed to the **specific** Phillips-curve included in those models. This relationship was however not considered integral to Keynesian economics. As noted by Gordon (1988), from the three elements of the Phillips relation - (i) gradual price adjustment, (ii) long-run tradeoff and (iii) no role for supply shocks - only (i) is necessary for the essence of the Keynesian approach, incomplete market clearing. Accordingly, the task for Neo-Keynesians was to reconstruct the formulation of wage-price dynamics on basis of the new evidence within the traditional IS-LM framework. The outcome of this effort was a specification of wage-price dynamics that combines the classical notion of long-run neutrality of money with the Keynesian idea of short-run disequilibria and at the same time incorporates shocks from the supply side. To be sure, this adjustment process lacks precise microfoundations and thus is in principle vulnerable to the Lucas critique. Extensive post-sample stability tests have however yielded quite favorable results; see

---

2. Policy could help if the government was better informed than the public; this assumption would however contradict rational expectations.

Gordon (1985) and Schultze (1986). Nevertheless, a convincing derivation of price and wage inertia from optimizing behavior would be highly welcomed by Keynesians as well (compare below for contributions in this vein). But the most important thing for Keynesians is that models be congruent with facts; in contrast to Lucas and his followers, they think that "rigorous optimizing explanations for what they observe can come later" [Blinder (1987)]. With respect to expectations formation, most Keynesians accept the general idea that expectations respond to policy changes; as to whether the narrow NCM-concept of 'rational expectations' is the right working premise, the Neo-Keynesian camp is however split.[3]

- Disequilibrium Economics - New Keynesian Macroeconomics (NKM): This line of research agrees with traditional Keynesian models in that prices and wages are assumed to adjust too slowly to clear markets permanently. On the other hand, there is a certain Walrasian flavor to the NKM-approach in that the consequences of gradual price adjustments are explored in a general equilibrium framework. Under the assumption of sticky prices, the general equilibrium method yields however results that are quite different from the usual Walrasian ones: If markets do not clear, agents on either the demand side or the supply side are not able to realize their initial plans (the so-called **notional** trade offers), i.e. they are rationed. Thus, they have to re-run their optimization programs, taking into account not only price signals and the usual budget constraint but also the **quantity constraints** they face. The resulting **effective** trade offers involve spillover effects across markets, introducing a specific interdependence of markets in disequilibrium. Indeed, as Clower (1965) and Leijonhufvud (1968) have

3. It has been argued that rational expectations are fundamentally anti-Keynesian since they transform uncertainty - a key element of Keynesian thought - into a situation of calculable risk; see Schelbert (1983).

shown, central concepts in Keynes' work like the consumption function and the multiplier process can be established on basis of such microeconomic 'non-Walrasian' reasoning. The rigorous formalization of non-Walrasian or 'fix-price' economics was carried out by Drèze (1975), Benassy (1977) and Grandmont (1977), among others.[4] The implications at the macroeconomic level have been studied in a two-market setting (labor and goods) by Barro and Grossman (1971, 1976), Muellbauer and Portes (1978) and Malinvaud (1977, 1980). In these models, the two aggregate markets may be in a state of either excess demand or excess supply. Hence, the economy can be located in one of four possible 'regimes'. These regimes are endogenously generated by the model. In each regime, the economy follows specific rules of behavior and is subject to specific spillover effects across markets. The regime of 'Keynesian unemployment', characterized by excess supply for both labor and goods, closely replicates the traditional IS-LM analysis with the

---

4. Two brief remarks as to the fix-price method and the associated equilibrium concept are in order here:
   - 'Fix-price' models do not actually assume that prices do not move at all. They rather posit that during the short period under consideration only quantities are free to vary while prices are subject to inter-period adjustments. This may be accepted as an approximation to the more general insight that prices are relatively inert. However, simply adding an ad hoc inter-period price adjustment equation to fix-price models is certainly not satisfactory. An integrated theory of how firms decide on quantities and prices would be highly desirable; compare Ramser (1987) on this point.
   - Within the period, a so-called **fix-price equilibrium** is established through a tâtonnement of quantities (temporary equilibrium with quantity rationing). The fixed point of this process is an equilibrium in the sense of a 'state of rest'. It is however in general not a market equilibrium in the usual sense of an equality of demand and supply. Hence the alternative labelling of fix-price models as **disequilibrium models**.

corresponding policy implications. The other regimes - classical unemployment, repressed inflation, underconsumption - show different behavior and imply other policy measures. For example, a stimulation of goods demand exerts its full multiplier effect only in the Keynesian regime. Income policy (a real wage restraint) may effectively cope with classical unemployment but would be counterproductive in a Keynesian situation. To summarize, by clarifying the relationship between Walrasian and Keynesian economics, the NKM school has developed a modelling approach in which formerly disjoint structures are endogenously generated as special cases of an integrated framework. In this sense, it may be claimed that the NKM-approach, while clearly rooted in the Keynesian tradition, provides a more general basis for analysing macroeconomic developments and policy issues than standard Neo-Keynesian models.[5]

1.2 Assessment of the controversy - Motivation of the present study

The attempt of this paper to construct an empirical model of the NKM variety for Switzerland was motivated by an appraisal of the above-mentioned conflicting approaches which is outlined in some detail in Stalder (1983) and Frick, Hollenstein, Loertscher and Stalder (1983). In the following, the main points of this assessment are restated.

The new classicals have no doubt raised the consciousness of economists as to the importance of expectations formation in macro modelling. However, whether the concrete NCM version of rational expectations (model-consistent expectations) is theoretically less arbitrary than other assumptions about

---

5. The claimed generalization refers to the narrow IS-LM representation of Keynes; broader (non-formalized) views of Keynesian theory, stressing the uncertainty aspect [see the survey in Rothschild (1981), chapter 7] are not covered by NKM models in the Barro-Grossman-Malinvaud line.

the forecasting behavior of agents must be questioned; the empirical evidence (directly based on survey data or derived from tests in connection with behavioral assumptions) is rather against rationality. Similarily, the demand for strict microfoundations is certainly respectable as a principle;[6] but whether a simple-minded transposition of a representative agent who solves an overly simplified optimization problem to the macro level produces more sensible macro relationships than an approach that builds on real-world decision problems and structural facts of the economy must be doubted as well. Further, in order to resolve the conflict between the stability arising from the basic assumption of market-clearing and the observed fluctuations in economic activity, the NCM has to graft auxiliary elements onto the market-clearing framework that are not rooted in optimizing behavior. In particular, the information delays and the asymmetries in the information sets of buyers and sellers that are required to reproduce the observed positive correlation between nominal and real variables are quite arbitrary and implausible. And even with these ad hoc elements, many well-documented stylized facts of the business cycle remain unexplained [Tobin (1980), p. 42].[7]

Additional doubt has been cast on the usefulness of the NCM-approach in recent years when it became clear that models of this type are not able to cope with the distressing problems of the day, especially mass unemployment

---

6. See however Hey (1981), p.252, as to the usefulness of microfoundations.
7. Of course, tractability of a model always requires simplifying assumptions. A model is useful when it reduces real world complexity in a way that allows us to analyse those aspects which are central to the subject under study. On this criterion, the market-clearing assumption can be regarded as an appropriate simplification in many applications (e.g. growth models, explanations of long-term structural change); but - as pointed out by Schelbert (1983) - the "comparative advantage" of market-clearing models is hardly in the field of business cycle analysis.

in Europe.[8] Stimulated by this failure, there was a revival of interest in Keynesian models, both of the standard Neo-Keynesian and the NKM variety. Many economists have taken up the challenge of the new classical school and attempted to provide microfoundations for price and wage stickiness, the distinctive feature of every Keynesian model. Explaining price setting behavior requires, first of all, a shift to the framework of imperfect (monopolistic) competition since agents in a fully competitive environment take prices as given.[9] Recent work on price and wage rigidities includes a refinement of the theory of implicit contracts,[10] efficiency wage models, models with staggered contracts, insider-outsider approaches and the theory of customer markets. However, while Keynesian models need an explanation for the slow adjustments in **nominal** wages and prices, the all these approaches imply rigidities in relative or **real** prices (prices relative to other prices,

---

8. In Switzerland unemployment remained low, even during the 1975 and 1982 recessions. This is however not primarily due to a more favorable development of employment but primarily to the high "flexibility" of labor supply (foreign workers and labor force participation of women).
9. One may argue that market disequilibria and price taking behavior are contradictory assumptions anyway. If markets do not clear, some agents must abandon the notion that they can sell or buy at the going price as much as they want. It seem most likely then that they form conjectures about how price changes might affect the quantity constraints they face. A model based on this idea has been developed by Hahn (1978). Hahn's framework is basically competitive, but monopoly power arises endogenously as a result of rationing.
10. Early models of implicit contracts only explain 'fixed-income' contracts and not the 'fixed-wage variable-employment' contracts actually observed. Extensions of the model, incorportating unemployment benefits and asymmetric information (workers do not know the true 'state of nature' of firms) may explain something which might be called "voluntary layoffs". But contract theory does not offer a rationale for involuntary unemployment. Compare, e.g., Rosen's (1985) survey of contract theory.

wages relative to prices, etc.). This is of course not surprising at all; it simply reflects the underlying proposition that optimizing agents care about real and not nominal magnitudes. But real rigidities do not rule out that prices and wages move in proportion to nominal demand - insulating thus real output from nominal fluctuations. Consequently, the task for Keynesians is to show why such a coordinated 'realignment' of all prices and wages does not take place in reality.

Considering the information problems created by the complex supplier-demander relationships in the real world - each firm buying inputs from a multitude of heterogeneous suppliers, each worker buying goods from a great number of firms whose prices in turn reflect wages of other workers - it is indeed not difficult to understand why a simultaneous and proportionate response of all prices and wages to a nominal disturbance remains a purely hypothetical possibility. In case of a contraction of nominal demand, for example, no individual has an incentive to contribute to aggregate stability by lowering the price (wage) in proportion to nominal demand without being sure that everybody else does the same: On the one hand, the potential losses incurred when acting alone are high; on the other hand, each individual can safely ignore his own contribution to the general price level. Aggregate stability can thus be viewed as a public good subject to a free-rider problem [Gordon (1988)]. This **input-output table** approach, which gives a rationale for both real and nominal rigidities, is due to Gordon (1981). It has been further elaborated by Blanchard (1987). Evidently, the basic idea is quite similar to Keynes' original explanation of wage rigidity: workers resist cuts in money wages because they do not know how general these cuts will prove to be, each worker fearing a fall in his own wage relative to others.

A related theory of price stickiness is based on **'menu costs'** (e.g. the small costs of printing new catalogues). In simple terms, the argument goes as follows [compare, e.g., Ball, Mankiw and Romer (1988)]: Ignoring first menu costs, it can be shown that the loss for a firm from not adjusting its price in response to a change in demand is small (second-order). Thus, even when menu costs are small, taking them into account may explain why it can be privately optimal for a firm to keep its price fixed. The beneficial aggregate externalities of price reductions in case of falling nominal demand (arising in particular from the real income effect) do not show up in the individual firm's optimization problem. According to menu-cost models, it is not only a high **variability** of money (reducing the informational content of price changes) but also a high **average rate** of money growth that affects the Phillips-curve tradeoff (because high inflation shortens the optimal interval of price changes).

With the input-output table approach and the new menu-cost models Keynesian economics has certainly made a significant step towards a reconciliation of sticky prices with optimizing behavior. Nevertheless, a lot remains to be done if one really wants to comply with the microfoundation principle. For instance, to strictly justify the fix-price method one would have to show why it is optimal for agents to adjust prices between periods in response to quantity constraints while behaving within the period as if prices were fixed. However, as far as empirical macroeconomics is concerned, no convincing alternative to the customary ad hoc specification of wage-price adjustments is at hand for the time being. One should also note in this respect that new research on microfoundations need not have macroeconomic implications which fundamentally contradict the traditional empirical formulation of wage-price dynamics, typically involving demand-pull, cost-push and expectational elements. Once such a pragmatical position is accepted, one is left with the choice between the standard Neo-Keynesian and NKM models.

The common basis of Neo-Keynesian and NKM models is incomplete market clearing due to price and wage stickiness. Neo-Keynesian models take then however for granted that product and labor markets, if not in equilibrium, are in a state of excess supply so that output and employment are demand-determined. To be sure, supply-side factors are not entirely absent from these models; they typically show up in the price and wage adjustment equations and may this way influence output and employment. But the only admissible rationing situation is 'Keynesian unemployment', i.e., a state of general excess supply where aggregate goods demand determines actual output and, via effective labor demand, actual employment. However, if prices and wages are sticky, other types of disequilibria may emerge in the business cycle as well: For example, there may be situations in which employment and output are constrained to a significant degree by 'profitable capacities' (classical unemployment). Or it may be that employment is limited by the available labor supply, implying a negative spillover onto goods supply which in turn constrains actual output (repressed inflation). As already noted above, by including these various possibilities as special cases, the NKM offers a more general framework for macro modelling and policy analysis than the demand-oriented Neo-Keynesian approach.

It may be argued, however, that prices and wages are more flexible upward than downward so that only 'Keynesian unemployment' is a candidate for a long-lasting disequilibrium whereas 'classical unemployment' and 'repressed inflation' would quickly set in motion self-correcting forces. This is potentially a strong argument in favor of the standard Neo-Keynesian approach. The point is even more noteworthy as the distinction in NKM models between different regimes and spillovers introduces non-linearities and discontinuities that are difficult to handle econometrically and call for restrictive assumptions in other respects. In other words, econometric **tractability** establishes a **tradeoff** between the rigorous modelling of disequilibria and spillovers à la NKM and the detailed demand-oriented analysis that is typical for Neo-Keynesian models. Of course, intermediate modelling approaches are possible as well. Which of the several possibilities is the most appropriate one can only be decided on basis of the relative success of alternative modelling efforts in practice. The answer is likely to differ from country to country and depend on the time period considered. Some general tentative conclusions may however be derived from recent empirical work on disequilibrium models for several European countries and the US:[11]

- In practically all countries for which NKM models have been estimated, the Keynesian regime turns out to be the dominant one over long periods of time. Nevertheless, other regimes prove empirically relevant as well, although they are in fact relatively short-lived.
- 'Classical unemployment' plays a quite important role in several European countries. In contrast to the original set-up of NKM models, the classical regime is however not to be associated with the notion that consumers get

---

11. Besides the models already mentioned compare the studies of Metha and Sneessens (1988), Entorf, Franz, König and Smolny (1988), Gagey, Lambert and Ottenwaelter (1988), Bean and Gavosto (1988), Neudorfer, Pichelmann and Wagner (1988) and Burda (1988). All these studies grew out of the **European Unemployment Program** which was undertaken in order to understand the forces behind the persistence of high unemployment in the 1980's. The common prototype model underlying this multicountry research effort is due to Sneessens and Drèze (1986) and the main empirical results are summarized in Drèze and Bean (1990).

rationed to any significant degree. In open economies, where for a large part of domestic products imported substitutes are available, 'classical unemployment' rather describes a situation that arises when - due for instance to deteriorating international competitiveness - profitability dwindles so that the capital stock becomes insufficient to absorb the available labor force while imports fill the gap on the goods market.

- Although a specific regime may be predominant in a certain phase of the cycle, in heterogeneous economies one always has to expect that the several sectors and industries (and even firms within industries) are facing quite different rationing situations. As a consequence, the transitions between different regimes at the aggregate level should be viewed as gradual.

These points clearly illustrate the usefulness of the NKM-approach for empirical macro modelling. This is not to say, however, that standard Neo-Keynesian models are futile. Indeed, the two approaches are not necessarily mutually exclusive but can, under certain circumstances, be regarded as **complementary** directions of research. It is conceivable for instance that the estimation of a NKM-modell leads to the conclusion that non-Keynesian rationing situations are limited to short time intervals or narrow subsectors of the economy. A standard Neo-Keynesian specification may then be considered to be an acceptable approximation (for a certain period of time). This being the case, one might in a second step dispense with the complicated story of changing regimes and spillovers in favor of a more detailed analysis of the demand side of the economy. Such a "double-tracked" approach - each track emphasizing some specific aspects of the business cycle while neglecting some others - may ultimately be the only way to do justice to the complex reality of business cycles. The strong appeal of the NKM-approach within in such a research strategy is that it does not impose untested regime assumptions on the theoretical structure a priori but infers the ruling regimes from empirical evidence.

1.3 Scope and limitations of the investigation

In view of official unemployment rates that hardly ever exceeded 1%, the attempt to construct an econometric two-market (labor and goods) disequilibrium model for Switzerland may at first glance appear as a somewhat far-fetched exercise. It is however a fact that output and employment have been extremely volatile in Switzerland over the past 20 years. The most dramatic event occurred in the mid-1970s when Switzerland experienced a recession that was stronger than in the majority of other countries, with employment and output falling from peak to trough by 9% and 14% respectively. It seems indeed very hard to interpret swings of this magnitude in a traditional manner as points of intersection of demand and supply curves, the more so as prices and wages moved rather sluggishly. Not surprisingly then, econometric studies in many fields have encounterd difficulties in explaining developments over longer periods of time on a common theoretical basis with stable parameters. The usual reaction to this kind of problem was to subdivide the estimation period, to introduce dummy variables or to resort to other constructs that account for "structural change" in a more or less ad hoc manner. Against this background, the potential of a modelling framework that allows for endogenous transitions between different regimes is quite obvious. Such a framework may be of great help in identifying more stable econometric relationships because - as Kooiman and Kloek (1985) put it - "supply and demand functions are no longer forced to accommodate observations they do not really apply to". Disequilibrium models thus offer an interesting new interpretation of the notorious problem of "parameter instability" in traditional macro models (as an alternative to the new classicals' view of the problem).

A first empirical indication of the usefulness of the disequilibrium approach for Switzerland is provided by several earlier investigations that were confined to the aggregate labor market. These models imply considerable amounts of both excess demand and excess supply along the business cycle [Büttler, Frei and Schips (1986), Stalder (1985a)]. In a labor market model that includes an exogenous Keynesian spillover from the goods market [Stalder (1985b, 1989a)], the short-run variations in labor demand and employment are traced back to a significant degree to this spillover while medium-term developments seem to depend strongly on classical determinants as well (real wages, relative factor costs).

The present study tries to overcome two limitations of existing empirical disequilibrium models. **First, investment** in productive capacity is determined - on basis of a vintage approach - along with labor demand and investment as an **endogenous** variable; this enhances the usefulness of the model for analysing longer-term developments.[12] **Second,** the model incorporates inventories and unfilled orders in their role as **buffer stocks**; this aims at an improved description of the short-term link between the goods market and the labor market.

Treating **investment** and the capital stock as exogenous - or rather predetermined - variables has been common practice in a first generation of disequilibrium models. This may be admissible from an econometric point of view (weak exogeneity). However, without an explanation of capital formation,

---

12. Meanwhile, parallel research in other countries has also produced empirical two-market disequilibrium models with endogenous investment [e.g. Metha and Sneessens (1988), Entorf, Franz, König and Smolny (1988), Burda (1988)]. Investment behavior has been analysed in a disequilibrium context by Artus and Muet (1984), Lambert and Mulkay (1986) and - theoretically - by Malinvaud (1987).

such models may give us only a very incomplete account of longer-term developments. This applies in particular to the distinction between the regimes of 'Keynesian' and 'classical' unemployment, which is one of the central themes of macro disequilibrium models. To be sure, it can be quite interesting to determine, conditional on a given capital stock, whether employment has been constrained in a certain period by insufficient goods demand (Keynesian unemployment: firms would increase employment at given relative prices if they were able to sell more goods) or by a lack of profitable jobs (classical unemployment: profitable capacities are fully utilized but too small to absorb the available labor supply). But such a static "snapshot" tells us little about the underlying causes of the imbalances. Consider for instance a prolonged slack of goods demand that entails low investment and eventually leads to a reduction in productive capacities. In a subsequent upswing, capacities may then become a binding constraint for output and employment before the labor market gets cleared again. The instantaneous rationing situation thus appears as 'classical unemployment', whereas the original cause is lack of goods demand. Or think of a sharp autonomous wage push. Since the technical coefficients on existing capital are largely fixed, the short-run response of labor demand is probably weak. But in the longer run we must expect significant negative effects of the wage increase on production capacities and labor demand, transmitted through capital accumulation, i.e. the impact of low profitability and high relative labor costs on the volume of investment and its labor intensity respectively. As the process of capital accumulation is a relatively slow, the resulting situation of 'classical unemployment' may persist in future periods even if wages return to normal levels. Further, since investment plays a role as demand component as well and since higher wages are likely to be passed onto prices, the wage push may also give rise to transitory states with "insufficient demand", i.e. situations in which the momentary rationing situation would appear as 'Keynesian'.

The process of capital accumulation will be specified in the model in form of a **vintage**-approach, involving the following features:

- The creation of new equipment is explained by an investment equation whose main determinants are excess demand, profitability and relative factor costs.
- The technical coefficients on new capital (the "labor requirements" of new vintages) depend on relative factor costs (ex ante). Once investment has become physical (ex post), technical coefficients remain however fixed.
- Existing "machines" differ with respect to labor productivity. They remain in operation down to a marginal productivity level which is related to the current level of real wages.

According to this specification, there are three dynamically quite different channels by which wages influence labor demand and output supply: First, via profitability and the volume of new investment; second, via relative factor costs and the capital intensity of new vintages; third, via the scrapping of old equipment. In addition, the model takes into account that labor demand may be subject to Keynesian spillover effects from the goods market (effective labor demand). Symmetrically, the specification of effective output supply involves a potential spillover from rationed labor demand.

The second improvement we try to achieve in this study concerns the "production smoothing" role of **buffer stocks** (output inventories and unfilled orders). It has been argued, e.g. by Blinder (1980, 1981), that the minimum-condition (i.e. the assumption that transacted quantities are given by the minimum of demand and supply), while being an adequate device for analysing the labor market of an economy, would make little sense for the goods market: If firms cannot sell all the output they want to, they do not immediately adjust production to demand but let the difference be absorbed by accumulating inventories (or reducing order backlogs). For similar reasons, an excess of goods demand over production is not tantamount with rationing of comsumption demand. According to Blinder, the existence of such buffer stocks largely prevents spillover effects and robs disequilibrium models much of their interest. We do not agree with this extreme conclusion but rather take the view that buffer stocks give rise to an dynamical modification of the short-run link between current demand and output that should be taken into account **within** the disequilibrium framework. The specification set forth in this paper assumes, roughly speaking, that firms let differences between current demand and predetermined output be absorbed within the period by buffers stocks, but, when deciding on next period's output, tend to gradually reduce the deviation of actual buffer stocks from target levels. This way, demand fluctuations produce delayed and smoothed movements in output and employment. However, as the production smoothing model is not unquestioned in the inventory literature, we shall regard this specification as an empirical variant to a model that neglects buffer stocks, i.e. posits the usual min-condition for the goods market.

As a remaining shortcoming, we must note that the model developed in this paper does not explain how prices (wages) are set, i.e. treats them as exogenous or predetermined variables. As noted above, the assumption of only slowly adjusting or predetermined prices is at the core of disequilibrium economics and forms the basis for the notion that consistency of plans is established, within the period, primarily by quantity adjustments. But this 'fix-price' assumption is a short-run concept. In the longer term, the development of the economy depends of course on how prices respond to current disequilibria and other factors. In particular, the persistence of the various rationing situations depends crucially on the adjustment speeds of prices and wages. Therefore, endogenizing price and wage setting behavior would be highly desirable for analysing longer-term developments. This task must however be left to future research.

Existing macroeconomic disequilibrium models may be distinguished into two broad groups, differing as to how the problem of **aggregating markets in disequilibrium** is tackled. In a **first** type of model, the minimum-condition is assumed to hold for the aggregates. This means, for instance, that the employment level of the economy is given by the smaller of aggregate labor demand and aggregate labor supply. According to this assumption, the whole economy switches, at specific dates of the cycle, from one regime into another.[13] Further, there are either unemployed workers or vacancies in a given period, but never both. These implications are not realistic. In order for an aggregate economy to exhibit such behavior, all individual markets (defined in terms of qualification, location, industry etc.) would have to be in the same rationing situation at a given point of time, which seems quite unlikely. A **second** type of model starts from the notion that aggregate markets like the labor and goods market of an economy consist of a multitude of 'micro markets' on which demand/supply ratios may differ. The minimum-condition is applied to these micro markets. Aggregation (by integrating over density functions that describe the distribution of demand/supply ratios across micro markets) converts the "sharp corners" of the micro level minimum-condition into continuous nonlinear macro relationships, mapping aggregate demand and supply onto aggregate transactions (output and employment). In this type of model, there are no unrealistic discrete switches from

---

13. Depending on whether or not the demand and supply equations contain separate disturbance terms, these regime switches are stochastic [e.g. Kooiman and Kloek (1985)] or deterministic [Sneessens (1983)].

purely demand-determined to purely supply-determined situations but the transitions between regimes become gradual. As a result, the assessment of the efficacy of alternative policy measures will be more differentiated as well. Further, depending on the degree of 'structural mismatch' at the micro level, aggregate transactions (actual output and employment) are always smaller than the minimum of aggregate demand and supply, implying positive amounts of unemployment and vacancies at the same time.[14]

While the first type of model may be appropriate for discussing certain theoretical issues, its usefulness as a device for empirical macro analysis seems rather questionable. To be sure, the discrete switches of regimes may be viewed as a handy simplification on a theoretical level. They do however not translate into an easy econometric formulation. Quite to the contrary, a model with aggregate min-conditions is more difficult to handle econometrically than a model with continuous regime transitions. In particular, in the second type of model the aggregation procedure leads to theoretical expressions that map the latent demand and supply variables onto the proportions of firms in the different regimes. These proportions can be related empirically to business survey data. Incorporating such information may considerably increase the efficiency of the econometric estimation [Lambert (1984), Drèze (1987)]. It further helps modelling dynamic structures since the lagged values of the latent demand and supply variables can be expressed in terms of past observables and regime proportions. In a model with discrete switches of regimes, on the other hand, dynamic specifications that involve lagged latent demand and supply variables entail practically intractable

---

14. The idea of applying a "smoothing-by-aggregation" procedure to markets in disequilibrium is due to Muellbauer (1978). The concept has been elaborated by Malinvaud (1982b), Kooiman (1984), Lambert (1984, 1988), Gourieroux and Laroque (1985), among others.

estimation problems. The "smoothing-by-aggregation" model thus proves both more realistic and easier to implement econometrically. Therefore, we shall base our investigation on this approach.

1.4 Set-up of the paper

The **set-up of the paper** is as follows. In section 2 we develop a theoretical model that describes the spillovers between goods and labor markets and the associated regimes at the level of the individual firm. Starting from this micro model, we derive in section 3 macroeconomic relationships, showing how aggregate demands and supplies (unobserved) are mapped onto aggregate transactions (observed output and employment) and regime proportions (measured by survey data). Section 4 introduces the buffer role of inventories and unfilled orders. In section 5 we specify the aggregate behavioral equations. While labor supply and goods demand are formulated more or less conventionally, the equations for the production sector (labor demand, output supply, investment) are based on a specific vintage approach. Section 6 summarizes the model, discusses the method of estimation and proposes some dynamical extensions. Section 7 presents the estimation results and tests several parameter restrictions. Section 8 addresses the question of structural parameter stability. In section 9 we perform simulations under various conditions in order to evaluate the model with respect to its fit, dynamic tracking performance, implied regimes and short-term and long-term multiplier effect arising from aggregate demand and wage shocks.

2. THE MICRO MODEL

In this section we discuss the connections between demand, supply and actual transactions at the level of single micro goods and labor markets. This 'micro model' will serve then in section 3 as starting point for the derivation of macroeconomic relationships by adopting a "smoothing-by-aggregation" technique. Generally speaking, goods and labor markets are linked through **(a)** firms' decisions on goods supply and labor demand, **(b)** households' decisions on goods demand and labor supply. When prices and wages adjust too slowly to clear markets in the period under consideration, these decisions are subject to quantity rationing and may involve spillover effects, so that a distinction between 'notional' and 'effective' trade offers becomes necessary. We focus our analysis on link (a), taking thus into account that firms rationed in labor demand curtail effective output supply and that firms facing a 'sales constraint' react by reducing effective labor demand. Spillovers in the household sector, although theoretically substantiated in an analogous manner, seem less relevant in practice:

- In Western industrialized countries, and in particular in a small open economy like Switzerland where a large part of consumption goods is imported, it seems unlikely that households get ever rationed in goods demand to an extent that induces them to reduce labor supply. Therefore, we need not distinguish between notional and effective labor supply.
- The spillover from involuntary unemployment to consumption demand, even though dampened by unemployment benefits, is surely more important. It is however only demand for domestically produced consumption goods, representing a rather small part of total sales, that is relevant to the output and employment decision of domestic firms. Furthermore, the spillover in question can be accounted for, without an explicit distinction between

notional and effective demand, by means of a traditional Keynesian consumption function with realized income as explanatory variable.[1]

Since we want to concentrate on link (a), it seems natural to define micro markets from the perspective of the individual firm. Firms are thus viewed as hypothetical production units (not necessarily real firms) that supply goods (y^s) and demand labor (l^d) on specific micro goods and labor markets, on which they face a certain demand y^d and a certain supply l^s respectively. We have to distinguish between a firm's **notional** and its **effective** trade-offers: First, given the short-run production function and the available capital stock, each firm is assumed to decide simultaneously on the optimal levels of output and employment, corresponding to what may be called 'profitable capacities'; these are the firm's notional output supply, $\tilde{y}^s$, and notional labor demand, $\tilde{l}^d$. The effective trade-offers, y^s and l^d, fall short of the notional ones if the firm is rationed in the "other" market. As noted above, such a distinction is not required with respect to households.

Depending on the values of y^d, $\tilde{y}^s$, $\tilde{l}^d$ and l^s, each firm is located in a specific 'regime'. In the following we discuss the corresponding spillovers and determine the transaction levels y and l. The variables y^d, $\tilde{y}^s$, $\tilde{l}^d$ and l^s are regarded as predetermined during the period (fix-price assumption), so that consistency of plans is established solely through quantity adjustments. In subsequent sections of this study, the aggregate values of y^d, $\tilde{y}^s$, $\tilde{l}^d$ and l^s will be explained by econometric equations. Due to the dispersion

1. Realized income can be smaller than or equal to 'planned' income. If the two are equal (no involuntary unemployment), effective consumption demand corresponds to the notional demand; otherwise, the involuntary income reduction captures the spillover effect.

of demand-supply ratios at the firm level (firm-specific factors), the different regimes - discrete states for individual firms - will in general coexist at the macro level, in varying proportions of course, depending on the development of the aggregates over time.[2]

2.1 Spillovers and transactions

In every period the firm is assumed to decide simultaneously, based on its short-run production function and available capital, on the notional levels of goods supply and labor demand, $\tilde{y}^s$ and $\tilde{l}^d$. The firm is then confronted on the output market with a certain demand y^d and on the labor market with a certain supply l^s. The following **effective functions** arise:

Effective labor demand:

If $y^d \geq \tilde{y}^s$ (firm able to sell notional goods supply): $l^d = \tilde{l}^d$

If $y^d < \tilde{y}^s$ (firm faces a 'sales constraint'): $l^d < \tilde{l}^d$ (spillover)

This may be specified, e.g., by writing

$$l^d = \tilde{l}^d \min(x^\gamma, 1) , \quad \text{where} \tag{1}$$

$$x = y^d/\tilde{y}^s \quad , \quad \gamma > 0 \quad \text{(spillover elasticity).}$$

Effective goods supply:

If $l^s \geq \tilde{l}^d$ (firm able to hire notional labor demand): $y^s = \tilde{y}^s$

If $l^s < \tilde{l}^d$ (firm constrained by labor supply): $y^s < \tilde{y}^s$ (spillover).

This may be specified, e.g., by writing

$$y^s = \tilde{y}^s \min(z^\delta, 1) , \quad \text{where} \tag{2}$$

$$z = l^s/\tilde{l}^d \quad , \quad \delta > 0 \quad \text{(spillover elasticity)}$$

---

2. Looking at micro labor and micro goods markets from the perspective of firms has the advantage that one can derive expressions for aggregate output and aggregate employment by integrating over one single population (firms), instead of having to deal with two populations (micro labor and goods markets). This has been pointed out by Kooiman (1984).

The **employment** level of the firm corresponds to the minimum of labor supply and demand:

$$l = \min(l^s, l^d) = \min[l^s, \tilde{l}^d \min(x^\gamma, 1)]$$

Taking $\tilde{l}^d$ out of the min-condition and using the definition of z, we obtain:

$$l = \tilde{l}^d \min(z, x^\gamma, 1) \tag{3}$$

To determine the firm's **output** level we proceed correspondingly and get:

$$y = \min(y^d, y^s) = \min[y^d, \tilde{y}^s \min(z^\delta, 1)] \quad \text{or}$$

$$y = \tilde{y}^s \min(z^\delta, x, 1) \tag{4}$$

If unconstrained on both markets ($x \geq 1$ and $z \geq 1$), the firm realizes as employment and output levels its notional trade offers $\tilde{l}^d$ and $\tilde{y}^s$; otherwise, l and y get reduced according to the 'minimum factor' in (3) and (4).

2.2 Discussion of the spillover elasticities

We assume that a firm constrained by labor supply ($z < 1$) moves along a concave production function, suffering thus a less than proportionate fall in effective output supply. This implies $0 < \delta < 1$.[3] If the firm in case of a 'sales constraint' ($x < 1$) stayed strictly on the efficient production frontier, its effective labor demand function would just correspond to the inverse of the effective output supply function, implying $\gamma = 1/\delta > 1$, so that labor productivity would increase in recessions. While such behavior is feasible in a technical sense, adjustment costs make it optimal for firms to hoard labor to some extent in recessions, and labor productivity is in fact

3. This restriction may arise from a traditional neoclassical production function or a vintage approach. In the latter case, each "machine" has a fixed labor productivity at a given point of time, but labor constrained firms will first stop producing on the least efficient machines.

Fig. 1: Notional and effective goods supply, $\tilde{y}^s$ and y^s

Notional and effective labor demand, $\tilde{l}^d$ and l^d

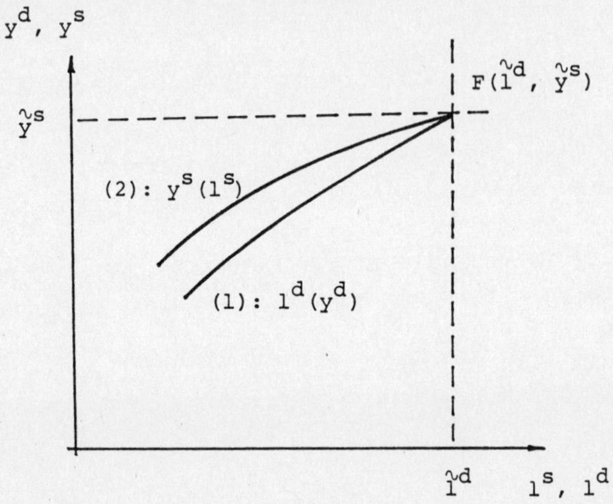

known to be procyclical. Labor hoarding can be identified in our model with the restriction $0 < \gamma < 1/\delta$.[4] To generate the empirical productivity cycle, we have the stronger requirement $0 < \gamma < 1$. Graphically - see **fig. 1** - labor hoarding implies an effective labor demand function (1) that lies below the effective output supply function (2) (production frontier), except in its maximum where (1) and (2) coincide (point $F(\tilde{l}^d, \tilde{y}^s)$).[5]

---

4. Labour hoarding is a rather complex dynamical phenomenon, involving longer-term demand expectations and other factors like anticipated difficulties of re-recruiting workers and the state of financial reserves of the firm as determinants. To capture hoarding behavior simply in the (static) form of the parameter restriction $\gamma < 1/\delta$ is certainly not fully adequate. One would expect that γ varies over time (tending to $1/\delta$ if demand is persistently low). So one might prefer to posit $\gamma = 1/\delta$ and to allow for hoarding by amending effective labor demand (1) by a dynamic adjustment scheme. We shall come back to this issue later in the paper.
5. For $\gamma < 1$ (procyclical labor productivity) the effective labor demand function (1) lies further below y^d and becomes convex.

2.3 Regimes

The goods and labor market of a firm can be in excess demand or in excess supply. Accordingly, each firm may find itself in one of four possible rationing situations, referred to usually as 'regimes' (boundary cases can be assigned arbitrarily):

$y^d > y^s = y$	$l = l^d < l^s$	Classical unemployment	C
$y = y^d < y^s$	$l = l^d < l^s$	Keynesian unemployment	K
$y^d > y^s = y$	$l^d > l^s = l$	Repressed inflation	R
$y = y^d < y^s$	$l^d > l^s = l$	Underconsumption	U

Given $0 < \gamma < 1/6$ (coherency condition), the occurrence of these regimes is uniquely related to inequality conditions in terms of x and z, corresponding to the 4 mutually exclusive regions in the (x,z)-plane shown in **fig. 2**. The

Fig. 2: Demand-supply ratios and possible regimes of the firm: C, K, R, U

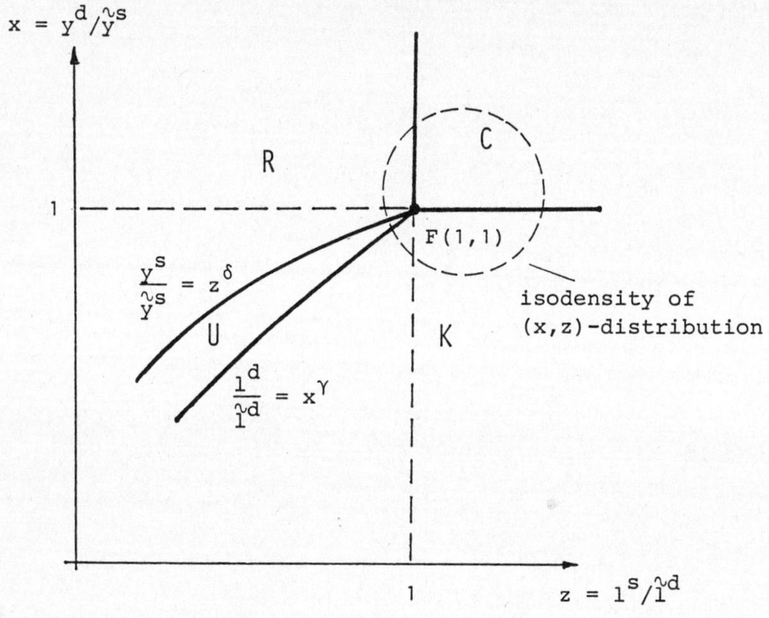

inequalities are easily derived from the min-conditions in eqs. (3) and (4), considering that the minimum factor in (3) and (4) - either a z-term, a x-term or 1 - indicates whether transactions l and y are constrained by labor supply, goods demand or the firm's notional trade offers respectively:

- If a firm has

$$x > 1 \quad \text{and} \quad z > 1 , \tag{5.1}$$

then 1 is the minimum in (3) and (4). The firm faces excess demand for goods and excess supply of labor. A **C-Regime** prevails and the firm realizes its notional trade offers:

$$y = \tilde{y}^s \quad \text{and} \quad l = \tilde{l}^d .$$

- If a firm has x and z values such that

$$x < 1 \quad \text{and} \quad x^{\gamma} < z , \tag{5.2}$$

x^{γ} is the minimum in (3) and - as is easy to see (using $\gamma < 1/\delta$) - x is the minimum in (4). Both employment and output are thus constrained by the x-terms, i.e. goods demand. The firm is in a **K-Regime** and we have

$$y = y^d \quad \text{and} \quad l = \tilde{l}^d x^{\gamma} .$$

- If a firm has x and z values such that

$$z < 1 \quad \text{and} \quad z^{\delta} < x , \tag{5.3}$$

z^{δ} is the minimum in (4) and - since $\gamma < 1/\delta$ - z is the minimum in (3). Both output and employment are thus constrained by labor supply. The firm is in a **R-Regime** and we have

$$y = \tilde{y}^s z^{\delta} \quad \text{and} \quad l = l^s .$$

- If a firm has x and z values such that

$$z < x^{\gamma} \quad \text{and} \quad x < z^{\delta}, \tag{5.4}$$

z is the minimum in (3) and x is the minimum in (4). The firm is thus in an **U-Regime**, i.e. constrained in both markets, and we have

$$y = y^d \quad \text{and} \quad l = l^s .$$

Rewriting (5.4) as $x^{1/\delta} < z < x^{\gamma}$, we see that the U-region narrows for $\gamma \to 1/\delta$ and disappears in the limiting case $\gamma = 1/\delta$.[6] It is further obvious that, given $0 < \gamma < 1/\delta$, the inequality for an U-Regime can only be met for x and z smaller than 1.

Appendix : Comparison with other spillover-formulations

There are three major alternative formulations of spillovers, associated in the literature with the names of Ito, Portes-Benassy and Gourieroux-Laffont-Monfort. They have been discussed by Portes (1977), Sneessens (1981) and Martin and Portes (1987), among others. We shall compare these spillover concepts now with our formulation, which is closely related to the one proposed by Kooiman (1984). Transposed to the framework of this paper, which neglects spillovers in the household sector, the three alternatives to (1) and (2) may be written as:

Ito:
$$l^d = \tilde{l}^d \left(\frac{y}{\tilde{y}^s}\right)^{\gamma} \qquad y^s = \tilde{y}^s \left(\frac{l}{\tilde{l}^d}\right)^{\delta} \qquad (6.1)$$

PB:
$$l^d = \tilde{l}^d \left(\frac{y}{y^s}\right)^{\gamma} \qquad y^s = \tilde{y}^s \left(\frac{l}{l^d}\right)^{\delta} \qquad (6.2)$$

GLM:
$$l^d = \begin{cases} \tilde{l}^d & \text{if } y = y^s \le y^d \\ \tilde{l}^d \left(\frac{y}{\tilde{y}^s}\right)^{\delta} & \text{if } y = y^d < y^s \end{cases}$$
$$y^s = \begin{cases} \tilde{y}^s & \text{if } l = l^d \le l^s \\ \tilde{y}^s \left(\frac{l}{\tilde{l}^d}\right)^{\delta} & \text{if } l = l^s < l^d \end{cases} \qquad (6.3)$$

6. In this case the effective labor demand function and the effective output supply function coincide.

Common to all formulations are the min-conditions

$$l = \min(l^d, l^s) \qquad \text{and} \qquad y = \min(y^d, y^s) \quad .$$

In Ito's spillover concept, the firm always responds to differences between notional trade offers and actual transactions in the "other" market, regardless of how these transactions are determined. For example, a firm in a Keynesian situation reduces effective goods supply y^s in relation to $\tilde{y}^s$ because actual employment l is less than $\tilde{l}^d$ - even though the labor market is in excess supply and employment is determined the firm's labor demand. The PB-formulation on the other hand stipulates that spillovers arise only if the effective trade offer in the other market is rationed, and the size of the spillover is assumed to reflect the relative difference between actual trade and effective trade offer. In GLM's formulation spillovers arise (as in PB) only if the firm cannot realize its effective trade offer in the other market, but the spillovers are then formulated in terms of the gap between actual transactions and notional trade offers (as in Ito).

Despite these differences, the definition of regimes in terms of notional trade offers are exactly the same for Ito, PB and GLM. All three versions produce further identical 'short sides' and thus the same levels of transactions l and y. These results, established in Portes (1977), extend to our specification. The formulations differ however with respect to the 'long sides' of the markets. All formulations are coherent in the sense of defining a one-to-one mapping from notional trade offers $v' = (y^d, \tilde{y}^s, \tilde{l}^d, l^s)$ to effective demands and supplies $w' = (y^d, y^s, l^d, l^s)$, provided that $\gamma < 1/\delta$.

In PB's, GLM's and our formulation, the limiting case $\gamma = 1/\delta$ (no labor hoarding) solely rules out the U-regime. If we combine however Ito's formulation with the assumption $\gamma = 1/\delta$, the model is moreover no longer able to generate positive excess supply of goods (K-regimes) or positive excess demand for labor (R-regimes). For example, we may let y^d fall to an arbitrarily small value but never get a K-regime with $y^s > y^d = y$. The reason for this is that y^s adjusts to actual employment and decreases thus exactly with $y^d = y$.

To further clarify the differences between the spillover concepts, consider **fig. 3**, showing effective labor demand as specified by Ito, PB, GLM and our eq. (1). In point H we have a R-regime and:

$$l^d_{Ito} = \tilde{l}^d\left(\frac{y}{\tilde{y}^s}\right)^{\gamma} < l^d_{eq.1} = \tilde{l}^d\left(\frac{y^d}{\tilde{y}^s}\right)^{\gamma} < l^d_{GLM} = l^d_{PB} = \tilde{l}^d$$

Moving from H to the right (relaxing the labor supply constraint), l, y and thus l^d_{Ito} increase. At point E, output y becomes demand-constrained, l^d_{Ito} reaches $l^d_{eq.1}$ and l^d_{GLM} jumps back to $l^d_{eq.1}$. Between E and G (U-regime) l^d_{PB}

Fig. 3: Effective labor demand according to Ito, Portes-Benassy, Gourieroux-Laffont-Monfort and eq.(1); positions referring to point H

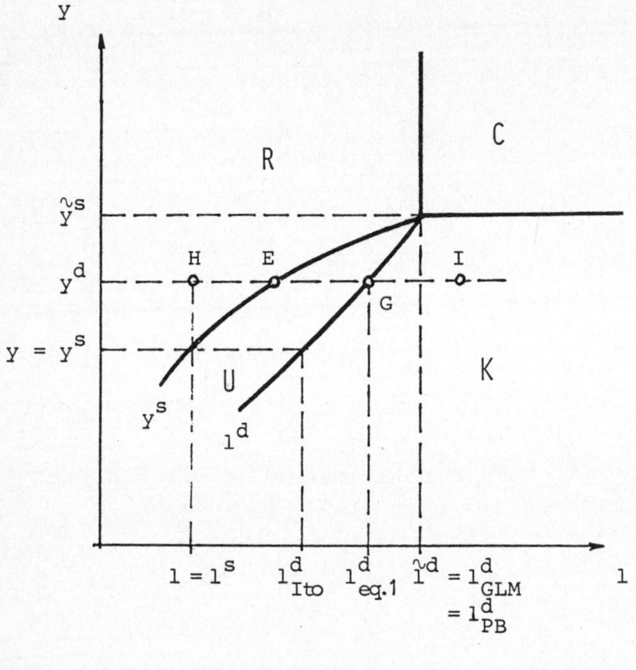

decreases with growing l^s (the firm feels more and more demand-constrained since y^s increases whereas $y = y^d$ remains constant). Beyond G, labor demand is on the 'short side' of the labor market (K-regime) and all four effective functions coincide (in G). Symmetrical consideration apply of course to effective goods supply.

What should we conclude from this discussion? Quandt (1982) for instance finds that the theory of rationing has been stated so far only in most general terms so that "it is not easy to see how any of the above formulations could claim preeminence on theoretical grounds". Still, we think that the negative response of effective labor demand to a relaxation of the labor supply constraint, as implied by GLM and PB, is difficult to substantiate. And that firms should increase labor demand when offered more labor (Ito) seems also rather counterintuitive. Such reactions are absent from our formulation since effective labor demand according to (1) is always a function of y^d (as long as $y^d < \tilde{y}^s$). On a more fundamental level, the various spillover concepts reflect conflicting views as to the information structure. In eq. (1) firms are assumed to be informed about the state of y^d (and thus to translate y^d into effective labor demand) even if they are not effectively constrained by y^d. In point H of fig. 3 for instance output y is labor supply constrained but the fact that $y^d < \tilde{y}^s$ is reflected in $l^d_{eq.1}$ nevertheless. One may argue that firms get demand information through order inflows, inventory changes, length of waiting lines etc. The other spillover concepts seem to assume that firms perceive y^d only when it is a binding constraint. As this is not the case in point H, firms according to GLM and PB exert notional labor demand. In Ito's formulation labor demand is reduced in point H not in response to y^d but since output is constrained by l^s.

3. DERIVATION OF THE AGGREGATE MODEL

3.1 Aggregation

Microeconomic behavioral assumptions are usually converted into aggregate relationships by invoking the concept of the 'representative' firm. Although rather unsatisfactory, such side-stepping of the aggregation problem is often the only procedure that leads to tractable macro models. It is basically also the way we pursue here. However, the assumption that the aggregate economy consists of identical firms in the sense that the micro model of eqs. (1) to (4) can directly be transposed to the macro level (identifying y^d with aggregate demand, etc.) would have quite unrealistic implications: The model would produce discrete switches of regimes for the economy as a whole, i.e. imply that aggregate output and employment are either purely demand-determined or purely supply-determined. Considering the actual heterogeneity of goods and labor markets, it seems much more likely that situations of excess demand and excess supply coexist and that transitions between regimes are gradual. This view is endorsed for example by business survey data, which, on the one hand, convey the existence of an overall business cycle but, on the other hand, clearly show that this 'common factor' is superimposed in the cross section of firms by 'firm-specific factors'. Sensible aggregate relationships should account for this micro level dispersion and exhibit a certain degree of 'continuity' or 'smoothness' in relation to the underlying discrete micro relationships.

In order to derive such a "streamlined" macro model - and to exploit the information provided by business surveys - we assume that firms **differ** as to the z and x-values they face (while being identical in all other respects). It is evident then from fig. 2 that the distribution of the z and x-ratios in the population of firms uniquely determines the proportions of firms in the different regimes. Assuming a very large number of firms we let the distribution of z and x across firms be approximated by a continuous density function g(z, x). Eqs. (3) and (4) define then the distribution of l and y across firms, which, as a result of the min-conditions, involves points of accumulation. On this basis, aggregate employment L and aggregate output Y can be expressed in form of expected values. For L we have:

$$L = n\,E(l) = n\,E\left[\tilde{l}^d \min(z, x^{\gamma}, 1)\right] \qquad \text{n: number of firms}$$

$$= n\,\tilde{l}^d\,E\left[\min(z, x^{\gamma}, 1)\right]$$

$$= \tilde{L}^d\,\underbrace{E\left[\min(z, x^{\gamma}, 1)\right]}_{Q^L} \tag{7}$$

where $\tilde{L}^d = n\,\tilde{l}^d$ is aggregate notional labor demand. For Y we have:

$$Y = n\,E(y) = n\,E\left[\tilde{y}^s \min(z^{\delta}, x, 1)\right]$$

$$= n\,\tilde{y}^s\,E\left[\min(z^{\delta}, x, 1)\right]$$

$$= \tilde{Y}^s\,\underbrace{E\left[\min(z^{\delta}, x, 1)\right]}_{Q^Y} \tag{8}$$

where $\tilde{Y}^s = n\,\tilde{y}^s$ is aggregate notional goods supply.

Shifting in the cycle, density g(z, x) will produce varying proportions of firms falling into the different regimes (see fig. 2) and - via the terms Q^L and Q^Y - varying levels of aggregate employment L and output Y. The term $Q^L = E\left[\min(z, x^{\gamma}, 1)\right]$ for example shows to what extent L is reduced in relation to notional labor demand $\tilde{L}^d$ due to insufficient labor supply ($z < 1$) and insufficient goods demand ($x' = x^{\gamma} < 1$). Q^L is given by

$$Q^L = E\left[\min(z, x', 1)\right] =$$

$$= \underbrace{\int_0^1\int_z^\infty z\, f(z, x')\, dx'dz}_{Q^L_{R+U}} + \underbrace{\int_0^1\int_{x'}^\infty x'f(z, x')\, dz\, dx'}_{Q^L_K} + \underbrace{\int_1^\infty\int_1^\infty f(z, x')\, dz\, dx'}_{Q^L_C} \tag{9}$$

where $f(z, x')$ is the density of z and x' (= x^γ). The ranges over which the integrals are taken are obvious from fig. 2 (see p. 29). The three components of Q^L - Q^L_{R+U}, Q^L_K and Q^L_C - reflect the employment shares of firms in the regimes R+U, K and C. In a completely analogous manner one may express Q^Y as

$$Q^Y = Q^Y_R + Q^Y_{K+U} + Q^Y_C ,$$

where the three components reflect output shares of firms in the respective regimes.

In order to derive concrete expressions for Q^L and Q^Y we assume that x and z are independent **lognormal:**

$$x = \exp(\mu_x + u_x\sigma_x) \qquad z = \exp(\mu_z + u_z\sigma_z) \qquad u_x, u_z \sim N(0, 1) \tag{10}$$

The variables $x' = x^\gamma$ and $z' = z^\delta$ are then also lognormal with $\mu'_x = \mu_x\gamma$, $\sigma'_x = \sigma_x\gamma$, $\mu'_z = \mu_z\delta$ and $\sigma'_z = \sigma_z\delta$. On this basis, Q^L and Q^Y can be defined as (relatively complicated) functions of the underlying distribution parameters μ_x, σ_x, μ_z, σ_z, γ and δ [Stalder (1989a)]. In short, we may write these functions as

$$Q^L = \xi_1(\bar{z}, \bar{x}; \gamma, \sigma_z, \sigma_x) \tag{11}$$

$$Q^Y = \xi_2(\bar{z}, \bar{x}; \delta, \sigma_z, \sigma_x) \quad , \tag{12}$$

where we have replaced the means μ_z and μ_x by the means $\bar{z}$ and $\bar{x}$, using

$$E(z) = \bar{z} = \exp(\mu_z + \sigma_z^2/2) \qquad \text{and} \qquad E(x) = \bar{x} = \exp(\mu_x + \sigma_x^2/2) \; . \tag{13}$$

The proportion of labor constrained firms ($l^s < l^d$), weighted by employment, is given by the labor share of the firms in regimes R and U and thus obtains as a function of the same arguments:

$$P_L = P_{R+U} = Q^L_{R+U}/Q^L = \xi_3(\bar{z}, \bar{x}; \gamma, \sigma_z, \sigma_x) \ . \tag{14}$$

Similar expressions define the other employment-weighted regime shares,[1]

$$P_K = Q^L_K/Q^L \quad \text{and} \quad P_C = Q^L_C/Q^L \ . \tag{15}$$

The mean $\bar{z}$ in (11), (12), and (14) can be identified with

$$\bar{z} = E(z) = E(l^s/\tilde{l}^d) = E(l^s)/\tilde{l}^d = L^s/\tilde{L}^d \ , \tag{16.1}$$

i.e. $\bar{z}$ can be equated to the ratio of aggregate labor supply $L^s = n\,E(l^s)$ to aggregate notional labor demand $\tilde{L}^d = n\,\tilde{l}^d$. For $\bar{x}$ we can substitute

$$\bar{x} = E(x) = E(y^d/\tilde{y}^s) = E(y^d)/\tilde{y}^s = Y^d/\tilde{Y}^s \ , \tag{16.2}$$

the ratio of aggregate goods demand to aggregate notional goods supply.

To demonstrate the general characteristics of these macro relationships we hold the 'dispersion parameters' σ_z and σ_x and the spillover elasticities γ and δ fixed and let $\bar{x}$ and $\bar{z}$ vary:

- First we let $\bar{x} = Y^d/\tilde{Y}^s$ assume progressively smaller values (smaller than $\bar{z}$ and 1), shifting the (x,z)-distribution downwards in fig. 2. As a result, Q^L_{R+U} and Q^L_C and hence P_L and P_C tend to 0, while Q^L_K and thus Q^L approach $E(x^\gamma)$ (consider the middle term in (9)), which is approximately equal to $\bar{x}^\gamma$.[2] In the limit we thus have $P_K = 1$ and $L \cong \tilde{L}^d\,\bar{x}^\gamma$; "all" firms

1. Output-weighted regime proportions can be defined correspondingly in terms of the components of Q^Y. Unweighted proportions are given by the three double integrals in (9) if the first and second one are written without z and x' in front of the density f(z, x').

2. $E(x^\gamma) = \bar{x}^\gamma \exp\left[\frac{\sigma_x^2}{2}(\gamma^2-\gamma)\right] \cong \bar{x}^\gamma$ for γ close to 1 and small σ_x.

are in a K-regime, i.e. constrained by goods demand.

- If we let $\bar{z} = L^s/\tilde{L}^d$ get sufficiently small compared to $\bar{x}$ and 1 (shifting the (x,z)-distribution to the left in fig. 2), we obtain in the limit $Q^L_K = Q^L_C = P_K = P_C = 0$, $Q^L = Q^L_{R+U} = \bar{z}$, $P_L = 1$ and $L = \tilde{L}^d\,\bar{z} = L^s$; "all" firms are are in the regimes R and U, i.e. constrained by labor supply.
- Finally, if we let both $\bar{x}$ and $\bar{z}$ become large compared to 1 (shifting the (x,z)-distribution north-east in fig. 2), we have in the limit $Q^L_K = Q^L_{R+U} = P_K = P_L = 0$, $Q^L = Q^L_C = 1$, $P_C = 1$ and $L = \tilde{L}^d$; "all" firms are in a C-regime, i.e. unconstrained (one may also say 'constrained by profitable capacities') so that L goes to its maximum value $\tilde{L}^d$.

The corresponding limiting situations for output determination are $Y = \tilde{Y}^s\,\bar{x} = Y^d$ (all firms in K+U), $Y \cong \tilde{Y}^s\,\bar{z}^{\delta}$ (all firms in R) and $Y = \tilde{Y}^s$ (all firms in C). In general, however, we expect to observe mixed situations where total employment and output are made up of contributions from firms in different regimes.

What is the role of the dispersion parameters σ_z and σ_x? Large σ_z and σ_x increase the smoothness of the transition between regimes at the aggregate level. Further $Q^L = \xi_1(.)$, $Q^Y = \xi_2(.)$ and thus L and Y are decreasing functions of σ_z and σ_x. Put differently, for given levels of aggregate demand and supply, strongly differing z and x values across firms have a negative impact on aggregate transactions in the labor and output markets. This property is usually termed 'structural mismatch' in the disequilibrium literature.

In the sequel we will also make use of the (unweighted) proportion of firms facing a goods demand y^d at least as large as notional supply $\tilde{y}^s$. This proportion $P_G(x > 1)$ is directly obtained from (10) and (13):

$$P_G = \Phi(\mu_x/\sigma_x) = \Phi[\ln(\bar{x})/\sigma_x - \sigma_x/2] \qquad \Phi(.): \text{ cumulative standard normal distribution function}$$

$$= \xi_4(\bar{x};\ \sigma_x) \qquad \text{(say).} \tag{17}$$

The aggregate model of this paper will be based on eqs. (7), (8), (11), (12), (14) and (17), which may be restated in the following form:

$$L = \tilde{L}^d\ \xi_1(\bar{z},\ \bar{x};\ \gamma,\ \sigma_z,\ \sigma_x) \tag{18.1}$$

$$Y = \tilde{Y}^s\ \xi_2(\bar{z},\ \bar{x};\ \delta,\ \sigma_z,\ \sigma_x) \tag{18.2}$$

$$P_L = \xi_3(\bar{z},\ \bar{x};\ \gamma,\ \sigma_z,\ \sigma_x) \tag{18.3}$$

$$P_G = \xi_4(\bar{x};\ \sigma_x)\ , \tag{18.4}$$

(18)

where $\bar{z} = E(z) = L^s/\tilde{L}^d$ and $\bar{x} = E(x) = Y^d/\tilde{Y}^s$.

These equations integrate all the preceding considerations, showing how the demands and supplies on the markets for labor and goods are related to aggregate transactions and regime proportions. The **mechanisms** described by system (18) are intuitively quite obvious and can be **summarized** as follows:

- $\tilde{L}^d$ and $\tilde{Y}^s$ in (18.1) and (18.2) are notional labor demand and notional output supply respectively; these magnitudes reflect total 'profitable capacities' in the economy, i.e., they correspond to the optimal labor input and output that firms would like to realize disregarding possible quantity constraints. The firms are confronted then on the labor market with a certain supply L^s and on the goods market with a certain demand Y^d. The ξ_1-function in (18.1) shows to what extent actual employment L gets reduced in relation to $\tilde{L}^d$ due to insufficient labor supply (low $\bar{z} = L^s/\tilde{L}^d$) and insufficient goods demand (low $\bar{x} = Y^d/\tilde{Y}^s$). For increasing $\bar{z}$ and $\bar{x}$ this function tends from below to 1 so that employment L converges to $\tilde{L}^d$; in the limit firms would fully realize notional labor demand. The ξ_1-function is "shaped" by the mismatch parameters σ_z and σ_x, expressing the diversity among firms with respect to $l^s/\tilde{l}^d$ and $y^d/\tilde{y}^s$, and the 'Keynesian' spillover elasticity γ, measuring how firms adjust effective labor demand in response to insufficient goods demand. In (18.2) the ξ_2-function shows, in a completely analogous manner, by how much aggregate output Y falls short of notional goods supply $\tilde{Y}^s$ due to insufficient goods demand and insufficient labor supply, δ being the the spillover elasticity that measures the reaction of effective goods supply to insufficient labor supply.

- Eqs. (18.3) and (18.4) define the mapping from $\bar{x}$ and $\bar{z}$ to P_L (proportion of labor-constrained firms) and P_G (proportion of firms with an excess of goods demand over notional supply). This mapping is illustrated in **fig. 4**,

Fig. 4: Location of (x,z)-distribution and regime proportions ($x = \tilde{y}^d/y^s$, $z = \tilde{l}^s/l^d$)

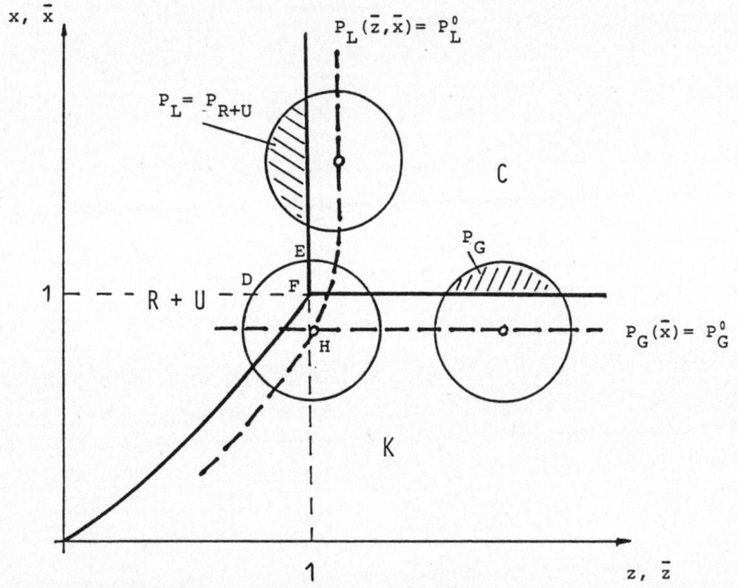

where the circle-like lines are to be viewed as isodensity lines that include say 99% of the total mass of a shifting (x,z)-distribution. The location of this distribution, depending on $\bar{x}$ and $\bar{z}$, determines P_L and P_G.[3] P_L tends to 0 (1) for increasing (decreasing) $\bar{z}$; if $\bar{x}$ increases, P_L tends towards a maximum value determined by $\bar{z}$. P_G depends only on $\bar{x}$ and is slightly below 0.5 at $\bar{x} = 1$ (assuming σ_x to be small, comp. (17)). For small values of σ_x and σ_z the mass of the distribution is concentrated close to $(\bar{x}, \bar{z})$, implying that P_L and P_G approach (0,1)-step functions.

Aggregate goods demand Y^d, aggregate notional goods supply and labor demand, $\tilde{Y}^s$ and $\tilde{L}^d$, and aggregate labor supply L^s will be explained in the empirical part of this study by more or less conventional econometric equations. The corresponding dependent variables are unobserved.[4] System (18) defines however a transformation which maps vector $V' = (Y^d, \tilde{Y}^s, \tilde{L}^d, L^s)$ onto vector $W' = (L, Y, P_L, P_G)$, whose components are assumed to be observable. Maximum likelihood estimation seems thus possible in principle. In the following we explain how P_L and P_G can be measured on basis of Swiss business survey data. Then we show that the mapping $V \to W$ is one-to-one, which is a prerequisite to the ML-estimation of the model.[5]

The main **Swiss business survey** (KOF-ETH Konjunkturtest) is organized somewhat differently from the harmonized EEC-surveys; in particular, firms

---

3. Strictly speaking, fig. 4 shows unweighted proportions whereas P_L as determined by (18.3) is an employment-weighted proportion.
4. In countries with reliable unemployment statistics labor supply could be calculated as the sum of employment and unemployment.
5. One might of course choose another set of transformation equations to relate the unobservable variables to observable ones. It is however essential to include (18.1) and (18.2) since all regime proportions are homogeneous of degree 0 in V whereas the output and employment equation are homogeneous of degree 1.

are not explicitly asked about the binding constraint of their operations (demand, capacity, supply of labor, other causes). Considering several proxies, it seems best to derive measures for P_L and P_G as follows:

- P_L, the proportion of firms rationed in the labor market ($l^s < l^d$), is measured as the proportion of firms reporting the available work force as "too small".
- P_G, the proportion of firms facing a goods demand y^d that is larger than their notional supply $\tilde{y}^s$ ('profitable capacities'), is measured as the proportion of firms reporting capacities as "too small". Note that we do not identify this answering proportion with the variable P_C of our model, although only firms in the C-Regime are effectively capacity-constrained ($y = \tilde{y}^s < y^d$). P_G additionally includes the D-E-F part of the R-region in fig. 4, i.e. firms for which demand y^d exceeds profitable capacities $\tilde{y}^s$ but whose actual output is given by effective supply y^s which is smaller than $\tilde{y}^s$ due to a labor shortage ($y = y^s < \tilde{y}^s$). It is not quite clear how firms in such a situation will assess their capacities. The assumption however that only firms in the C-regime will report capacities as "too small" is empirically untenable since in boom periods this answering proportion usually adds up with P_L to more than 1. The two regions must therefore overlap (in one way or another).

Both surveys (assessment of the work force and capacity) involve a "sufficient"-category besides the answering possibilities "too small" and "too large". The model of this paper on the other hand is bipartite, i.e. the events $l^s = l^d$ and $x = 1$ ($y^d = \tilde{y}^s$) are included only as borderline cases with mass 0. To bring the survey into line with the model, the empirical answering proportions in the "sufficient"-category must be allotted to the other two categories. A natural way to do this is to assume that firms choose the "sufficient"-answer when $\ln(l^s/l^d)$ and $\ln(y^d/\tilde{y}^s)$ respectively lie in a symmetrical indifference interval around 0 $[-c,c]$. The proportion $P_G\ (y^d > \tilde{y}^s)$ for instance is then given as $P_G = \Phi\left[[\Phi^{-1}(P^-) - \Phi^{-1}(P^+)]/2\right]$, where P^- and P^+ are the proportions of firms reporting capacities as "too small" ($\ln(y^d/\tilde{y}^s) > c$) and "too large" ($\ln(y^d/\tilde{y}^s) < -c$) respectively.

We show now that the mapping defined by (18) is one-to-one, i.e. that there exists an unique inverse $W' = (L, Y, P_L, P_G) \rightarrow V' = (Y^d, \tilde{Y}^s, \tilde{L}^d, L^s)$. As a monotonically increasing function, $\xi_4(.)$ in (18.4) can be inverted:

$$\bar{x} = \xi_4^{-1}(P_G; \sigma_x) = \psi_4(P_G, \sigma_x) \quad \text{(say)} . \tag{18.4'}$$

For given $\bar{x}$, $\xi_3(.)$ in (18.3) decreases monotonically with $\bar{z}$ and has thus an inverse as well; inserting (18.4') for $\bar{x}$, we may write

$$\bar{z} = \psi_3(P_L, P_G; \gamma, \sigma_z, \sigma_x) . \tag{18.3'}$$

Eqs. (18.3') and (18.4') map (P_L, P_G) uniquely on $(\bar{x}, \bar{z})$, as visualized by the intersection H of the two loci $P_G(\bar{x}) = P_G^o$ and $P_L(\bar{z}, \bar{x}) = P_L^o$ in fig. 4. Substituting (18.3') and (18.4') into (18.1) and (18.2) and solving for $\tilde{L}^d$ and $\tilde{Y}^s$, we obtain (19.1) and (19.2) below; inserting (18.3') and (19.1) into the definition $\bar{z} = L^s/\tilde{L}^d$, we get the unique expression (19.3) for L^s; finally, (18.4') and (19.2) and the definition $\bar{x} = Y^d/\tilde{Y}^s$ uniquely determine Y^d (19.4):

$$\left.\begin{aligned}
\tilde{L}^d &= L\,\psi_1(P_L, P_G; \gamma, \sigma_z, \sigma_x) && (19.1)\\
\tilde{Y}^s &= Y\,\psi_2(P_L, P_G; \gamma, \delta, \sigma_z, \sigma_x) && (19.2)\\
L^s &= L\,\psi_5(P_L, P_G; \gamma, \sigma_z, \sigma_x) && (19.3)\\
Y^d &= Y\,\psi_6(P_L, P_G; \gamma, \delta, \sigma_z, \sigma_x) && (19.4)
\end{aligned}\right\} \quad (19)$$

We have thus established that the mapping $V \rightarrow W$ is one-to-one, (19) being the inverse of (18).

3.2 Introduction of error terms

Transformation (18) or (19) relate the unobservable variables Y^d, $\tilde{Y}^s$, $\tilde{L}^d$ and L^s to the observables L, Y, P_L and P_G. On this basis, the parameters of the structural equations for Y^d, $\tilde{Y}^s$, $\tilde{L}^d$ and L^s (to be specified in section 5 below) can be estimated by maximum likelihood. Beforehand, we must however discuss how to properly introduce macroeconomic error terms. Errors can arise in the present context from different sources:

a) The micro model (especially the assumption of constant spillover elasticities γ and δ) and the aggregation procedure (the assumption of log-normal and independent x and z) may be not fully adequate.

b) The business survey proxies P_L and P_G (and possibly other variables) may be subject to measurement errors.

c) The structural equations for Y^d, $\tilde{Y}^s$, $\tilde{L}^d$ and L^s are likely to involve specification errors.

Due to the nonlinearity of the transformation equations, these different types of errors do not translate themselves into simple econometric disturbances that capture all potential inadequacies simultaneously. Two tractable solutions are available:

A) On may add error terms $\omega_1,..\omega_4$ to the right-hand side of (18) and substitute deterministic equations for Y^d, $\tilde{Y}^s$, $\tilde{L}^d$ and L^s (deterministic expressions are henceforth marked by "hats", the transformation parameters γ, δ, σ_z, σ_x are dropped if not important in the context):

$$L = \hat{\tilde{L}}^d\, \xi_1\left[\hat{L}^s/\hat{\tilde{L}}^d,\ \hat{Y}^d/\hat{\tilde{Y}}^s\right] + \omega_1$$

$$Y = \hat{\tilde{Y}}^s\, \xi_2\left[\hat{L}^s/\hat{\tilde{L}}^d,\ \hat{Y}^d/\hat{\tilde{Y}}^s\right] + \omega_2 \tag{18*}$$

$$P_L = \xi_3\left[\hat{L}^s/\hat{\tilde{L}}^d, \hat{Y}^d/\hat{\tilde{Y}}^s\right] + \omega_3 \qquad P_G = \xi_4\left[\hat{Y}^d/\hat{\tilde{Y}}^s\right] + \omega_4$$

System (18*) is the **'reduced form'**-representation of the observable endogenous variables L, Y, P_L and P_G. It can be estimated my ML, assuming that $\omega' = (\omega_1, \omega_2, \omega_3, \omega_4)$ is i.i.d. as $N(0, \Omega)$. Numerous cross-equation restrictions must be taken into account (the same structural and transformation parameters show up in different equations). This approach accounts in an appropriate manner for errors of type b) and possibly a) above. Errors of type c) however are troublesome. Such errors, which must realistically be expected (all the more so since one is forced to parametrize the structural equations parsimoniously), will translate themselves into ω in a highly nonlinear fashion. The resulting residuals are heteroscedastic and correlated across equations and may even have nonzero means that depend on the values of the explanatory variables.

B) Alternatively, one may specify the equations for Y^d, $\tilde{Y}^s$, $\tilde{L}^d$ and L^s stochastically, e.g. with lognormal errors, and use (19) to link the unobserved dependent variables with the oberservables L, Y, P_L and P_G:

$$\begin{aligned} Y\,\psi_6(P_L, P_G) &= Y^d = \hat{Y}^d \exp(u_1) \\ Y\,\psi_2(P_L, P_G) &= \tilde{Y}^s = \hat{\tilde{Y}}^s \exp(u_2) \\ L\,\psi_1(P_L, P_G) &= \tilde{L}^d = \hat{\tilde{L}}^d \exp(u_3) \\ L\,\psi_5(P_L, P_G) &= L^s = \hat{L}^s \exp(u_4) \end{aligned} \tag{19*}$$

Assuming that $u' = (u_1, u_2, u_3, u_4)$ is i.i.d. $N(0, \Omega)$, it is again possible to estimate the structural parameters in $\hat{Y}^d$, $\hat{\tilde{Y}}^s$, $\hat{\tilde{L}}^d$ and $\hat{L}^s$, along with the transformation parameters in the ψ-functions, by ML. Cross equation restrictions appear now only in form of the latter (unless the structural equations are subject to cross restrictions). The problem with this approach is that errors of type a) and b), in particular measurement errors in the proxies P_L and P_G, are not adequately represented by the u's. To be sure, P_L and P_G are stochastic endogenous variables. But because of the nonlinearity of the model with respect to P_L and P_G, measurement errors in these variables are not appropriately captured by he u's. On the other hand, measurement errors in L and Y (which are less likely though) can be interpreted as common components in (u_1, u_2) and (u_3, u_4) respectively.

There is no clear advantage of one of the above approaches over the other. Forced to make a choice, we opt for (19*) as basis of our empirical model for the following reasons. As the theoretical foundation of the structural equations is notoriously weak and parsimonious specifications will be a necessity, it is probably wise to put the emphasis on specification errors. Moreover, (19*) lends itself in a straightforward manner to dynamic specifications that involve lagged values of the latent variables Y^d, $\tilde{Y}^s$, $\tilde{L}^d$ and L^s, since these can easily be expressed in terms of past observables and transformation parameters (lagged left-hand sides of (19*)).

3.3 Adopting an econometrically tractable approximation

It is evident from the derivation of (19*) that the ψ-functions do not exist in closed form. They arise from inverting (18), where the ξ-functions contain several integrals that can be evaluated only numerically. The residuals in (19*) are thus only defined as outcomes of relatively complicated numerical iteration routines. Dealing with such algorithms (for $4 \cdot T$ residuals) within a likelihood function whose maximization requires itself a large number of function evaluations would make things numerically very tedious. We shall adopt therefore a closed-form approximation to (19*). By considering how the ψ-functions depend on P_L and P_G, it may be shown that (19*) can be approximated by

$$Y\,(1-P_L)^{-\alpha_Y}\,(1-P_G)^{-\kappa_Y} = Y^d = \hat{Y}^d\, e^{u_1} \qquad (19^o.1)$$

$$Y\,(1-P_L)^{-\alpha_Y}\,P_G^{-\kappa_Y} = \tilde{Y}^s = \hat{\tilde{Y}}^s\, e^{u_2} \qquad (19^o.2)$$

$$L\,(1-P_L)^{-\alpha_L}\,P_G^{-\kappa_L} = \tilde{L}^d = \hat{\tilde{L}}^d\, e^{u_3} \qquad (19^o.3) \qquad (19^o)$$

$$L\,P_L^{-\alpha_L} = L^s = \hat{L}^s\, e^{u_4}\,, \qquad (19^o.4)$$

with $\alpha_Y, \alpha_L, \kappa_Y, \kappa_L > 0$.

This formulation corresponds largely to the one suggested by Lambert (1984). Note however that P_G is defined here as $P_G\,(y^d > \tilde{y}^s)$ whereas Lambert uses the proportion of micro markets in excess demand $(y^d > y^s)$ as an indicator of tension in the goods market. As a result, our P_G is given as $\bar{x} = Y^d/\tilde{Y}^s$ and thus - unlike Lambert's indicator - independent of rationing in the labor market. This entails a different formulation of (19°.1) and, neglecting stochastic terms, introduces a certain recursivity into the model (see next section).[6]

System (19°) lends itself to the following **intuitive interpretation.** On the right-hand side of (19°) we have the stochastic equations for goods demand Y^d, notional goods supply and labor demand, $\tilde{Y}^s$ and $\tilde{L}^d$, and labor supply L^s. On the left-hand side, the expressions involving P_L and P_G can be viewed as 'disequilibrium correction terms', linking the unobserved demands

6. On a more basic level, our aggregation procedure differs from Lambert's in that we have introduced spillovers between the labor and goods market at the micro (firm) level whereas Lambert first aggregates over labor and goods markets without spillovers and introduces then spillovers in a more ad hoc-fashion at the aggregate level. This difference in the theoretical model is however blurred in the final approximate formulation.

and supplies to the realized levels of output and employment. For instance, if "all" firms are labor constrained ($P_L \to 1$), (19°.4) implies that L tends to L^s, i.e., households could fully realize their labor supply (in the limit). If $P_L < 1$, we have $L < L^s$ and there is some unemployment. In order for L to correspond to $\tilde{L}^d$ - and for Y to correspond to $\tilde{Y}^s$ - we must have $P_L \to 0$ ("no" firm is labor constrained) and $P_G \to 1$ ("all" firms face sufficient demand). Finally, output Y corresponds to goods demand Y^d if both P_G and P_L go to zero. Notice that P_G and P_L are endogenously determined in (19°), and the functional forms ensure that these proportions are confined to the unit interval. It is further instructive to note that P_G and P_L take the role which, in a usual equilibrium model, is played by the price and the wage: P_G for example adjusts in each period in such a way that the first to equations imply the same level of transactions, Y.

3.4 Accuracy of the approximation

In the following we want to check how well the terms involving P_L and P_G in (19°) approximate the exact ψ-functions in (19*). However, instead of directly comparing (19°) with (19*), we draw another parallel which is absolutely tantamount but easier to establish and more instructive as to the functioning of (19°): We solve (19°) for the endogenous variables L, Y, P_L and P_G and compare the resulting reduced-form expressions with the original exact system (18).

Determination of P_L and P_G :

To derive the approximate reduced form for P_G we simply have to devide (19°.1) by (19°.2), yielding

$$\left(\frac{P_G}{1 - P_G}\right)^{\kappa_Y} = \frac{Y^d}{\tilde{Y}^s} = \bar{x} \qquad \text{or} \qquad P_G = \left(1 + e^{-(\ln \bar{x})/\kappa_Y}\right)^{-1} . \tag{20}$$

With a suitable choice of κ_Y - related to parameter σ_x of the exact model - this 'logistic' function is a good approximation to (18.4).[7]

To derive the reduced form for P_L, we devide (19°.3) by (19°.4), yielding

$$\left(\frac{P_L}{1 - P_L}\right)^{\alpha_L} = \frac{\tilde{L}^d \, P_G^{\kappa_L}}{L^s} = \frac{P_G^{\kappa_L}}{\bar{z}} \quad . \tag{21}$$

Replacing P_G by (20), we obtain P_L as a function of $\bar{x}$ and $\bar{z}$. This function mimics the basic properties of (18.3): P_L goes asymtotically to 1 (0) for small (large) values of $\bar{z}$; P_L is an increasing function of $\bar{x}$ but cannot exceed a certain maximum, defined by setting $P_G = 1$ in (21). Note in this respect that the term $P_G^{\kappa_L}$ measures in (19°) the spillover from the goods market onto labor demand; the expression $\tilde{L}^d \, P_G^{\kappa_L}$ in (21) represents thus effective labor demand L^d. For large $\bar{x}$ ("all" firms have $x > 1$) P_G tends to 1 so that $L^d = \tilde{L}^d \, P_G^{\kappa_L}$ converges to $\tilde{L}^d$. In the limit there are no Keynesian spillovers and the proportion P_L is solely a function of $L^s/\tilde{L}^d = \bar{z}$, parametrized by α_L. In general, however, α_L captures the firm level dispersion with respect to l^s/l^d, l^d being **effective** labor demand. According to (1), l^d depends on x^γ. Therefore, α_L not only takes the role of parameter σ_z of the exact model (dispersion of $l^s/\tilde{l}^d$) but also depends on parameters σ_x (dispersion of x) and γ. This is increasingly the case if $\bar{x}$ is low. Consequently, treating α_L in the approximate model as a constant parameter seems

---

7. It is well-known that the standard normal distribution $\Phi(h)$ is closely approximated by the logistic distribution $L(h) = [1 + \exp(-h\lambda)]^{-1}$ with λ set to 1.6 [Amemiya (1981)]. This suggests $\kappa_Y = \sigma_x/1.6$. Note however from (17) that the approximation neglects the 'correction term' $\sigma_x/2$ arising from lognormality (which can be assumed to be small though).

somewhat problematical.[8]

Determination of L and Y:

To derive the reduced forms for L and Y we first rearrange the third and second equation of (19°) as follows:

$$L = \tilde{L}^d \, (1 - P_L)^{\alpha_L} \quad P_G^{\kappa_L}$$

$$Y = \tilde{Y}^s \, (1 - P_L)^{\alpha_Y} \quad P_G^{\kappa_Y} \quad .$$

If we look now at the exact formulations (18.1) and (18.2), it is evident that assessing the accuracy of the approximation amounts to comparing

$$Q^L = \xi_1(\bar{z}, \bar{x}; \gamma, \sigma_z, \sigma_x) \quad \text{with} \quad \overset{o}{Q}{}^L = (1 - P_L)^{\alpha_L} \quad P_G^{\kappa_L} \quad \text{and}$$

$$Q^Y = \xi_2(\bar{z}, \bar{x}; \delta, \sigma_z, \sigma_x) \quad \text{with} \quad \overset{o}{Q}{}^Y = (1 - P_L)^{\alpha_Y} \quad P_G^{\kappa_Y} \quad , \tag{22}$$

where P_G and P_L have to be expressed via (20) and (21) in terms of $\bar{z}$ and $\bar{x}$. We know that Q^L and Q^Y are increasing functions of $\bar{x}$ and $\bar{z}$, tending asymtotically to 1 for large $\bar{x}$ and $\bar{z}$ (limiting situation of a pure C-regime). The approximations $\overset{o}{Q}{}^L$ and $\overset{o}{Q}{}^Y$ exhibit the same characteristics since P_G and P_L, according to (20) and (21), tend to 1 and 0 respectively for increasing $\bar{x}$ and $\bar{z}$. To examine the relationship between the approximation and the exact model in some more detail, we consider three particular situations (a, b and c below) and then perform a small numerical experiment.

(a) We set labor supply $\tilde{L}^s$ equal to effective labor demand $L^d = \tilde{L}^d \, P_G^{\kappa_L}$. In such an "aggregate labor market equilibrium" the third and forth equation of (19°) imply (see (21)):

---

8. Put differently, all combinations of $\tilde{L}^d$ and P_G that result in the same L^d imply in the approximation the same P_L. This is not exactly so in the theoretical model as the dispersion of l^s/l^d changes with P_G.

$$(1 - P_L) = P_L = 0.5, \quad L/L^s = 0.5^{\alpha_L} < 1 \quad \text{and} \quad \frac{L^s - L}{L^s} = 1 - 0.5^{\alpha_L} > 0 \;. \qquad (23)$$

Adopting the terminology of Sneessens and Drèze (1986), the last expression in (23) is labelled 'structural unemployment rate at equilibrium', SURE. It measures unemployment that arises not from a lack of aggregate demand but from the dispersion, or mismatch, of demand and supply at the micro level. SURE is an increasing function of the 'mismatch parameter' α_L.

(b) We rule out Keynesian spillovers by setting $\bar{x}$ to a large value ($P_G \to 1$) and choose $\bar{z}$ such that a certain proportion of firms is constrained by labor supply ($0 < P_L < 1$). The resulting reduction of employment L in relation to $\tilde{L}^d$ (rationing) is captured in the approximation by the factor $(1 - P_L)^{\alpha_L}$. The associated reduction of output Y in relation to $\tilde{Y}^s$ ('repressed inflation' spillover) is measured by $(1 - P_L)^{\alpha_Y}$. Consequently, according to the restriction $\delta < 1$ of the exact model (concave production function; see section 2.2), we should expect in the approximation $\alpha_Y < \alpha_L$. A proportional spillover ($\delta = 1$) would imply $\alpha_Y = \alpha_L$.

(c) We exclude rationing of labor demand by setting $\bar{z}$ to a large value ($P_L \to 0$) and choose $\bar{x}$ such that a certain proportion of firms is rationed by goods demand ($0 < P_G < 1$). This leads to a reduction of output in relation to $\tilde{Y}^s$ by factor $P_G^{\kappa_Y}$. The resulting 'Keynesian' spillover on employment is represented by $P_G^{\kappa_L}$. In order for the approximate model to generate the empirical productivity cycle (labor hoarding), corresponding to the restriction $\gamma < 1$ in the exact model, we must have $\kappa_L < \kappa_Y$.[9]

9. Compare however footnote 4, p. 28. In the empirical model we shall set $\kappa_L = \kappa_Y$ and allow for the productivity cycle by amending the labor demand equation by a dynamical adjustment mechanism.

We want to check now the goodness of the approximation quantitatively by performing a numerical experiment. To simplify things somewhat (without neglecting important numerical aspects) we set $\gamma = \delta = 1$ (proportional spillovers). With this assumption, the two comparisons in (22) coincide, i.e. we only have to compare

$$Q = \xi(\bar{z}, \bar{x}; \sigma_z, \sigma_x) \quad \text{with} \quad \mathring{Q} = (1 - P_R)^{\alpha} \; P_G^{\kappa} .$$

Calculating Q is a rather tedious because the double integrals in (9), even though x and z are assumed to be independent across firms, cannot be split into univariate normal integrals for which standard numerical routines are available.[10] To evaluate Q we must therefore implement a method of numerical integration. We employ **Simpson's Rule.**[11] Fixing the dispersion parameters at $\sigma_z = 0.05$ and $\sigma_x = 0.075$, we let $\bar{z} = L^s/\tilde{L}^d$ and $\bar{x} = Y^d/\tilde{Y}^s$ assume the following values:

---

10. This, after all, was the reason to adopt an approximation in the first place. Based on (10) and (13), the middle double integral in (9) for example can be brought into the form $Q_K^L =$

$$\bar{x} \int_{-\infty}^{\frac{-\ln \bar{x}}{\sigma_x} + \frac{\sigma_x}{2}} \frac{1}{\sqrt{2\pi}} e^{-(u_x - \sigma_x)^2/2} \, \Phi\left(\frac{\ln \bar{z} - \sigma_z^2/2 - \ln \bar{x} + \sigma_x^2/2 - u_x \sigma_x}{\sigma_z} \right) du_x,$$

where $\Phi(.)$ is the standard normal integral.

11. The method, to be applied to terms like the one reported in footnote 10, can be described in short as as follows: We subdivide the range of integration into N equally wide intervalls (starting at a lower limit where the integrand is virtually zero), replace the integrand in each intervall by a quadratic polynominal that agrees with the exact function at the end points and in the middle of the intervall and finally add up the integrals of the N adjoining polynominals. This is of course an approximation of Q as well; setting N = 30 the result can however be regarded as 'exact' for all practical purposes.

$\bar{z} = (0.85, 0.9, 0.95, 1.0, 1.05, 1.1)$

$\bar{x} = (0.85, 0.9, 0.95, 1.0, 1.05, 1.1)$

This produces 36 constellations of excess supply of labor and excess demand for goods for which the 'exact' Q-values are computed using the above-mentioned numerical method. The values range from 0.819 to 0.995 and are displayed in fig. 5.[12] Next, using (20) and (21), we replace P_R and P_G in $\mathring{Q}$ by $\bar{z}$ and $\bar{x}$, yielding an expression of the form

$$\mathring{Q} = \mathring{\xi}(\bar{z}, \bar{x}; \alpha, \kappa) .$$

The approximate $\mathring{Q}$-values are calculated then for the same 36 constellations of $\bar{z}$ and $\bar{x}$ with a 'suitable' choice of α and κ. One might, for instance, derive κ from σ_x (see footnote 7) and adjust α in such a way as to make the approximation $\mathring{Q}$ exactly equal to Q at $\bar{z} = \bar{x} = 1$ (an average situation); this implies $\kappa = \sigma_x/1.6 = 0.047$ and $\alpha = 0.040$. We prefer however to adjust κ and α optimally by regressing the exact Q-values on $\mathring{Q} = \mathring{\xi}(\bar{z}, \bar{x}; \alpha, \kappa)$ over the 36 pairs of $\bar{z}$ and $\bar{x}$. This nonlinear regression produces $\kappa = 0.039$, $\alpha = 0.042$ and $R^2 = 0.997$. The RMSE of $\mathring{Q}$ in relation to Q is 0.003. The values of $\mathring{Q}$ are confronted in fig. 5 with the exact Q-values.[13] The high agreement between the two series suggests that the approximation works satisfactory.

---

12. P_L and P_G, calculated on basis of (14) and (17), range from 0.001 to 0.997 and 0.016 to 0.895 respectively.
13. As a by-product, fig. 5 gives a good grasp of the functioning of the model (effect of insufficient labor supply ($\bar{z}$) and lack of goods demand ($\bar{x}$) on aggregate output and employment).

FIG. 5: 'Exact' values of Q (x) (numerical integration) and approximation by the model (+)

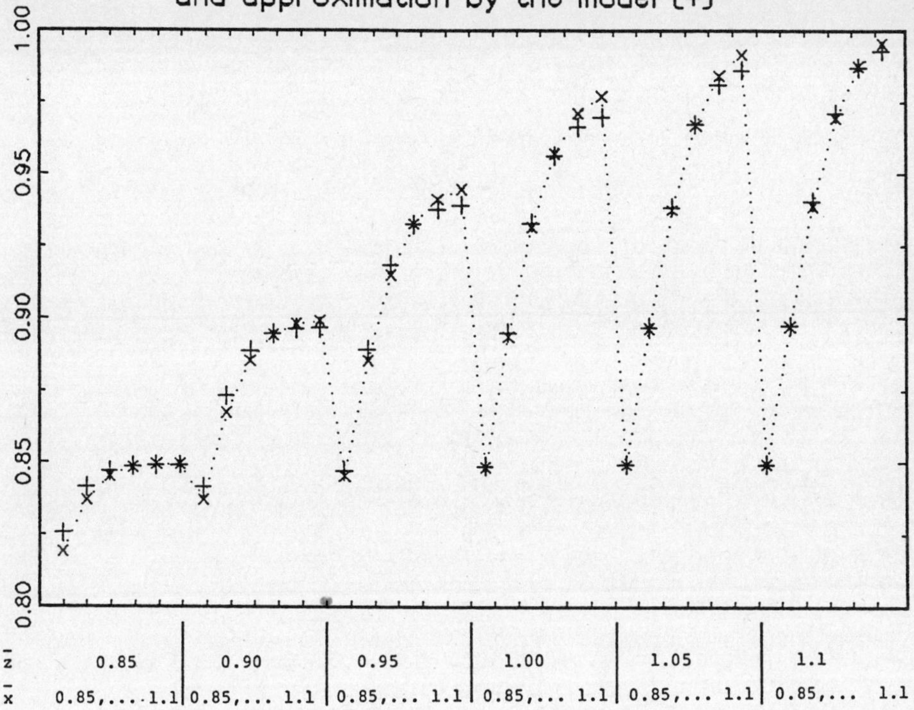

4. MODIFIED VERSION: BUFFER ROLE OF INVENTORIES AND UNFILLED ORDERS

According to the firm level model, goods demand y^d acts as a potential constraint on output and - if smaller than $\tilde{y}^s$ - spills over onto labor demand. Such immediate rationing and spillover effects, captured in the aggregate model by the P_G-terms, may seem somewhat unrealistic in a quarterly model because firms should be expected to smooth production in relation to current demand, using output inventories and unfilled orders as buffer stocks. It has been argued, e.g. by Blinder (1980, 1981), that this kind of behavior calls in question the min-condition: output y can be temporarily larger than current demand y^d, and $y < y^d$ does not necessarily mean that demand gets rationed.

It is certainly true that buffer stocks interfere with the short-run link between current demand and output. Blinder's conclusion however that this robs disequilibrium models much of their interest goes too far. To be sure, firms may at first tend to interpret a negative demand shock as a transitory event and hold constant or even keep on expanding production. But if the slack of demand turns out to be more sustained than expected, the combination of low current demand, persistent unfavorable demand expectations and by then excessive inventories or insufficient unfilled orders may well result in an even more drastic cutback of production and spill over into the labor market. Conversely, in situations where output is constrained by profitable capacities $\tilde{y}^s$ or effective supply y^s, drawing down inventories may prevent a rationing of goods demand.[1] But as far as **output** determination is concerned, supply constraints remain relevant nevertheless. The

1. Imports introduce additional flexibility so that a notable rationing of demand and an associated spillover onto labor supply seem indeed quite unlikely. Therefore, our model has been specified without such a spillover effect to begin with.

conclusion from these considerations is that the existence of buffer stocks will probably give rise to a dynamic modification of the short-run link between current demand and output but does not call in question the disequilibrium framework fundamentally. In the following, we shall amend the model of the preceding pages along these lines.

Before turning to the concrete specification of buffer behavior, some brief remarks as to the general empirical record of the production smoothing model are in order. It is well known that production has often been found to be more volatile than sales [Blinder (1986)]. To reconcile the smoothing model with this finding, cost shocks and accelerator effects were introduced. But the extended models did still not perform well when overidentifying restrictions were tested with aggregate time series [Christiano and Eichenbaum (1987), Miron and Zeldes (1988)]. On the other hand, several studies using disaggregated data have supported the hypothesis of production smoothing [Ghali (1987), Seitz (1988), Rahiala and Terasvirta (1988)]. Fair (1989) claims that previous negative results were mainly due to unreliable data. Recent studies for Swiss manufacturing based on survey data also provide strong evidence for production smoothing, especially when unfilled orders are taken into account as buffer stocks (besides output inventories) and demand is accordingly measured as order inflow (instead of sales); see Etter, Nerlove and Willson (1989), Salzgeber (1989) and Stalder (1990). However, despite these more favorable recent results, the overall evidence for production smoothing still looks rather ambiguous. Therefore, we shall regard the specification of buffer behavior set forth below as a variant to the basic disequilibrium model. It remains to be seen whether the buffer version of the model or the original specification without buffer stocks, as summarized in eqs. (19°) above, prove superior in the empirical application.

The production smoothing role of buffer stocks can be substantiated, in the context of imperfect competition, with convex cost functions or specific costs of changing the output level (a). In addition, firms usually have to decide on output and prices before they know demand (b); note in this respect that for the individual firm demand typically involves a considerable random element, entailing the problem of a low 'signal to noise' ratio. For both reasons (a and b), firms must be assumed to decide on output and prices on basis of some concept of 'expected demand' $E(y^d)$, which - due to motive (a) - will refer to the longer term. Differences between actual demand y^d and output y are absorbed by buffer stocks. Assuming that firms use either output inventories (iv) or unfilled orders (uo) as buffers, we have the following firm-level definitions of beginning-of-period stocks:

$$iv = iv_{-1} + y_{-1} - y^d_{-1} \qquad uo = uo_{-1} + y^d_{-1} - y_{-1}. \tag{24}$$

Demand y^d corresponds to sales and order inflow respectively.

Firms' demand expectations are of course interlinked with their price decision[2] and will influence - through the investment process - the time path of 'profitable capacities' $\tilde{y}^s$. In the longer run, firms can be expected to aim at an equilibrium of the form

$$E(y^d) = \tilde{y}^s \tag{25}$$

by setting prices and adjusting capacities accordingly. As an extreme form of production smoothing one might think of a policy in which firms keep output y always at the level of profitable capacities $\tilde{y}^s$. Such behavior is however hardly optimal: First, the more complete the detachment of y from

2. The following discussion elicits some implications as to how prices are set. However, as noted in the introduction, we do not formally endogenize the price decision of firms, which is admittedly a limitation of the present model.

fluctuations in y^d, the larger are the buffer stocks required on average, which is either costly (iv) or likely to deter customers (uo). Second, as can be seen from (24), the random element in y^d would give rise to non-stationary processes of iv and uo. It is thus clear that optimizing behavior implicates a certain feedback from iv and uo - in relation to 'normal' or 'desired' levels (*) - onto the output and price decision. For example, if a firm has iv > iv* it will tend to reduce output y in relation to $\tilde{y}^s$ and lower prices in order to raise expected sales. This renders the process of iv stationary. A stronger feedback increases the variance of output and prices but reduces the variance of iv and thus allows the firm to operate with a lower target level iv*.[3]

We show now how the micro model of eqs. (1) to (4) can be amended in order to account for production smoothing and turn then to the consequences of this modification in the macro model.

The feedback from iv and uo to 'desired production' y^{des} (to be distinguished from actual y, which may be subject to capacity or labor supply constraints) can be specified as

$$y^{des} = \begin{cases} E(y^d)(iv/iv^*)^{-\eta_1} & \text{(firms producing to stock)} \\ E(y^d)(uo/uo^*)^{\eta_2} & \text{(firms producing to order)} \end{cases} \qquad \eta_1, \eta_2 > 0 \quad (26.1)$$

The target levels iv* and uo* are treated as constants. As far as output inventories are concerned, this assumption is supported by empirical studies showing that desired inventories are related to expectations of longer-term

3. This intuitive result of a negative (positive) impact of beginning-of-period inventories on production (sales) can be derived more rigorously; see e.g. Blinder (1981) who argues with differences between the shadow value of inventories and the going market price.

'normal' sales and possibly 'normal' levels of some other variables.[4]

To clarify the essence of this modelling approach, note that buffer stocks (iv and uo) as defined by (24) reflect accumulated past differences between demand y^d and output y. Within the period, y^{des} is thus predetermined with respect to current demand y^d, which is a realistic assumption in a quarterly model. In the long run, y^{des} according to (26.1) basically follows the path of expected demand, $E(y^d)$. However, accumulated buffer stocks function as kind of an error correction term, entailing deviations of desired output from expected demand that prevent buffer stocks from becoming non-stationary. Transitory fluctuations in y^d that offset one another over short time periods will leave y^{des} largely unaffected. Persistent swings in y^d however produce stronger adjustment in y^{des}.

Using (25), we can replace $E(y^d)$ in (26.1) by $\tilde{y}^s$. Demand expectations do then no longer show up in the model explicitly but are assumed to be reflected in the development of profitable capacities. This substitution is not quite innocuous since demand expectations relevant to the output decision may involve a shorter time horizon than those relevant to the formation of production capacities. To the extent that the former are more volatile than the latter, our specification will overstate the degree of production

---

4. Compare e.g. Maccini and Rossana (1981). The question of "slow adjustment to rapidly changing inventory targets" (a) vs. "rapid adjustment to slowly changing inventory targets" (b) has been studied for Switzerland by Fluri and Spörndli (1981) on basis of qualititive micro-level survey data. Although somewhat inconclusive, their results are rather in line with view (b).

smoothing.[5] To introduce now the buffer mechanism into the original **firm model** we simply have to redefine x in (3) and (4) as $x = y^{des}/\tilde{y}^s$, which, according to (25) and (26.1) is

$$x = \frac{y^{des}}{\tilde{y}^s} = \begin{cases} (iv/iv^*)^{-\eta_1}, & iv = iv_{-1} + y_{-1} - y^d_{-1} \\ (uo/uo^*)^{\eta_2}, & uo = uo_{-1} + y^d_{-1} - y_{-1}. \end{cases} \tag{26.2}$$

Whereas firms can always produce less than $\tilde{y}^s$ - in order to get rid of excessive inventories or to restore insufficient unfilled orders - it is more difficult for them to do the opposite, i.e. to push y beyond $\tilde{y}^s$ in order to build up too low inventories or to reduce unacceptably long delivery lags. Actually, by combining (26.2) with (4), we are ruling out such a possibility completely; y^s and $\tilde{y}^s$ are treated as rigid upper bounds for y. Consequently, firms with $iv < iv^*$ or $uo > uo^*$ dispose of only one short-run channel by which they can bring iv and uo into line with target levels: By increasing next period's price, thereby reducing expected order inflow. Although such an asymmetry between the reaction of firms in recessions (reducing output, possibly lowering prices) and in booms (increasing prices) seems plausible in principal, it may be overemphasized in our specification; in particular, the possibility of overtime work is neglected. In the longer run, of course, profitable capacities $\tilde{y}^s$ are not rigid but are

5. According to this argument there might be situations, for example in a long-lived recession, where inventories iv have returned to iv* but y^{des} is still below $\tilde{y}^s$ due to persistent unfavorable demand expectations (not reflected in $\tilde{y}^s$). While conceivable theoretically, situations of this sort seem to be rare in practice judged on basis of business survey data: Firms assessing output inventories as "too large" or unfilled orders as "too small" typically regard capacities as "too large" and report low degrees of capacity utilization.

likely to respond to pressure of demand. This adjustment process will be taken into account in form of an aggregate investment equation that includes $\bar{x}$, the mean of $x = y^{des}/\tilde{y}^s$ in the population of firms, as one explanatory variable.

We turn now to the modifications in the **aggregate model** (19°) arising from the redefinition of x. Eqs. (19°.2), (19°.3) and (19°.4) remain unchanged with the only difference that the tension indicator P_G (proportion of firms with current demand exceeding notional supply) is defined now as the proportion of firms with 'desired output' y^{des} larger than notional supply $\tilde{y}^s$. Note that the micro variable x, which has been assumed to be lognormally distributed in the population of firms, stems now from two subsets of firms (using iv or uo as buffer stocks). This implicates that $(iv/iv^*)^{-\eta_1}$ and $(uo/uo^*)^{\eta_2}$ in (26.2) have to be identically distributed in the respective subsets of firms. The only information available to check the appropriateness of this assumption comes from a related survey: The proportions of firms reporting output inventories as "too small" and unfilled orders as "too large" show in fact quite similar developments during the sample period 1967.1 to 1985.4 ($R^2 = 0.81$, RMS-difference = 0.06). This constitutes some weak evidence in favor of the assumption.

The survey on the assessment of inventories and unfilled orders may at the same time be used to derive a proxy for P_G. As the two sub-groups of firms are of about equal size, we measure P_G as

$$P_G(x > 1) = \frac{P_{iv}(iv < iv^*) + P_{uo}(uo > uo^*)}{2} \quad . \tag{27}$$

As the answering proportions P_{iv} and P_{uo} differ only slightly, the weights employed in (27) are of minor importance. On the other hand, one should note that the survey is confined to manufacturing and that some service industries operate without buffer stocks. In view of the cyclical coherence of sectors one may argue that P_G is representative for the tension in goods markets outside manufacturing as well, at least in an approximate sense. Still, considerable measurement errors in P_G must be expected and should be accounted for when the model is estimated (by endogenizing P_G).

The first equation of (19°) has to be replaced by an equation that determines P_G as a function of aggregate demand Y^d on the micro basis of (26.2). Before going into details, it may be helpful to sketch the general principle: For instance, if aggregate demand Y^d exceeds output Y, firms will enter next period with on average lower output inventories and higher unfilled orders, implying that $\bar{x}$, the mean of $x = y^{des}/\tilde{y}^s$ in the population of firms, increases. This suggests an equation that might roughly look like

$$\bar{x} = \bar{x}_{-1} + a(Y^d_{-1} - Y_{-1}) ,$$

where unobserved $\bar{x}$ has to be replaced via (17) by $P_G(x > 1)$ and Y^d is to be explained by an aggregate demand equation. To derive this mapping from Y^d to P_G more rigorously, we have to make some simplifying assumptions. Lognormality of x in the population of firms - i.e. $\ln x \sim N(\mu_x, \sigma_x^2)$ - implies that

$$P_G(x > 1) = \Phi(\mu_x/\sigma_x) \tag{28}$$

and further requires, by (26.2), that iv/iv* and uo/uo* are lognormal as well. Setting in $\eta_1 = \eta_2 = \eta$ (a rather arbitrary assumption), we have:

$$\begin{aligned} &\ln(iv/iv^*) \sim N(-\mu_x/\eta, \sigma_x^2/\eta^2) \\ &\ln(uo/uo^*) \sim N(\mu_x/\eta, \sigma_x^2/\eta^2) . \end{aligned} \tag{29}$$

Assuming that firms are identical with respect to the targets iv* and uo*, E(iv/iv*) and E(uo/uo*) are equal to the corresponding ratios of aggregates, IV/IV* and UO/UO*, and can be expressed via (29) in terms of μ_x and σ_x:

$$IV/IV^* = E(iv/iv^*) = \exp(-\mu_x/\eta + \sigma_x^2/2\eta^2) .$$

$$UO/UO^* = E(uo/uo^*) = \exp(\mu_x/\eta + \sigma_x^2/2\eta^2) .$$

Combining now these two equations we obtain

$$\ln(UO/UO^*) - \ln(IV/IV^*) = 2\mu_x/\eta$$

or - linking with (28) -

$$\eta\left[\frac{\ln(UO/UO^*) - \ln(IV/IV^*)}{2\sigma_x}\right] = \mu_x/\sigma_x = \Phi^{-1}(P_G) .$$

Adopting a first order approximation ($\ln a \cong a - 1$ in the neighborhood of $a = 1$), assuming that UO* and IV* remain constant over time and condensing the various constants into a single constant k, we get

$$(UO - IV)/k = \Phi^{-1}(P_G) ,$$

or - defining **aggregate buffer stocks** as BU = UO - IV:

$$BU/k = \Phi^{-1}(P_G) , \quad k > 0 . \tag{30}$$

This equation implies $P_G = 0.5$ in a situation where aggregate buffer stocks (unfilled order minus inventories) are zero. Aggregate demand Y^d, output Y (real GNP) and buffers BU are further related by the definition

$$BU = BU_{-1} + Y^d_{-1} - Y_{-1} , \tag{31}$$

which is the aggregate form of (24). If data for BU were at hand, one could compute Y^d from this definition and directly estimate the aggregate demand equation, say $Y^d = \hat{Y}^d + u_1$, where $\hat{Y}^d$ stands for the systematic part. Equation (30), with k adjusted optimally, would then only be used to establish the link from BU to P_G. Reliable quantitative data for overall buffer stocks are however not available for Switzerland. Therefore, we have to combine (30), (31) and the aggregate demand equation, yielding

$$\Phi^{-1}(P_G) = \Phi^{-1}(P_{G_{-1}}) + \frac{1}{k}(\hat{Y}^d_{-1} - Y_{-1}) + u_1 \; . \qquad (19^o.1')$$

This equation, which replaces (19°.1) of the original model, can be looked at from two angles. First, with regard to the estimation of aggregate demand, (19°.1') defines unobserved demand Y^d in terms of observed aggregate output Y and the change in buffer stocks, proxied by $k\Phi^{-1}(P_G)$. Second, in the framework of the complete model, (19°.1') serves to determine P_G, which appears then in (19°.2) and (19°.3) as rationing and spillover variable. As P_G depends on **lagged** values of demand and output only, it can be considered predetermined in the rest of the model, provided that u_1 is not autocorrelated and independent of the other error terms of the model. Such a recursivity does not hold in the original model, where P_G is jointly determined by (19°.1) and (19°.2).

5. SPECIFICATION OF THE AGGREGATE ECONOMETRIC EQUATIONS

In the following we specify the deterministic parts of the aggregate econometric equations (to be linked via (19°) to observables). As our focus is on the production sector, i.e. firms' decisions on goods supply, labor demand and investment, we keep the specification of labor supply and goods demand as simple as possible. The **labor supply** equation is in the spirit of the intertemporal substitution approach (section 5.1); as all its determinants are exogenous and no spillover effect is involved, it plays a rather peripherical role in the model. **Goods demand** is assumed to depend on aggregate income Y, the real interest rate, an activity indicator for the world economy and the ratio of Swiss output prices to prices of foreign competitors (section 5.2). This equation can be viewed as reduced form of a more detailed specification of goods demand and foreign trade. It incorporates - by the inclusion of Y as an explanatory variable - a Keynesian spillover or "multiplier" effect whose strength varies however depending on the aggregate rationing situation. The equations for **notional labor demand** and **goods supply** are formulated on basis of vintage production function. The adaptation of the production apparatus to changing factor costs is thus specifically connected to investments in new equipment and scrapping of old equipment. In the short run, capital equipment can be regarded as given; firms have to decide "down" to which marginal productivity level they can operate existing equipment profitably. However, as we want to explain the development of labor demand and output supply beyond the short run, we have to analyse the **investment** process itself. This is done in connection with a Malinvaud-type investment equation, involving "pressure of demand", "profitability" and "relative prices" as determinants (section 5.3).

5.1 Labor supply

Labor supply is specified exactly as in Stalder (1989). Total labor supply L^s is split into two parts, the labor supply of Swiss residents L^s_{SW} and foreign labor supply 'controlled' by immigration policy L^s_F (exogenous). Following the approach of intertemporal substitution, we postulate for Swiss labor supply:[1]

$$\hat{L}^s_{SW_t} = d_1' \, POP_t \, e^{d_2 t} \, wr^{*\,d_3'}_t \, (\frac{wr}{wr^*})^{d_4}_t ,$$

or equivalently ($d_3 = d_3' - d_4$):

$$\hat{L}^s_{SW_t} = d_1' \, POP_t \, e^{d_2 t} \, wr^{*\,d_3}_t \, wr^{d_4}_t , \qquad d_4 > 0 \text{ (elasticity of intertemporal substitution).} \qquad (32)$$

POP is the potential labor force (Swiss residents, age 16 to 64), wr is 'net real wage' (nominal wage after taxes, deflated by CPI), and wr* is 'permanent net real wage'. The term d_2t is to capture trend factors like increasing labor force participation of women, longer periods of education, earlier retirement etc. Parameter d_3 (and even d_3') may have either sign (possibility of a backward bending supply curve due to a negative 'income effect'). Wage anticipations are modelled adaptively as:

$$wr^*_t = wr_t^{d_5} \, wr^{*\,(1-d_5)}_{t-1} = wr_t^{d_5} \, wr_{t-1}^{d_5(1-d_5)} \, wr_{t-2}^{d_5(1-d_5)^2} \ldots , \quad 0 < d_5 < 1 . \qquad (33)$$

By applying a Koyck-transformation to (32) and (33) we obtain

$$\hat{L}^s_{SW_t} = d_1 \, POP_t \, POP_{t-1}^{-(1-d_5)} \, e^{d_2 d_5 t} \, wr_t^{d_3 d_5 + d_4} \, wr_{t-1}^{-d_4(1-d_5)} \, L^{s\,(1-d_5)}_{SW_{t-1}} . \qquad (34)$$

As labor supply is unobserved (Swiss unemployment figures are very incomplete), the inclusion of foreign labor supply in an exogenous manner,

---

1. The hat-symbol is used to denote deterministic parts of equations.

without specifying a corresponding behavioral equation, is somewhat delicate. Under the assumption that L_F^s is equal to observed employment of foreigners, L_F, one could derive total labor supply by adding L_F to (34). This implies that foreign workers, once laid off, would no longer supply labor in Switzerland. A presumably preferable alternative is to assume that the unemployment rates of foreign and Swiss workers are identical. This amounts to defining total labor supply - which will be substituted into (19°.4) - by augmenting Swiss labor supply by a 'foreign worker factor' as:

$$\hat{L}^s{}_t = \hat{L}^s_{SW_t} \, (1 + RFS_t) \; . \tag{35}$$

where $RFS = L_F/L_{SW}$ is the observed ratio of foreign to Swiss employment. RFS will be treated econometrically as predetermined or weakly exogenous. This is probably not fully adequate since immigration may have responded - even within the period - to labor market disequilibria. Modelling Switzerland's foreign labor policy is however beyond the scope of this study.

5.2 Demand for domestic output

The relevant definition of Y^d - to be substituted into the transformation equation (19°.1) or (19°.1') - is 'demand for value-added produced by domestic firms' or in short 'demand for domestic output'. In general terms, Y^d can be viewed as being determined by **(a)** the development of **total demand** on domestic and foreign markets and **(b)** the **relative share** in these markets taken by **domestic firms** in competition with foreign producers. We shall propose now a simple specification for Y^d along these lines.

(a) As to the specification of **domestic demand,** we separate firms' investment demand, I^d (gross fixed business investment, excluding residential construction), from the remaining part of domestic demand, D^d, comprising private consumption, residential construction and government demand.

This partition is motivated as follows. Investment demand I^d shows up on the production side of the model as well and will be specified there on basis of a vintage approach. To ensure a consistent formulation of the model, we have to use the same (relatively sophisticated) specification of I^d on the demand side of the model. For the rest of domestic demand, D^d, we postulate (with less ambition) a positive impact of "aggregate income" Y and a negative impact of the real interest rate i^r (= nominal interest rate minus expected inflation rate; definition see section 5.3.3).

$$D^d = D^d(\underset{+}{Y}, \underset{-}{i^r}) ,$$

The development of **foreign demand** F^d, relevant to Swiss exports, is explained by an appropriately weighted index of GDP in Switzerland's major trading partners, denoted by Y^F:[2]

$$F^d = F^d(\underset{+}{Y^F}, \underset{+}{\Delta Y^F}) .$$

ΔY^F is included because foreign investment demand, accounting for about 45% of Swiss exports, can be expected to be more strongly related to changes in foreign activity than its level.

(b) The allocation of I^d, D^d and F^d to Swiss and competing foreign firms is considered to be governed by relative prices. To keep things as simple as possible, we apply to all markets the same weighted price ratio p/p^F.[3]

---

2. Comp. 'Konjunktur', Monatsbericht der Konjunkturforschungsstelle, Eidgenössische Technische Hochschule, Zürich.
3. The weights are designed to capture the relative importance of Switzerland's main competitors on home, foreign and third countries' markets. Considering several alternatives, we decided to measure p/p^F as 'relative export unit values' as published by the IMF (International Financial Statistics). Export unit values are thus assumed to be representative not only of prices of exports but of the Swiss and foreign tradables output supplied to the respective home markets as well.

Positing furthermore an identical price elasticity a_6, we may write 'demand for domestic output' as

$$\hat{Y}^d = (k_1 D^d + k_2 I^d + k_3 F^d)(p/p^F)^{a_6} .$$

Assuming that $D^d(.)$ and $F^d(.)$ are linear functions of their determinants, we obtain

$$\hat{Y}^d = (a_0 + a_1 Y + a_2 i^r + a_3 I^d + a_4 Y^F + a_5 \Delta Y^F)(p/p^F)^{a_6} , \qquad (36)$$

$$a_1,\ a_3,\ a_4,\ a_5 > 0, \quad a_2,\ a_6 < 0 .$$

We shall estimate this composite demand equation by linking it via (19°.1) or (19°.1') to actual Y - and do not estimate in the usual manner separate equations for the individual demand components with actual transactions used as dependent variables. The purpose of this is to allow for demand rationing or - in the buffer version - to reconstruct unobserved demand from observed output and changes in inventories and unfilled orders. Consequently, one should substitute the equation for investment demand I^d into (36) as well. While feasible for a simple investment equation, such a procedure is bound to lead to a hopeless over-parametrization of (36) for the detailed explanation of investment demand developed in section 5.3 below. A careful representation of investment behavior is however crucial in the present context. Therefore, we shall estimate the I^d-equation of section 5.3 detached from (36), using observed investment as dependent variable, i.e. assuming $I^d = I$. The neglect of possible supply constraints on the investment market can be considered a minor flaw in view of an import share of about 50%. To be sure, investment goods are strongly differentiated so that the high import share does not absolutely guarantee that firms can always realize investment demand. But it certainly means that the contribution of investment to total demand for domestic output is small (about 7%).

Thus, while the assumption $I^d = I$ may cause some distortion in the equation for investment demand, it seems unproblematical with respect to the estimation of total demand for domestic output in (36).[4]

In a quarterly model the formation of goods demand must be expected to be subject to dynamic adjustment lags. The several demand components implicit in (36) and the response of the market shares to p/p^F may of course involve rather different lag patterns. However, since we are forced to economize on empirical parameters, we simply augment (36) by a partial adjustment mechanism:

$$\begin{aligned} \hat{Y}^d_t &= \lambda_G (a_0 + a_1 Y_{t-1} + a_2 i^r_{t-1} + a_3 I_t + a_4 Y^F_t + a_5 \Delta Y^F_t)(p/p^F)_t^{a_6} \\ &\quad + (1-\lambda_G) Y^d_{t-1}, \qquad 0 < \lambda_G < 1. \end{aligned} \tag{37}$$

To allow for some extra inertia in consumption, government and residential construction demand, represented in (37) by the variables Y and i^r, we have introduced - as an empirical option - a one-quarter lag on these variables.

In the context of the entire model (19°), eq. (37) - through the inclusion of Y and I as endogenous explanatory variables - implies Keynesian multiplier effects. For example, an increase in foreign activty Y^F acts directly on Y^d, leading to a higher Y. This induces, in next period, an additional rise in Y^d and Y, etc. ... In contrast to traditional Keynesian models, we do however do not equate Y^d with Y but take into account that Y may be subject to supply constraints. As a result, the size of the multiplier effect depends on the rationing situation: It is largest if both P_G and P_L are low (in a predominantly 'Keynesian' situation); it disappears if

4. If we distinguished between I^d and I we would further have to specify a rationing scheme for the goods market, since for production capacities it is actual I and not I^d that matters.

either $P_L \rightarrow 1$ ("all" firms are labor-supply constrained) or $P_G \rightarrow 1$ ("all" firms are capacity constrained) since then actual Y does no longer respond to Y^d. Note however that Y^d will further increase because capacity constraints induce firms to boost investment demand (see the specification of investment behavior in the in next section).[5]

5.3 Notional labor demand, notional goods supply and investment

5.3.1 Preliminaries

Notional labor demand $\tilde{L}^d$ and notional goods supply $\tilde{Y}^s$ are defined as the levels of employment and output that correspond to a full utilization of profitable capacities, profitability being determined by relative prices. According to this definition, equipment which is momentarily idle because of insufficient goods demand or labor supply bottlenecks but - in absence of these constraints - could be operated profitably at prevailing prices is included in $\tilde{L}^d$ and $\tilde{Y}^s$. On the other hand, there may be capacities that physically still exist but are out of operation because profitability is insufficient at current prices; these capacities are excluded from the definition of the notional trade offers.

In the very short run, one may formulate $\tilde{L}^d$ and $\tilde{Y}^s$ conditional on a given exogenous capital stock. In order to discuss longer-term issues, we must however analyse the development of $\tilde{L}^d$ and $\tilde{Y}^s$ in connection with the **invesment decision.** In a disequilibrium model like the one of this paper, firms may find themselves in different regimes. Therefore, one might consider modelling investment conditional on the prevailing regime or the regime-mix in the aggregate economy, taking thus into account that labor constrained, demand constrained and capacity constrained (unconstrained)

5. The question of dynamic stability of the model will be addressed by means of simulations on basis of the empirical parameter estimates.

firms show different investment behavior.[6] However, while the **current rationing situation** is undoubtedly relevant to the short-term employment and output decision of firms, its impact on investment is less clear. Investment decisions are typically of a longer-term nature and largely irreversible, with respect to the amount invested as well as the chosen technical coefficients. It can thus be argued that firms regard disequilibria as transitory states relative to the time horizon of investment projects: Current disequilibria tend to be eliminated through adjustments and new, possibly different disequilibria may arise from future random shocks. According to this view, investment decisions, rather than being contingent on the momentary regime, would be based on **longer-term expectations**, including an assessment of future demand, prices and factor costs. Empirically, however, investment is known to be large when current goods demand is high in relation to capacities. This well-established stylized fact contradicts a specification of investment demand which is completely uncoupled from the momentary regime. It rather suggests an approach that emphasizes the importance of longer-term expectations but models these expectations in connection with the current rationing situation.

To simplify the following considerations we neglect (anticipated) labor constraints. This seem acceptable because the dependence of investment on labor constraints is theoretically ambiguous and appears to be weak empirically anyhow.[7] We concentrate thus on demand constraints and - as their complement - capacity constraints.[8] Over the time horizon relevant to in-

---

6. Compare e.g. Artus and Muet (1984).
7. In a study for France, Artus and Muet (1984) find a weak negative impact of labor supply constraints on investment.
8. At the aggregate level, the corresponding proportions of firms are $(1 - P_G)$ and P_G.

vestment decisions, demand expectations are subject to a considerable degree of uncertainty. Consequently, when deciding on investment, firms must always take into account that future demand may be larger or smaller than capacities. Put more precisely, the investment decision is subject to a tradeoff in the sense that the creation of large capacities involves a high risk of ending up with excess capacities and thus - due to irreversibility - bearing "excessive" fixed capital costs, whereas small capacities are associated with a high risk of missing profitable future production opportunities.

5.3.2 Malinvaud's investment model

The investment decision of firms has been analyzed in such a framework of "irreversibility" and "demand uncertainty" by Malinvaud (1987). Compare also Lambert (1986) who refers to an earlier but similar study by Malinvaud. In the following we outline the main elements of this theoretical approach and develop then the specifications of investment demand, notional goods supply and labor demand to be used in our model. As Malinvaud's analysis aims at the longer run, i.e. deals only with the "desired" levels of capital, output and employment, we will have to amend the approach by specifying the mechanisms of short-run dynamics.

In Malinvaud's model, the representative firm is assumed to face, ex ante, a traditional 'neoclassical' production function but to dispose of no substitution possibilities once capital has been physically installed (putty-clay assumption). Determinants of the investment decision are prices, factor costs and demand expectations. The price level p and relative capital costs $C = uc/w$ (uc: user cost of capital, w: nominal wage) are assumed to be known with certainty and to reflect longer-term averages. Demand expectations are stochastic and defined by a subjective normal distribution with mean E and coefficient of variation $H = \sigma/E$. The problem of the firm, which is assumed to maximize expected profits, is to choose the optimal point on the ex ante production function

$$\bar{Y} = \bar{Y}(L, K) \ . \tag{38}$$

This point can be characterized for instance in terms of the optimal production capacity $\bar{Y}$ and the optimal capital coefficient $K/\bar{Y}$; once these two variables are determined, the derivation of K, L and K/L (optimal capital intensity) is straightforward. Malinvaud's analysis produces, loosely stated, the following relationships:[9]

$$\begin{aligned} \bar{Y} &= f_1(\underset{+}{E}, \underset{+}{PFT}, \underset{+}{C}, \underset{\pm}{H}) \\ K/\bar{Y} &= f_2(\underset{-}{C}, \underset{-}{PFT}, \underset{-}{H}) \ . \end{aligned} \tag{39}$$

PFT is a measure for profitability or - more precisely - the influence of p, w and uc on profitability. The positive impact of expected demand E on $\bar{Y}$ and the negative impact of relative capital costs C on $K/\bar{Y}$ are traditional. The other explanatory factors arise from the "new" elements of uncertainty and irreversibility. In fact, if demand was known with certainty (H = 0), optimal $\bar{Y}$ would be equal to E and $K/\bar{Y}$ would solely depend on C. Whereas the dependence of $\bar{Y}$ on H is ambiguous, H affects $K/\bar{Y}$ negatively. The intuition behind this is the following: Since labor input, in contrast to capital, is assumed to be fully flexible, a firm facing higher demand uncertainty will shift towards a more labor intensive technology in order to substitute fixed capital costs by variable labor costs.[10] If profitability PFT improves, the

---

9. These relationships have to be interpreted in a comparative-static manner; they are obtained by differentiating the first-order conditions for a profit maximum. We indicate beneath the variables the signs of the corresponding partial derivatives.

10. Treating capital as a completely fixed factor and labor as a completely flexible one certainly overstates the case to some extent.

firm will increase its production capacity $\bar{Y}$ in relation to E - in order to reduce the probability of missing future opportunities of profitable production (in other words: if profitability is high, it is worth-while for the firm to take a greater risk of ending up with excess capacities). This positive impact of PFT on $\bar{Y}$ is especially strong if H is large. It is accompanied by a reduction in $K/\bar{Y}$; the motivation for this is again enhancing cost flexibility.

If we view H as a positive constant (since demand uncertainty is difficult to capture empirically) and further suppress the determinants whose impacts on $\bar{Y}$ and $K/\bar{Y}$ are likely to be weak numerically (see Malinvaud's discussion), we obtain the following simplified relationships:

$$\begin{aligned} &\bar{Y} = f_1(\underset{+}{E}, \underset{+}{PFT}) , \\ &K/\bar{Y} = f_2(\underset{-}{C}) , \text{ or via (38): } K/L = f_3(\underset{-}{C}) . \end{aligned} \qquad (40)$$

Practical empirical studies have of course since long considered profitability an important determinant of investment. The contribution of Malinvaud's analysis is to establish the role of profitability within a precise theoretical framework. It should be mentioned, however, that Malinvaud's model involves a rather special demand curve: Firms are treated as price takers, but - unlike firms in perfect competition - face a stochastic upper bound with respect to quantities. This may actually be a fairly realistic approximation for firms supplying undifferentiated products on international markets; such firms have hardly any influence on the price but are typically used to do business with a fixed group of customers to whom they cannot sell unlimited quantities. Technically, this assumption of a "rectangular" demand curve allows Malinvaud to draw a clear distinction between profitability in terms of relative prices and demand expectations. Such a distinction obtains as well under the less restrictive assumption of a "kinked" demand curve as introduced by Sweezy (1939) for oligopolistic competition. Interestingly, risk averse firms that have imperfect knowledge about the price elasticity of demand can be shown to behave under quite general conditions "as if" operating at a kink [Drèze (1979)].

In all these cases, Malinvaud's analysis is valid. In the traditional model of monopolistic competition with a smooth demand curve, however, the distinction between "profitability" and "expected demand" becomes somewhat vague since the optimal price-quantity combination of the firm reflects continuously cost conditions and the position of the demand schedule. But this model deals only with the long-term equilibrium of the firm. In the short run, a distinction between profitability and demand may still be meaningful. For example, think of an exporting firm that is confronted with a sudden increase in the exchange rate. If prices are quoted in foreign currency, demand will at first remain unaffected. The immediate effect is to depress prices in domestic currency and thus profitability. It is only in the medium term that the firm will pass the higher exchange rate onto prices in foreign currency, thereby partly restoring profitability and at the same time reducing sales. Quite a different dynamical pattern emerges if a firm is hit by a drop in demand: Profitability (in terms of relative prices) will then at first remain unchanged; it only deteriorates later if the firm tries to stimulate sales by reducing prices.

We may conclude from this discussion that it is reasonable, under a wide set of circumstances, to distinguish between expected demand and profitability (in terms of relative prices) when modelling the investment decision of firms. However, leaving price setting behavior unexplained is certainly a flaw of both Malinvaud's theoretical approach and our related specification set forth below.

5.3.3 Adopting a vintage-approach

Taking (40) as point of departure, we shall develop now the concrete econometric equations for investment demand, notional goods supply and notional labor demand. In addition, we must specify the process of short-run dynamic adjustment. This can be done most naturally in a vintage framework, i.e. by applying (40) only to new equipment and specifying a "scrapping rule" for old equipment. In such a framework, the adjustment of production capacities and technical coefficients to changing demand expectations and relative prices is connected specifically to the amount invested in new "machines" and the extent to which old ones are shut down.

Under the vintage assumption, notional goods supply and notional labor demand can be defined by the following 'updating'-equations:

$$\tilde{Y}^s_t = \tilde{Y}^s_{t-1} - Y^\nabla_t + Y^\Delta_t$$

$$\tilde{L}^d_t = \tilde{L}^d_{t-1} - L^\nabla_t + L^\Delta_t \;.$$

Y^∇_t and L^∇_t (Y^Δ_t and L^Δ_t) are output and employment on equipment taken out of operation (newly installed) in period t. We assume that existing machines differ with respect to labor productivity π and let the corresponding productivity distribution be described by a continuous density function. At any point of time, machines are are assumed to be in use down to a marginal productivity level π^{min}_t. Consequently, from period t-1 to period t machines with productivity levels between π^{min}_{t-1} and π^{min}_t are taken out of operation. Defining $\Pi_t = \pi^{min}_t/\pi^{min}_{t-1}$, we can reformulate the above two equations as[11]

11. We introduce again the "hat"-symbol to denote deterministic parts.

$$\hat{\tilde{Y}}^s_t = \tilde{Y}^s_{t-1} F^Y(\Pi_t) + Y^\Delta_t \,, \qquad (41.1)$$

$$\hat{\tilde{L}}^d_t = \tilde{L}^d_{t-1} F^L(\Pi_t) + L^\Delta_t \,, \qquad (41.2) \qquad (41)$$

where the functions $F^Y(\Pi_t)$ and $F^L(\Pi_t)$ are continuously decreasing in Π_t. These functions are henceforth referred to as 'scrapping functions' (although equipment taken out of operation is not necessarily scrapped) and will be discussed in more detail below.

We apply now the Malinvaud-approach to new equipment, associating thus $\bar{Y}$ with Y^Δ, L with L^Δ and K with I (gross investment of the period). Adopting a Cobb-Douglas form, the ex ante production function (38) reads as

$$Y^\Delta_t = c\, L^{\Delta\,\beta_1}_t \, I_t^{1-\beta_1} \, e^{\beta_2 t} = c\, I_t \left(\frac{L^\Delta}{I}\right)_t^{\beta_1} e^{\beta_2 t} \qquad (42.1)$$

or - interpreting technical progress as labor augmenting ($\beta_3\beta_1 = \beta_2$) -

$$Y^\Delta_t = c\, (L^\Delta_t \, e^{\beta_3 t})^{\beta_1} \, I_t^{1-\beta_1} = c\, I_t \left(\frac{L^\Delta e^{\beta_3 t}}{I}\right)_t^{\beta_1} \qquad (42.2)$$

On this basis, the problem of the optimizing firm can be viewed as a decision on three variables: The production capacity of the new vintage t, Y^Δ_t, its labor intensity $(L^\Delta/I)_t$, and the increase in marginal productivity Π_t on old equipment (by scrapping). Once these variables are determined, (42.1) implies I_t and L^Δ_t, and (41) defines $\hat{\tilde{Y}}^s_t$ and $\hat{\tilde{L}}^d_t$. We discuss first the decision on Y^Δ_t and $(L^\Delta/I)_t$ and turn then to Π_t.

Considering (40) we postulate

$$Y^\Delta_t = Y^\Delta_t(E_t, PFT_t) \,, \qquad (43)$$

$$\left(\frac{L^\Delta}{I}\right)_t = c_1 \left(\frac{w}{uc}\right)_t^{-c_2} , \quad c_1, c_2 > 0 \,. \qquad (44)$$

The concrete form of (43) will be developed below. w is nominal wage; uc is the user cost of capital, measured in the usual way as

$$uc = p_c(\zeta + r - \dot{p}^e) \;, \tag{45}$$

where p_c is the price of investment goods, ζ is a constant depreciation rate (set to 0.1 per year), r is the long-term nominal interest rate, and $\dot{p}^e$ is the 'long term expected inflation rate', specified adaptively as a weighted average of actual inflation rates over the past 12 quarters as proposed by Ando et al. (1974). In a purely static environment, the Cobb-Douglas function would imply $c_2 = 1$ (elasticity of substitution); however, as the underlying optimization problem involves additional elements (uncertainty, irreversibility), we do not impose this constraint. Substituting (44) into (42.1) and restating (43) we obtain the following vintage-equations:

$$I_t = Y_t^{\Delta}(E_t, PFT_t)\; c_1' \left[\frac{w}{uc}\right]_t^{c_2\beta_1} e^{-\beta_2 t} \;, \tag{46.1}$$

$$L_t^{\Delta} = Y_t^{\Delta}(E_t, PFT_t)\; c_1'' \left[\frac{w}{uc}\right]_t^{c_2(1-\beta_1)} e^{-\beta_2 t} \;, \tag{46.2}$$

$$Y_t^{\Delta} = Y_t^{\Delta}(E_t, PFT_t) \;, \tag{46.3}$$

(46)

defining capital I, and labor input L^{Δ} and output Y^{Δ} on a new vintage in terms of expected demand E, profitability PFT and relative factor costs w/uc. This system can be recast in various tantamount ways. With regard to estimation, note that the determination of Y^{Δ} in (46.3) is likely to involve a large error term since we cannot expect to find a precise econometric representation of firms' "scale decision" (animal spirits). Technical ratios like L^{Δ}/I or Y^{Δ}/I on the other hand presumably are much easier to model. This suggests that we specify L^{Δ} and Y^{Δ} conditional on I, thereby capturing the scale component in form of an observed variable, and enclose (46.3) only in the investment equation. (46.1) is simply recast below as (47.1) with b_2 replacing $c_2\beta_1$; once I is explained, we can use (44) to determine L^Δ, yielding (47.2) below; inserting (47.2) into the production function (42.1) we obtain (47.3):

$$I_t = Y_t^\Delta(E_t, PFT_t)\ c_1' \left[\frac{w}{uc}\right]_t^{b_2} e^{-\beta_2 t} \qquad (47.1)$$

$$L_t^\Delta = c_1 I_t \left[\frac{w}{uc}\right]_t^{-c_2} \qquad (47.2) \qquad (47)$$

$$Y_t^\Delta = b_1 I_t \left[\frac{w}{uc}\right]_t^{-b_2} e^{\beta_2 t}, \quad b_2 = c_2\beta_1 \ . \qquad (47.3)$$

This system is equivalent to (46) but easier to handle econometrically: Eqs. (47.2) and (47.3), to be inserted into (41) and then linked to observables via (19°), are quite simple. Eq. (47.1) is more complicated and is likely to involve a relatively large error; it has however a directly observable dependent variable (by assumption, comp. section 5.2 above). This equation must be estimated jointly with the other equations to allow for cross-equation restrictions (b_2, β_2), the endogeneity of I in (47.2) and (47.3) and the occurence of presumably contemporaneously correlated disturbance terms (due to common specification errors).

The model treats **technical progress** in a rather restrictive manner. All technical change is assumed to be embodied. Moreover, it is introduced in (42) in such a way that the shape of the isoquants and thus the optimal labor intensity L^Δ/I remain unaffected while capital productivity Y^Δ/I as well as labor productivity Y^Δ/L^Δ are enhanced. As a result, technical progress does not show up in labor demand (conditional on capital I) but exerts a positive impact on output supply (conditional on I) and a negative impact on investment (conditional on capacity Y^Δ); see (47) above. Of course, (47.1) includes a positive counter-effect from technical progress on I via the profitability term in Y^{Δ}, and this effect will prove dominant empirically. A more general treatment of technical progress seems desirable but is beyond the scope of the present paper.

For $Y^{\Delta}(E, PFT)$ in (47.1), the scale of new capacities, we postulate:

$$Y^{\Delta}_t = \underbrace{Y_t\left[e_1 + e_2\Phi^{-1}(P_{G_t})\right]}_{E} \underbrace{\exp\left[e_3\left[\ln\frac{(w/p)_t}{(w/p)_0} - \beta_3 t\right]\right]}_{PFT} \qquad (48)$$

$e_2, \beta_3 > 0$
$e_3 < 0$

This specification is motivated as follows:

- The PFT-term is an index of profitability on new equipment. The formulation assumes that profitability on new equipment remains unchanged over time if the real wage w/p increases exactly with the rate of labor augmenting technical progress β_3 in the vintage production function (see (42.2)). On such a hypothetical growth path, wage costs take a constant share in value added. The course of actual w/p in relation to this implicitly estimated trend determines profitability, positive deviations of w/p implying a deterioration of PFT ($e_3 < 0$). This specification of profitability takes into account wage costs and costs of material inputs (as p is price of value added) but neglects capital costs. Variants including capital costs have been tried but capital costs turned out insignificant.
- Firms are assumed to assess uncertain future demand in relation to presently available capacities on basis of actual excess demand.[12] In the framework of our model, relative excess demand is defined, averaging

12. As outlined above, the uncertainty of demand expectations is reflected in the impact of profitability on investment.

across firms, as $E[\ln(y^d/\tilde{y}^s)] = E[\ln(x)] = \mu_x = \sigma_x \Phi^{-1}(P_G)$.[13] This gives rise to the E-term in (48), where e_2 is a positive parameter (including σ_x) and e_1 is probably also positive since firms, in a situation of zero excess demand ($\mu_x = \sigma_x \Phi^{-1}(P_G) = 0$), can be expected to create a certain amount of new capacities to replace scrapped equipment. Since $\sigma_x \Phi^{-1}(P_G)$ measures excess demand in relative terms, we finally multiply by Y (a more sophisticated solution might be to use latent $\tilde{Y}^s$ as scaling factor).

We insert now (48) into (47.1). To account for the various probable lags (with respect to perception, formation of expectations, decision, installation) we back-shift all explanatory variables one quarter and augment the investment equation by a simple partial adjustment mechanism. After this manipulation, eqs.(47) read as:[14,15]

$$I_t^* = Y_{t-1}\left[e_1 + e_2 \Phi^{-1}(P_{G_{t-1}})\right] \exp\left\{e_3\left[\ln \frac{(w/p)_{t-1}}{(w/p)_0} - \beta_3 t\right]\right\} \left[\frac{w}{uc}\right]_{t-1}^{b_2} e^{-\beta_2 t}$$

$$\hat{I}_t = \lambda_I I_t^* + (1 - \lambda_I)\, I_{t-1} \tag{49.1}$$

$$L_t^{\Delta} = c_1 I_{t-1} \left[\frac{w}{uc}\right]_{t-2}^{-c_2} \tag{49.2}$$

$$Y_t^{\Delta} = b_1 I_{t-1} \left[\frac{w}{uc}\right]_{t-2}^{-b_2} e^{\beta_2 t} \tag{49.3}$$

---

13. Compare (10) and (17) and the redefinition of $x = y^d/\tilde{y}^s$ as $x = y^{des}/\tilde{y}^s$ in the buffer version of section 4.
14. c_1' becomes redundant, i.e. is included in e_1 and e_2.
15. b_2 and β_2 will be estimated as common parameters of (49.1) and (49.3) (cross-equation restriction). Note further that the ratios β_2/β_3 and b_2/c_2 are both equal to β_1, i.e. $\beta_2/\beta_3 = b_2/c_2$ (= β_1) (comp. (42) and (47)). This restriction will not be imposed in estimation but used to check plausibilty.

5.3.4 Scrapping of old equipment

We turn now to the 'scrapping functions' appearing in (41). First, we discuss F^L. In each period firms have to determine down to which minimal productivity level they can operate existing 'machines' profitably. This minimal or 'marginal' productivity level required by firms, i.e. real value-added per unit of labor on the least productive machine still in use in period t, is denoted by π_t^{min}.[16] We let now the distribution of π across existing machines - in the sense of 'places of work' - be described in every period t by a continuous density function $f(\Pi)$, where $\Pi = \pi/\pi_{t-1}^{min}$ relates π to the previous period's marginal productivity.[17] Let $f(\Pi)$ be defined such that $\int_1^\infty f(\Pi)d\Pi = 1$. One might then first tend to express F_t^L as

$$F^L(\Pi_t) = \int_{\Pi_t}^\infty f(\Pi)d\Pi \quad , \tag{50}$$

where $\Pi_t = \pi_t^{min}/\pi_{t-1}^{min}$ measures the relative increase in marginal productivity.[18] This specification implies $F^L = 1$ for $\Pi_t = 1$, i.e. "all" machines from period t-1 would be carried over to period t provided that firms do not require a higher marginal productivity on old equipment. This seems however not quite realistic since profitability on existing equipment will dwindle over time so that a certain set of machines, those with π just a little above π_{t-1}^{min} in the previous period, must be taken out of operation in period t if marginal productivity is to remain constant, implying $F_t^L < 1$ at $\Pi_t = 1$.

16. Under perfect competition, the labor productivity of the least productive machine is equal to the real wage, i.e. $\pi_t^{min} = (w/p)_t$; see below.
17. For the general idea of describing efficiency differences among production units (firms, machines, places of work) by means of continuous density functions compare, e.g., Houthakker (1955) or Sato (1975).
18. Density $f(\Pi)$ will of course go to zero at a certain maximum value of Π. One might thus replace ∞ by this value as upper integration limit.

We assume that productivity on all existing equipment decreases from period to period by a factor (1-s), where s is a small positive constant. A machine with productivity π last period will thus show productivity $\pi' = \pi(1-s)$ this period. Accordingly, the variable Π is mapped onto $\Pi' = \Pi(1-s)$ - graphically amounting to a proportional shift of the density to the left - and (50) has to be replaced by

$$F^L(\Pi_t) = \int_{\Pi_t}^{\infty} f(\frac{\Pi'}{1-s})\,\frac{d\Pi'}{1-s} \quad . \tag{51}$$

A first-order approximation to (51) for Π_t near (1-s) yields:

$$F^L(\Pi_t) \cong F^L(1-s) - \frac{f(1)}{1-s}[\Pi_t - (1-s)]$$

$$= \quad 1 \quad - \quad f(1)[\Pi_t/(1-s) - 1] \ .$$

Substituting $\pi_t^{min}/\pi_{t-1}^{min}$ for Π_t and replacing f(1) by a constant r, [19] we finally obtain:

$$F^L(\Pi_t) = 1 \ - \ r\left[\frac{\pi_t^{min}}{\pi_{t-s}^{min}(1-s)} - 1\right] . \tag{52}$$

The scrapping function F^Y can be developed in a similar manner. From density $f(\Pi)$, describing the productivity distribution on existing equipment with respect to 'places of work', we obtain the density of Π with respect to 'value-added' as $(\pi_{t-1}^{min}/\approx{\pi}_{t-1})\Pi\, f(\Pi)$, where $\approx{\pi}_{t-1}$ is 'average productivity' in the previous period. The resulting expression is

19. The assumption of a constant f(1) means - loosely stated - that the relative share of 'working places' located in a critical range around marginal productivity must be constant over time. At other points the "shape" of the density may change.

$$F^Y(\Pi_t) = (1-s)\left[1 - \frac{\pi_{t-1}^{min}}{\tilde{\tilde{\pi}}_{t-1}} r\left(\frac{\pi_t^{min}}{\pi_{t-1}^{min}(1-s)} - 1\right)\right] . \tag{53}$$

We do not go into details about the derivation of (53) but explain it intuitively in comparision with (52). Assume that firms choose to reduce marginal productivity just by factor (1-s), i.e. $\pi_t^{min} = \pi_{t-1}^{min}(1-s)$. In this case, (52) implies $F^L = 1$, i.e. all machines operated in period t-1 are carried over to period t and there is no reduction in notional labor demand. However, as productivity on all machines has decreased by factor (1-s), notional output supply must fall by this factor. This is in fact exactly what (53) says, namely $F^Y = (1-s) < 1$. Parameter r in (52) can roughly be viewed as elasticity of F^L with respect to π_t^{min}. The elasticity of F^Y with respect to π_t^{min} must be weaker since value-added per unit of labor on marginal machines is below average. This is accounted for in (53) by the factor $\pi_{t-1}^{min}/\tilde{\tilde{\pi}}_{t-1}$, which will be set in the estimation to a fixed value of 0.6, corresponding to the average share of labor costs in value-added.

Under perfect competition on output and input markets, it would be optimal for firms to take machines out of operation when they no longer yield positive quasi-rents. This 'scrapping point' can be defined in various equivalent ways, for instance (a) by equating **unit labor costs** (labor costs per unit of real value added) with the **price** p (price of value-added) or (b) by setting **labor productivity** (real value-added per unit of labor) equal to the **real wage** w/p. Formulation (b) suggests that we replace the marginal productivities π^{min} in (52) and (53) with the real wage of the respective periods:

$$F^L(\Pi_t) = 1 - r\left[\frac{(w/p)_t}{(w/p)_{t-1}(1-s)} - 1\right] \quad (54.1)$$

$$F^Y(\Pi_t) = (1-s)\left\{1 - 0.6\, r\left[\frac{(w/p)_t}{(w/p)_{t-1}(1-s)} - 1\right]\right\}. \quad (54.2)$$

(54)

These equations apply to perfect competition. Under any form of imperfect competition - where sales and/or the supplies of production factors are not unlimited at going prices - it may pay a firm to replace old machines by new ones even if the old ones still yield positive quasi-rents. In terms of formulation (a) above, firms do not compare unit labor costs on existing machines to prices but to total costs on new machines: A machine gets replaced as soon as unit labor costs on that machine (LUC) become equal to 'total unit costs' (labor and capital) on new machines (TUC). As TUC measures costs on the most efficient machines while p rather reflects average costs on all machines, TUC can be expected to be smaller than p, implying that the marginal productivities π_t^{min} are higher under imperfect competition. An obvious way to adapt (54) to this case is to replace p by TUC. However, if we posit a constant relative mark-up of p over TUC and take into account that it is the ratio of marginal productivities, $\pi_t^{min}/\pi_{t-1}^{min}$, that matters, we may simply stick to (54). To judge the appropriateness of this specification under imperfect competition consider an old machine with LUC just a little below TUC. An increase in w/p will affect LUC relatively more than TUC, therefore push LUC beyond TUC and imply scrapping - exactly as stated in (54). On the other hand, scrapping of marginal machines may be induced by TUC falling below LUC due to reduced capital costs. If the decrease in TUC is accompanied by a proportional fall in p (constant mark-up), this case is also appropriately captured by (54). If not, then specification (54) is not fully adequate.

6. STRUCTURE OF THE MODEL, METHOD OF ESTIMATION AND DYNAMIC EXTENSIONS

In this section we recapitulate the equations retained for estimation, discuss the structure of the overall model, outline the appropriate method of estimation and consider some reparametrizations and dynamical extensions.

6.1 Allowing for a trend in labor market mismatch

A first reformulation concerns the mismatch parameters α_L and α_Y in the transformation equations (19°) (p. 48). As empirical studies for several countries, including Switzerland, have found evidence for a growing mismatch on the aggregate labor market [Stalder (1989)], we introduce some flexibility in this respect as well and respecify

$$\alpha_L = \alpha_0 e^{\nu t} \qquad \alpha_Y = \alpha_L \tau = \alpha_0 e^{\nu t} \tau \ . \tag{55}$$

Instead of α_L and α_Y we thus estimate α_0, ν and τ. Increasing mismatch shows up as $\nu > 0$, and the restriction $\alpha_Y < \alpha_L$ (implied by a concave production function, see point b, p. 52) is translated into $\tau < 1$.

6.2 Summary of the model

The **transformation equations** (19°), modified to allow for a trend in mismatch, read as:

$$Y_t(1 - P_{L_t})^{-\alpha_L \tau}(1 - P_{G_t})^{-\kappa_Y} = Y_t^d = \hat{Y}_t^d e^{u_{1t}} \qquad [19°.1]$$

$$\text{or:} \quad \Phi^{-1}(P_{G_t}) = \Phi^{-1}(P_{G_{t-1}}) + \frac{1}{k}(\hat{Y}^d_{t-1} - Y_{t-1}) + u_{1t} \qquad [19°.1'] \text{ buffer version}$$

$$Y_t(1 - P_{L_t})^{-\alpha_L \tau} P_{G_t}^{-\kappa_Y} = \tilde{Y}_t^s = \hat{\tilde{Y}}_t^s e^{u_{2t}} \qquad [19°.2]$$

$$L_t(1 - P_{L_t})^{-\alpha_L} P_{G_t}^{-\kappa_L} = \tilde{L}_t^d = \hat{\tilde{L}}_t^d e^{u_{3t}} \qquad [19°.3] \qquad [19°]$$

$$L_t P_{L_t}^{-\alpha_L} = L_t^s = \hat{L}_t^s e^{u_{4t}}, \qquad [19°.4]$$

where $\alpha_L = \alpha_0 e^{\nu t}$.

These equations serve to map the latent demand and supply variables (Y^d, $\tilde{Y}^s$, $\tilde{L}^d$, L^s) onto the observables (L, Y, P_L, P_G). In detail:

- The **vintage equations** (employment and output on a new vintage)

$$L^{\Delta}_t = c_1 I_{t-1} \left[\frac{w}{uc}\right]^{-c_2}_{t-2} , \tag{49.2}$$

$$Y^{\Delta}_t = b_1 I_{t-1} \left[\frac{w}{uc}\right]^{-b_2}_{t-2} e^{\beta_2 t} , \tag{49.3}$$

and the **scrapping functions**

$$F^L_t = 1 - r\left[\frac{(w/p)_t}{(w/p)_{t-1}(1-s)} - 1\right] \tag{54.1}$$

$$F^Y_t = (1-s)\left[1 - 0.6r\left[\frac{(w/p)_t}{(w/p)_{t-1}(1-s)} - 1\right]\right] \tag{54.2}$$

are inserted into the definitions for **notional goods supply** and **notional labor demand**,

$$\hat{\tilde{Y}}^s_t = \tilde{Y}^s_{t-1} F^Y_t + Y^{\Delta}_t \quad \text{and} \quad \hat{\tilde{L}}^d_t = \tilde{L}^d_{t-1} F^L_t + L^{\Delta}_t , \tag{41}$$

and the resulting expressions are linked by [19.°2] and [19°.3] to actual output, employment and regime proportions.

- The equation for **goods demand**

$$\hat{Y}^d_t = \lambda_G(a_0 + a_1 Y_{t-1} + a_2 i^r_{t-1} + a_3 I_t + a_4 Y^F_t + a_5 \Delta Y^F_t)(p/p^F)_t^{a_6} + (1 - \lambda_G) Y^d_{t-1} \tag{37}$$

is substituted into [19°.1] or - in the buffer model - into [19°.1'].

- The **labor supply** equation (Swiss workers)

$$\hat{L}^s_{SW_t} = d_1' \, POP_t \, e^{d_2 t} \, wr^{*}{}_t^{d_3} \, wr_t^{d_4} , \tag{32}$$

$$\text{where} \quad wr^*_t = wr_t^{d_5} \, wr_{t-1}^{d_5(1-d_5)} \, wr_{t-2}^{d_5(1-d_5)^2} \ldots, \tag{33}$$

is augmented by foreign workers,

$$\hat{L}^s_t = \hat{L}^s_{SW_t} \, (1 + RFS_t) \, , \tag{35}$$

and inserted then into [19°.4].

The model is completed by **investment demand** (49.1). This equation, supplied with an error term u_{5t}, is directly related to observed investment:

$$I^*_t = Y_{t-1} \left[e_1 + e_2 \Phi^{-1}(P_{G_{t-1}}) \right] \exp \left[e_3 \left[\ln \frac{(w/p)_{t-1}}{(w/p)_0} - \beta_3 t \right] \right] \left[\frac{w}{uc} \right]_{t-1}^{b_2} e^{-\beta_2 t}$$

$$I_t = \lambda_I I^*_t + (1 - \lambda_I) \, I_{t-1} + u_{5t} \tag{49.1}$$

The model contains thus five stochastic **observable endogenous variables:**

Y (aggregate output, i.e. real GDP), L (aggregate employment), the regime proportions P_L and P_G, and investment I.

As **explanatory variables** (econometrically treated as weakly exogenous) we have:

w (nominal wage), p (GDP-deflator), uc (user cost of capital), t (time), i^r (real interest rate), Y^F (weighted foreign GDP), p^F (foreign price index), POP (potential labor force), wr (net real wage), RFS (ratio of foreign to Swiss employment).

The remaining variables of the model are either **latent endogenous** (Y^d, $\tilde{Y}^s$, $\tilde{L}^d$, L^s) or **deterministic functions** of predetermined observable variables and unknown parameters.

6.3 Method of estimation

In the present context, joint estimation by **maximum likelihood** is advisable because of **cross-equation restrictions, contemporaneous correlation** of the error terms and **simultaneous endogenous variables.** We discuss these points now in more detail and sketch the derivation of the likelihood function.

For the moment we disregard the investment equation. All other equations are connected by [19.°] to observables. When estimating this system, cross-equation restrictions in form of the common parameters α_0, ν , τ, κ_Y, κ_L, r and s must be taken into account. Furthermore, the same theoretical specifications show up at different places in the model, which will most likely give rise to contemporaneous correlation of the error terms; this applies especially to u_{2t} and u_{3t} since (49.2) and (49.3) as well as (54.1) and (54.2) must be expected to involve substantial common specification errors.

Turning to the simultaneity of endogenous variables and the derivation of the **likelihood function,** we have to distinguish between the original model as set out in sections 2 and 3, and the version with buffer stocks as described in section 4. In the final aggregate structure, the buffer version differs from the original model only in two points: (i) Transformation equation [19°.1] is replaced by [19°.1'] (see page 88) and (ii) the tension indicator P_G is derived from the assessment of buffer stocks instead of capacities. All other equations are exactly the same in the two versions.

In the original **model without buffers** the variables L, Y, P_L and P_G are jointly endogenous. We assume that the errors $u = (u_1, u_2, u_3, u_4)'$ in [19°] are i.i.d. normal with covariance matrix Ω. Parameters to be estimated are: The 'transformation parameters' α_0, ν , τ, κ_Y and κ_L, the 'structural parameters' c_1, c_2, ... through d_5, henceforth collected in a vector Θ; the elements of Ω. The likelihood function thus reads in general terms as

$$\ln \pounds(\Theta, \alpha_0, \nu, \tau, \kappa_Y, \kappa_L, \Omega)$$

and can be set up in the usual manner; the (time-varying) Jacobian of transformation from u to (L, Y, P_L, P_G) - defined by [19°] - is

$$|\det J_t| = \frac{\kappa_Y \alpha_0 e^{\nu t}}{Y_t L_t P_{G_t}(1-P_{G_t})P_{L_t}(1-P_{L_t})} \quad \text{or} \quad \ln|\det J_t| = C_t + \nu t + \ln(\kappa_Y \alpha_0), \tag{56}$$

where C_t collects all terms not dependent on unknown parameters.

In the **buffer version**, the variable P_G, reflecting beginning-of-period buffer stocks, according to [19°.1'] depends only on lagged values of demand and output. The likelihood function is based on differently defined residuals u_{1t} and involves the Jacobian

$$|\det J_t| = \left(\frac{\partial \Phi^{-1}(P_G)}{\partial P_G}\right)_t \frac{\alpha_0 e^{\nu t}}{Y_t L_t P_{L_t}(1-P_{L_t})} \quad \text{or} \quad \ln|\det J_t| = C_t + \nu t + \ln(\alpha_0) \tag{57}$$

If u_1 is independent of (u_2, u_3, u_4), which is not implausible and can be tested as a constraint on Ω,[1] and furthermore non-autocorrelated (which is assumed throughout), the model becomes recursive: [19°.1'] determines P_G, and this variable can be considered predetermined in the other equations of the model. As no cross-restrictions are involved, P_G is also weakly exogenous to the rest of the model, i.e. the likelihood function factorizes into a marginal one for P_G and a conditional one for Y, L and P_L (given P_G) with no common parameters. In this case, single-equation estimation of (37),

1. Note however that measurement errors in P_G may give rise to correlation between u_1 and the other error terms.

connected via [19°.1'] to observables, is admissible.[2]

We now bring in the **investment equation** (49.1). Although this equation contains only exogenous and lagged endogenous variables as determinants, estimation by a single-equation technique would be inappropriate: Eq.(49.1) shares parameters b_2 and β_2 with (49.3). Further, investment cannot be treated as predetermined in the vintage equations (49.2) and (49.3) since firms must be assumed to decide simultaneously on capital, employment and output associated with a new vintage.[3] Common specification errors will thus entail correlation between u_{5t-1}, u_{3t} and u_{2t}. Therefore, the proper procedure is to estimate the investment equation (one period lagged) jointly with the other equations. The extended likelihood function is then based on the assumption that the five error terms are jointly i.i.d. normal. It is easy to see that Jacobians (56) and (57) remain unchanged.

6.4 Labor hoarding, partial adjustment and error correction dynamics

We consider now a dynamical modification of the model concerning the specification of labor hoarding and the related productivity cycle. As yet, labor hoarding has been taken into account in [19°.2] and [19°.3] only in form of the restriction $\kappa_L < \kappa_Y$. Accordingly, a certain reduction of output Y in relation to notional supply $\tilde{Y}^s$, caused by insufficient goods demand and captured in the model by P_G, is always associated with a fixed less-than-proportionate spillover onto labor demand. As noted earlier, modelling hoarding behavior in such a "static" fashion is rather problematical. It seems more realistic to assume that the response of effective labor demand

2. Compare Engle, Hendry and Richard (1983).
3. The one-quarter lag of investment in (49.2) and (49.3) is to be interpreted as a technical installation lag and does not make the **decision** on I_{t-1} predetermined with respect to L_t^{Δ} and Y_t^{Δ}.

to insufficient goods demand is weak in the short run but becomes larger if goods demand stays low for a prolonged period of time. To allow for such behavior, we shall introduce some simple dynamics of the 'partial adjustment' or 'error correction'-type (and confront it in the empirical part with the original formulation). Although one may regard a dynamic specification of this sort as an improvement, the various factors that may influence the extent to which firms hoard labor (demand expectations, anticipated difficulties of re-recruiting qualified workers, financial constraints, etc.) are of course still represented in a rather superficial manner.

Before turning to the concrete specification, notice that labor hoarding alters the way how firms translate demand constraints into effective labor demand but leaves the impact of the "classical" factors onto notional labor demand unaffected. To be sure, the development of notional labor demand (and likewise notional output supply) may be subject to short-run adjustment lags as well, reflecting that firms need some time to bring employment and output into line with 'profitable capacities'. But, as long as firms are not constrained by demand, they will always have the actually employed workers produce the technically feasible output.[4] This means that lags referring to "classical" factors (scrapping due to a rise in real wages, creation of new equipment) necessarily affect notional labor demand **and** notional output supply to the same extent and cannot be associated with labor hoarding. Only

4. Suppose for instance that existing capacities become unprofitable due to a real wage increase and that no offsetting creation of new equipment takes place. It is quite likely then that workers are dismissed only with a certain delay, be it for contractual reasons or because the deterioration of profitability is regarded as only temporary. But there is no reason why firms should not have the workers who are still employed produce the maximum feasible output as long as demand is sufficient to sell the output.

demand-constrained firms are likely to hoard labor in the sense of employing more workers than technically needed to produce current output. Consequently, when specifying labor demand, we have to distinguish between two types of adjustment lags: The first one concerns the formation of **notional** labor demand (and notional output supply); the second one refers to labor hoarding, i.e. the the way how firms adjust **effective** labor demand when goods demand is insufficient.

Labor hoarding in the model without buffer stocks:

First, we discuss the modification in the context of the original model neglecting buffer stocks. To specify the adjustment of the **notional trade offers**, we reinterpret the variables defined in (41) as "desired" levels, denoted by $\hat{\tilde{Y}}^{*s}_t$ and $\hat{\tilde{L}}^{*d}_t$, and postulate:

$$\hat{\tilde{Y}}^{s}_t = \hat{\tilde{Y}}^{*s\,\lambda_n}_t \, \tilde{Y}^{s\,(1-\lambda_n)}_{t-1}$$

$$\hat{\tilde{L}}^{d}_t = \hat{\tilde{L}}^{*d\,\lambda_n}_t \, \tilde{L}^{s\,(1-\lambda_n)}_{t-1} \, , \qquad 0 < \lambda_n < 1 \, . \qquad (58)$$

The appearance of lagged values of the latent variables $\tilde{Y}^s$ and $\tilde{L}^d$ in (58) does not pose a particular problem since - in the framework of the transformation equations [19°.2] and [19°.3] - they can be expressed in terms of past observables and unknown parameters.[5] We turn now to the formulation of **effective** labor demand L^d. By moving the spillover-term in [19°.3] to the right-hand side, we obtain

5. This is one of the advantages of the adopted stochastic formulation (comp. section 3.2). It has already been utilized in the dynamical specification of goods demand and labor supply.

$$L_t(1 - P_{L_t})^{-\alpha_L} = L_t^d = \tilde{L}_t^d \, P_{G_t}^{\kappa_L} = \hat{\tilde{L}}_t^d \, P_{G_t}^{\kappa_L} \, e^{u_{3t}} \, . \tag{59}$$

Thus far, we have captured labor hoarding behavior by allowing κ_L to differ from κ_Y in [19°.1] and [19°.2], expecting $\kappa_L < \kappa_Y$; compare point (c), page 52. As an alternative to this static form of labor hoarding, we impose the constraint $\kappa_L = \kappa_Y = \kappa$ (proportional long-run spillover) and modify (59) in that we let L^d adjust dynamically according to:

$$L_t^d = (\tilde{L}_t^d \, P_{G_t})^{\kappa \lambda_h} \, L_{t-1}^{d \; (1-\lambda_h)} \, , \qquad 0 < \lambda_h < 1 \, . \tag{60.1}$$

Slightly more general than such a 'partial adjustment' model is an 'error correction'-mechanism of the form

$$L_t^d = (\tilde{L}_t^d \, P_{G_t})^{\kappa \lambda_h} \, (\tilde{L}_{t-1}^d \, P_{G_{t-1}})^{\kappa \, (\gamma_h - \lambda_h)} \, L_{t-1}^{d \; (1-\gamma_h)} \, , \qquad 0 < \lambda_h, \, \gamma_h < 1, \tag{60.2}$$

where λ_h measures short-term adjustment and γ_h parametrizes the gravitation of labor demand towards its 'long-term equilibrium value', $\tilde{L}^d P_G^{\kappa}$. If $\lambda_h = \gamma_h$, (60.2) specializes to (60.1).

Labor hoarding in the model including buffer stocks:

According to the logic of the buffer model, firms are never demand-constrained in the sense that output would be directly rationed by current goods demand. The notion in this model is rather that firms enter the period with a certain (predetermined) level of buffer stocks (inventories, unfilled orders), reflecting accumulated past differences between output and demand, and - tending to partially reduce the deviation of buffer stocks from desired levels - decide on output and employment of the current period. The "feedback" from buffer stocks to output and employment can be made more apparent in [19°.2] and [19°.3] by moving the buffer variable P_G (proportion of firms assessing inventories as "too low" or unfilled orders as "too large") to the right-hand side and introducing the symbol Y^{sp} for 'planned output supply':

$$\begin{aligned} Y_t(1 - P_{L_t})^{-\alpha_L \tau} &= Y_t^{sp} = \tilde{Y}_t^s \, P_{G_t}^{\kappa_Y} \\ L_t(1 - P_{L_t})^{-\alpha_L} &= L_t^d = \tilde{L}_t^d \, P_{G_t}^{\kappa_L} , \end{aligned} \tag{61}$$

According to this formulation, firms reduce Y^{sp} in relation to profitable capacities $\tilde{Y}^s$ as a function of the aggregate buffer variable P_G. P_G at the same time captures the spillover onto effective labor demand L^d.[6] In this formulation, labor hoarding is again associated with $\kappa_L < \kappa_Y$. As an alternative, we propose the following 'partial adjustment'-specification:

$$\begin{aligned} Y_t(1 - P_{L_t})^{-\alpha_L \tau} &= Y_t^{sp} = \left[\tilde{Y}_t^s \, P_{G_t}^{\kappa}\right]^{\lambda_Y} Y_{t-1}^{sp\,(1-\lambda_Y)} \\ L_t(1 - P_{L_t})^{-\alpha_L} &= L_t^d = \left[\tilde{L}_t^d \, P_{G_t}^{\kappa}\right]^{\lambda_L} L_{t-1}^{d\,(1-\lambda_L)} , \quad 0 < \lambda_L < \lambda_Y < 1. \end{aligned} \tag{62.1}$$

As compared to (61), we have imposed the long-term constraint $\kappa_L = \kappa_Y = \kappa$ but allow now for different adjustment speeds λ_Y and λ_L. Note that the response of output to buffers is considered to be subject to an adjustment

---

6. Firms are confronted then on the labor market with a certain supply L^s. If L^s is large enough so that "every" firm can realize labor demand, (61) implies (in the limit) $P_L = 0$, $L = L^d$ and $Y = Y^{sp}$. If however a certain proportion of firms is rationed by labor supply ($P_L > 0$), L falls short of L^d, and this entails a less-than-proportional spillover onto actual output Y ($\tau < 1$).

lag as well ($\lambda_Y < 1$). By contrast, in the model without buffers, demand-constrained firms have no option whatsoever as to how fast to adjust output; therefore, introducing an adjustment mechanism for output in that model would not have made sense. As a somewhat more general form of dynamic adjustment one may again consider an 'error correction'-specification:

$$Y_t(1 - P_{L_t})^{-\alpha_L \tau} = Y^{sp}_t = \left[\tilde{Y}^s_t \, P^{\kappa}_{G_t}\right]^{\lambda_Y} \left[\tilde{Y}^s_{t-1} P^{\kappa}_{G_{t-1}}\right]^{(\gamma_Y - \lambda_Y)} Y^{sp\,(1-\gamma_Y)}_{t-1}$$

$$L_t(1 - P_{L_t})^{-\alpha_L} = L^d_t = \left[\tilde{L}^d_t \, P^{\kappa}_{G_t}\right]^{\lambda_L} \left[\tilde{L}^d_{t-1} P^{\kappa}_{G_{t-1}}\right]^{(\gamma_L - \lambda_L)} L^{d\,(1-\gamma_L)}_{t-1} , \qquad (62.2)$$

$$0 < \lambda_L < \lambda_Y < 1$$

$$0 < \gamma_L, \gamma_Y < 1 .$$

The λ's are the parameters of short-run adjustment, and the γ's measure how strongly output supply Y^{sp} and labor demand L^d are attracted by the respective long-run equilibrium values, $\tilde{Y}^s P^{\kappa}_G$ and $\tilde{L}^d P^{\kappa}_G$. This 'error correction'-mechanism may be seen more clearly if we rewrite (62.2) as

$$\Delta\ln(Y^{sp}_t) = \lambda_Y \Delta\ln(\tilde{Y}^s_t P^{\kappa}_{G_t}) + \gamma_Y\left[\ln(\tilde{Y}^s_{t-1} P^{\kappa}_{G_{t-1}}) - \ln(Y^{sp}_{t-1})\right]$$

$$\Delta\ln(L^d_t) = \lambda_L \Delta\ln(\tilde{L}^d_t P^{\kappa}_{G_t}) + \gamma_L\left[\ln(\tilde{L}^d_{t-1} P^{\kappa}_{G_{t-1}}) - \ln(L^d_{t-1})\right]$$

The 'partial adjustment'-model (62.1) arises as special case if $\lambda_Y = \gamma_Y$ and $\lambda_L = \gamma_L$.

7. ESTIMATION RESULTS

The several versions of the model are estimated with quarterly data over the period 1967.2 to 1985.4 (while the data from 1986.1 to 1989.4 will be used to test post-sample parameter stability). The appropriate likelihood functions, discussed in the preceding section, are concentrated with respect to Ω and maximized using the Davidon-Fletcher-Powell algorithm as implemented in the computer package GQOPT (R.E. Quandt). Starting values for the parameters can be obtained by setting the transformation parameters in [19°] to plausible values, calculating the latent demand and supply variables and regressing them on the explanatory variables of the corresponding equations by single-equation nonlinear least squares. The subsequent ML-estimation accounts for simultaneity of the endogenous variables, cross-equation parameter restrictions and contemporaneous correlation of error terms. Standard errors of the estimated parameters are derived in the usual manner from the approximate inverse of the Hessian at the maximum of $\ln \mathcal{L}$.

7.1 Empirical versions - Models 1 to 4

For all the variants of the model considered, the vintage equations, the scrapping functions and the equations for goods demand, labor supply and investment demand are specified identically, as stated in the summary of section 6.2 (pp. 88-90). The models differ however as to whether they allow for buffer stocks and the concrete specification of dynamics in the equations for output supply and labor demand. To begin with the simplest case, we first neglect buffer stocks and disregard the investment equation, i.e. treat investment as predetermined in the rest of the model. We proceed then to the version with buffer stocks and finally endogenize investment. In detail, the empirical work is organized as follows:

- First, we estimate the model without buffer stocks and a 'static' formulation of labor hoarding ($\kappa_L < \kappa_Y$). This model, henceforth referred to as **Model 1**, consists just of the equations summarized on pp. 88-90 and additionally allows for a dynamic adjustment of the notional trade offers as specified in (58), p. 95.
- Next, we represent labor hoarding dynamically according to the 'partial adjustment'-specification (60) ($\lambda_h < 1$); this version is called **Model 2.**
- We then turn to the buffer model. As Model 2 proves empirically superior to Model 1, we skip a potential combination of the buffer model with static hoarding - see (61) - and proceed directly to the dynamic specification (62.1) ($\lambda_L < \lambda_Y$). This model, referred to as **Model 3**, turns out to be more convincing than the models without buffer stocks. It will therefore be used as basis for the further analysis.
- Autocorrelated residuals in the equations for output supply and labor demand indicate that the dynamics in these equations need improvement. Replacing the 'partial adjustment'-scheme (62.1) by the more flexible 'error correction'-formulation (62.2) gives rise to a more satisfactory error process. We thus incorporate the investment equation into this structure, yielding **Model 4.** The parameter changes in the remaining equations, as compared to Model 3, are minor. This suggests that endogenizing investment in Models 1 and 2 would not lead to a notable improvement of the estimation results. Therefore, we leave it at that and regard Model 4 as the final outcome.
- In the framework of Model 4, we test several a priori restrictions and also check the sensitivity and structural stability of the parameter estimates.

For the following discussion of the estimation resulte, compare the **summary tables** on pages 102 and 121.[1]

7.2 Model 1: No buffer stocks, 'static' labor hoarding

The standard errors of residuals (SER) and the DW-statistics reported in **column 1** of the table indicate a satisfactory fit of the model.[2] As to the plausibility of the parameter estimates, there is a marked difference between the goods demand equation, where there seems to be a severe problem, and the remaining equations of the model, for which the obtained values look quite reasonable. We first give a brief interpretation of this second group of parameters (which will turn out to be fairly stable across models) and examine then the rather questionable goods demand equation. For the following discussion, the reader should refer to the summary of the model (pp. 88-90) and further keep in mind that we are commenting on point estimates, which are partly subject to substantial standard errors.

Transformation parameters (mismatch, spillovers):

The values obtained for α_0 and ν indicate a **growing labor market mismatch** ($\alpha_L = \alpha_0 e^{\nu t}$). The implied SURE (structural unemployment rate, definition see (a) on pp. 51-52) - increases from 1.20% in 1967.2 to 1.79% in 1985.4. This outcome contrasts with Switzerland's extremely low official unemployment figures (which are known to be incomplete though) and is more in line

1. For parameters a_0 and d_1 comparisons across models are uninteresting since they just compensate for differences in the optimal values obtained for the other parameters (similar to the constant term in a linear regression). Therefore, a_0 and d_1 are not reported in the tables.
2. Note that the error terms in [19°] are in multiplicative lognormal form so that the corresponding SER are in relative terms; labor demand for instance is explained with a standard error of 1.03%.

SUMMARY TABLE: Estimation Results (standard errors in parenthesis, insignificance at 5%-level indicated by *)

		Model 1 (1)	Model 1 (2)		Model 2 (1)	Model 2 (2)	Model 2 (3)		Model 3
mismatch spillovers	α_0	.0174 (.00388)	.0183 (.00358)	α_0	.0144 (.00302)	.0160 (.00315)	.0151 (.00305)	α_0	.0133 (.00325)
	ν	.00542* (.00404)	.00405* (.00357)	ν	.0105 (.00395)	.00699* (.00372)	.00811 (.00392)	ν	.0116 (.00423)
	τ	.699* (.418)	-.728 (.172)	τ	.465* (.237)	-.717 (.167)	-.765 (.0230)	τ	.618 .260)
	κ_Y	.0359 (.00949)	.0315 (.00538)	κ	.0431 (.00466)	.0330 (.00455)	.0332 (.00489)	κ	.149 (.0178)
	κ_L	.0236 (.00578)	.0268 (.00494)						
output demand	a_1	-17.4 (8.25)	.798 (.0495)	a_1	-8.12* (4.10)	.771 (.0589)	→ .7	a_1	.693 (.116)
	a_2	-951.* (1637.)	-4.88* (22.8)	a_2	-957.* (638.)	-9.80 (29.2)	-19.6 (35.1)	a_2	-110.* (62.9)
	a_3	31.2* (18.3)	.388 (.168)	a_3	14.0* (7.29)	.399* (.178)	.528* (.225)	a_3	.0890* (.281)
	a_4	3156.* (1779.)	52.2 (13.5)	a_4	2153. (932.)	57.1 (16.2)	75.0 (17.3)	a_4	76.5 (33.6)
	a_5	10908. (3774.)	138. (43.8)	a_5	5679. (2469.)	177. (53.3)	245. (96.3)	a_5	458. (104.)
	a_6	-1.31* (.836)	-.0612 (.0219)	a_6	-1.37 (.382)	-.0694 (.0265)	-.0907 (.0364)	a_6	-.0714* (.0541)
	λ_G	.0206 (.00694)	→ 1.	λ_G	.0594 (.0210)	→ 1.	.736 (.138)	λ_G	.706 (.0819)
output supply labor demand	b_1	.408 (.119)	.367 (.124)	b_1	.414 (.0409)	.348 (.0767)	.365 (.0797)	b_1	.413 (.0436)
	b_2	.637 (.250)	.525 (.200)	b_2	.439 (.0831)	.391 (.127)	.383 (.121)	b_2	.426 (.0830)
	β_2	.00424 (.00196)	.00358 (.00159)	β_2	.00258 (.00069)	.00253 (.00103)	.00269 (.0989)	β_2	.00259 (.000579)
	c_1	.0353 (.0127)	.0300 (.0140)	c_1	.0366 (.00678)	.0256 (.0109)	.0272 (.0117)	c_1	.0305 (.00879)
	c_2	.764 (.174)	.813 (.262)	c_2	.719 (.0890)	.845 (.237)	.803 (.219)	c_2	.722 (.110)
	r	.790 (.229)	.664 (.253)	r	.767 (.147)	.538 (.237)	.549 (.246)	r	.590 (.191)
	s	.0271 (.0102)	.0270 (.0119)	s	.0283 (.00319)	.0278 (.00746)	.0295 (.00775)	s	.0286 (.00348)
	λ_n	.233 (.0780)	.226 (.0587)	λ_n	.587 (.0954)	.355 (.0785)	.336 (.0818)	λ_Y	.669 (.0934)
				λ_h	.399 (.0714)	.580 (.120)	.596 (.122)	λ_L	.276 (.0524)
labor supply	d_2	-.00397 (.00117)	-.00373 (.00113)	d_2	-.00366 (.00038)	-.00326 (.00087)	-.00322 (.00087)	d_2	-.00442 (.00174)
	d_3	.177* (.205)	.179* (.196)	d_3	.178* (.122)	.129* (.175)	.126* (.169)	d_3	.301* (.289)
	d_4	.201 (.0927)	.154* (.0917)	d_4	.189* (.106)	.144* (.103)	.140* (.0986)	d_4	.179* (.106)
	d_5	.126 (.0624)	.129 (.0567)	d_5	.159 (.0247)	.162 (.0596)	.152 (.0594)	d_5	.0976* (.0614)
ln £		-657.72	-661.23		-649.05	-657.31	-656.37		-642.77
$\hat{u}_1$		.0152/2.12	.0140/2.24		.0142/2.04	.0140/2.13	.0139/2.21		.0562/1.87
$\hat{u}_2$		.0187/2.32	.0186/2.44		.0191/1.84	.0183/2.25	.0184/2.28		.0156/1.66
$\hat{u}_3$		.0103/1.58	.0108/1.68		.0080/2.05	.0086/2.11	.0087/2.11		.0072/1.32
$\hat{u}_4$		.0079/1.75	.0078/1.77		.0080/1.65	.0079/1.69	.0078/1.71		.0078/1.71

with estimates obtained, on basis of similar models, for other countries.[3] Note that SURE is not to be interpreted as a lower bound of total unemployment but is defined for a situation of aggregate equilibrium ($L^s = L^d$); the model will thus imply unemployment rates smaller than SURE in situations with positive aggregate excess demand for labor.

According to the estimate of τ, rationing of labor demand leads - as expected - to a less-than-proportionate **spillover onto effective output supply** (see (b) on p. 52, considering that α_Y is reparametrized as $\alpha_L \tau$). Numerical magnitudes can be demonstrated as follows: As point of reference we choose an **aggregate** labor market equilibrium, $L^s = L^d$ (= $\tilde{L}^d P_G^{\kappa_L}$), implying $P_L = 0.5$ (proportion of labor constrained firms), and calculate the associated values of employment L and output Y (α_L set to its mean value in the sample period). We let then L^s decrease by 1% ($L^s = 0.99\ L^d$). As a result, P_L increases to 0.616, entailing reductions in L and Y of 0.56% and 0.39% respectively.

As to the **Keynesian spillover,** first note that the condition for 'static' labor hoarding ($\kappa_L < \kappa_Y$) is fulfilled (see (c) on p. 52). To determine the size of the spillover effect, we set $Y^d = \tilde{Y}^s$, implying $P_G = 0.5$ (proportion of firms **un**constrained by goods demand) and compute Y and L (point of reference). We reduce then Y^d by 1%. As a result, P_G decreases to 0.430, and Y and L fall by 0.53% and 0.36% respectively.

All these implications of the transformation parameters seem plausible.

---

3. We shall come back to this point when discussing Model 4.

<u>Notional labor demand and goods supply</u> (vintage and scrapping equations):

Parameter c_2, corresponding to the elasticity of substitution of the underlying vintage production function, assumes a reasonable value of 0.764. The estimate for c_1, saying that about 35 new jobs were created with an investment volume of 1 million SFr. in 1970.1 (when w/uc = 1), seems rather high. Parameter b_2, the elasticity of the 'capital coefficient' I/Y^{Δ} with respect to relative factor costs, is - as expected on theoretical grounds - somewhat lower than c_2. The value obtained for b_1, indicating a capital productivity on new equipment of 0.408 at w/uc = 1 and t = 0, is probably overestimated. According to β_2, the technical progress on new equipment is 0.42% per quarter, which seems a bit low.

Parameter r measures the impact of real wages on notional labor demand due to scrapping of old equipment and can be interpreted roughly as an 'elasticity'; the value of 0.79 seems reasonable. According to the estimate for s, the deterioration of labor productivity on existing equipment is 2.71% per quarter, implying scrapping factors F_t^L and F_t^Y of 0.978 and 0.960 if $(w/p)_t = (w/p)_{t-1}$. In other words, if the real wage remains constant and no new equipment is installed, notional labor demand and output supply fall by 2.2% and 4% per quarter respectively as a result of the efficiency loss on existing equipment. This effect seems again rather strong, possibly compensating for the probable overestimation of c_1 and b_1 (labor input and output per unit of investment in new equipment).

All these impacts on notional labor demand and notional output supply are dampened in the short run by a partial adjustment mechanism; according to λ_n, the elasticity of short-term adjustment is 0.233 per quarter.

<u>Labor supply</u>:

The estimate of d_5 implies that variations in the actual net real wage are translated into the permanent one to an extent of approximately 50% in 5 quarters. The elasticity of intertemporal substitution (d_4) and the elasticity with respect to the permanent net real wage (d_3) are estimated at 0.201 and 0.177 respectively, implying a total 'wage elasticity' of 0.378. These estimates appear quite reasonable. Net real wages held constant, parameter d_2 indicates a negative time trend in labor supply relative to the potential labor force of about 0.4% per quarter, i.e. a rather strong tendency for the participation rate to decrease (ceteris paribus). In view of the rising share of young people participating in higher education and the steady decline in the average retirement age, this result is not implausible though. As far as female labor supply behavior is concerned (not separately modelled here), one should mention a special factor in Switzerland: Foreign women with comparatively high participation rates seem to adapt to Swiss women's bahavior in the course of time. This prevents the overall female participation rate from rising (as it does in most other countries).

The estimated labor supply parameters can be regarded as quite plausible. They correspond by-and-large to the values reported in Stalder (1989), where an identically specified labor supply equation was estimated in the context of a simpler model confined to the labor market. Note however that the standard errors of the supply parameters are relatively large.[4]

4. For Model 4 below, a sensitivity analysis of the likelihood function is performed, showing that the individual supply parameters cannot be determined with due precision. In particular, it turns out that it is not possible to separate statistically the 'income effect' of real wages from long-term socioeconomic developments captured by the time trend: For instance, if one suppresses the negative time trend, the income effect becomes negative and the loss in likelihood is insignificant.

Goods demand (demand for domestic output):

Estimation results for this equation turn out totally unsatisfactory. Most parameters are insignificant. Parameter a_1, measuring the 'marginal propensity to consume' (including government spending and residential construction), assumes a large negative value. The estimates for a_2 to a_5 have the correct sign but are all implausibly large in absolute value. The adjustment parameter λ_G is close to zero (random walk).[5]

One may suspect multicollinearity to be the reason for the unfavorable results. If this were the case, it should be possible to obtain more reasonable estimates by imposing a priori constraints - without causing a significant loss in likelihood. Several such experiments were performed. As an example, consider **column** 2 in the summary table on p. 102, where parameter λ_G is forced to a value of 1 (instantaneous adjustment of goods demand). The following points are worth noting about this experiment:

- All demand parameters assume now reasonable values. In particular, a_1 (marginal propensity to comsume) looks entirely plausible with a value of about 0.8. The price elasticity a_6, although considerably smaller than in the unconstrained estimation, becomes significant.

5. For a detailed interpretation, which is left to the reader, the following is useful to know: Y, I and Y^d are measured in millions of Swiss Francs at prices of 1970 and have sample means of 24185, 3417 and 24965 respectively; the price ratio p/p^F is 1 in 1970 and has a sample mean of 1.43; the real interest rate i^r is measured in percentage points and its sample mean is 0.3%; Y^F (foreign GDP) is an index (1980=100) with a sample mean of 89.3. Thus, for example, if Y^F increases by 1 point or 1.12% at its sample mean, Y^d according to a_4 increases by 3156 or 12.6% at its sample mean in the long run; due to the low λ_G, the short-run response is only 65 or 0.26%.

- The constraint on λ_G is however rather strongly rejected on a likelihood ratio criterion ($-2\Delta\ln \pounds = 7.02$ vs. $\chi^2_{.95} = 3.84$ or $\chi^2_{.99} = 6.63$). A test based on the estimated standard error of λ_G in the unconstrained estimation would lead to an even stronger rejection.[6]
- Constraining λ_G to a value of 1 entails only minor changes in the parameters of the other equations, with one important exception however: The transformation parameter τ becomes significantly negative, implying a wrongly-signed positive spillover from rationed labor demand onto output.

To sum up, by imposing the constraint $\lambda_G = 1$, we obtain reasonable parameters for goods demand; the constraint is however rejected in a LR-test and has moreover unrealistic implications as to the transformation parameter τ. Other experiments (not presented here), involving various constraints on a_1, λ_G and τ, lead to similar conclusions: It is not possible in the framework of Model 1 to obtain parameter values that are at the same time plausible and accepted by the data.

7.3 Model 2: No buffer stocks, dynamic labor hoarding

This model differs from Model 1 in that we impose $\kappa_L = \kappa_Y = \kappa$ and represent labor hoarding alternatively by a dynamic partial adjustment mechanism with $\lambda_h < 1$. This being the only change, there is little hope that the problem with Model 1, which seems to be rooted in the specification of goods demand and/or the associated transformation equation, can be resolved.

---

6. This demonstrates that the estimated standard errors, which only reflect the local curvature of the likelihood function near the maximum (approximate inverse Hessian), may give a misleading picture of the likelihood surface over more distant points in parameter space. This is typical for nonlinear models and shows that LR-tests are more reliable than tests that are based only on local properties of the likelihood function.

Indeed, an almost identical picture emerges: In the unconstrained estimation (column 1 for Model 2 in the summary table on p. 102), the parameters of goods demand assume again highly implausible values. With the constraint $\lambda_G = 1$ (column 2), plausible demand parameters are obtained, the constraint is however again rejected on a LR-criterion and entails a negative value of τ. Virtually the same happens if a_1 is forced to a plausible value of 0.7 (column 3). It is of course not impossible to reduce the parameter space still further in such a way that plausible values for all parameters result. For example, if we set $\lambda_G = 1$ and in addition impose $\tau = 1$, implying a proportional spillover from rationed labor demand to output supply, all parameters assume reasonable values (not reported in the table). However, the log-likelihood decreases drastically by 29.51. Moreover, the demand residuals $\hat{u}_1$ become notably larger and show strong autocorrelation (SER = 0.0199, DW = 1.11).

Comparing the unconstrained estimates of Model 2 with Model 1, and putting aside for the moment the problem with goods demand, the following differences show up (columns 1). In Model 2 the labor market mismatch is somewhat smaller at the beginning of the estimation period (α_0) but increases faster (ν). The spillover from rationed labor demand onto output supply (τ) becomes weaker but almost significant at the 5%-level. The Keynesian spillover from rationed goods supply to effective labor demand is stronger in the long run (κ) but dampened to a notable degree by labor hoarding in the short run (λ_h). On the other hand, the adjustment speed of notional trade offers increases substantially (λ_n). The response of the optimal capital coefficient to relative factor costs and the technical progress on new equipment become weaker (b_2, β_2). The remaining parameters show only minor changes.

As to 'model selection', note that Model 1 and Model 2 are nested in a more general specification that allows both for different values of κ_L and κ_Y and 'dynamic' labor hoarding (adjustment parameter λ_h). Model 1 obtains as special case for $\lambda_h = 1$, Model 2 imposes $\kappa_L = \kappa_Y$. Thus, each model involves just one constraint. The selection can therefore be made directly by comparing the respective likelihood values. This criterion gives preference to Model 2. Associated with the increase in likelihood is an improved fit of the labor demand equation (see SER and DW-statistic for $\hat{u}_3$), indicating that the dynamic specification of labor hoarding is indeed more appropriate. However, the implausible parameter values of the goods demand equation cast doubts on both models altogether.

At this point, two ways to proceed are conceivable. First, one may call in question the equation for goods demand (37) and try to find a more appropriate specification. Second, one may suspect the manner how latent goods demand is related to observed output to be at the root of the trouble and modify the corresponding transformation equation. This second route is of course the obvious one in our case since replacement of [19°.1] by the buffer equation [19°.1'] is just the essence of Model 3.

7.4 Model 3: Allowing for buffer stocks

In this model, demand for domestic output (37) is estimated in connection with transformation equation [19°.1'], which can be recast as

$$\Delta BU_t = k\Phi^{-1}(P_{G_t}) - k\Phi^{-1}(P_{G_{t-1}}) = Y^d_{t-1} - Y_{t-1} \quad , \quad k > 0 \; . \tag{63}$$

The term $k\Phi^{-1}(P_G)$ is a proxy for unobserved 'aggregate buffer stocks' BU (unfilled orders minus output inventories). The proportion P_G is derived from firms' assessment of unfilled orders and output inventories reported in business surveys and can be interpreted as proportion of firms with 'desired output' larger than 'profitable capacities' (section 4). Eq. (63) determines buffer changes ΔBU in terms of P_G and serves to derive unobserved demand Y^d from actual output Y. The basic idea behind the buffer model is that demand Y^d fluctuates around 'smoothed' output Y, leading to positive (negative) buffer changes ΔBU in booms (recessions). These - accumulated as BU - are assumed to work back on the output decision. Inspection of the series for P_G shows that the implied series of buffer stocks in fact exhibits the expected cyclical pattern. It is then clear from (63) that the parameter estimates for goods demand (37) will crucially depend on the calibration of 'scaling parameter' k: A large value of k implies more pronounced fluctuations of Y^d around Y and is thus likely to increase the estimated coefficients of the cyclical determinants in (37).

There are in principal two ways to calibrate k: (a) one may set k to a value which produces a series for ΔBU which seems plausible in view of extraneous information about buffer stocks ; (b) one may try to determine k by optimizing the fit of the demand equation. Ideally, this two methods should lead to similar conclusions about k.

We first proceed according to (a). Quantitative data about buffer stocks are sparse in Switzerland.[7] Some information as to how a reasonable series for ΔBU might look like is available nevertheless. For example, unfilled orders are reported quantitatively for the important machines industry. Further, national accounts contain the item 'inventory change', which however includes all types of inventories and 'errors and omissions'. While partial information of this sort is certainly not sufficient to construct a

7. This of course was the reason to resort to the proxy $k\Phi^{-1}(P_G)$ for buffers BU in the first place.

series for ΔBU, it may help to reasonably fix k once the course of ΔBU has been derived from P_G up to the scaling factor k. Since buffer changes relative to GDP are likely to be of similar magnitude in other countries, one may also get some hint regarding the value of k from foreign statistical sources. We cannot go into details about these considerations here but simply state that we regard values of k in a range of 3000 to 9000 as realistic (output Y being measured in millions of Swiss Francs at prices of 1970). Setting k = 6000, for instance, we obtain a series for ΔBU that has a standard deviation of about 2% in terms of average GDP in the sample period (the mean of ΔBU is close to zero). The resulting values of Y^d (calculated via (63)) are plotted against actual Y in fig. 6. In view of the introductory remarks to section 4 (p. 55), this figure looks quite plausible: Whereas short-run fluctuations in Y^d are smoothed out to some degree, the more sustained swings in Y^d entail - with some delay - changes in Y of comparable size. Over the whole sample period, the standard deviation of ΔY is slightly

FIG. 6: Actual output Y and goods demand Y^d

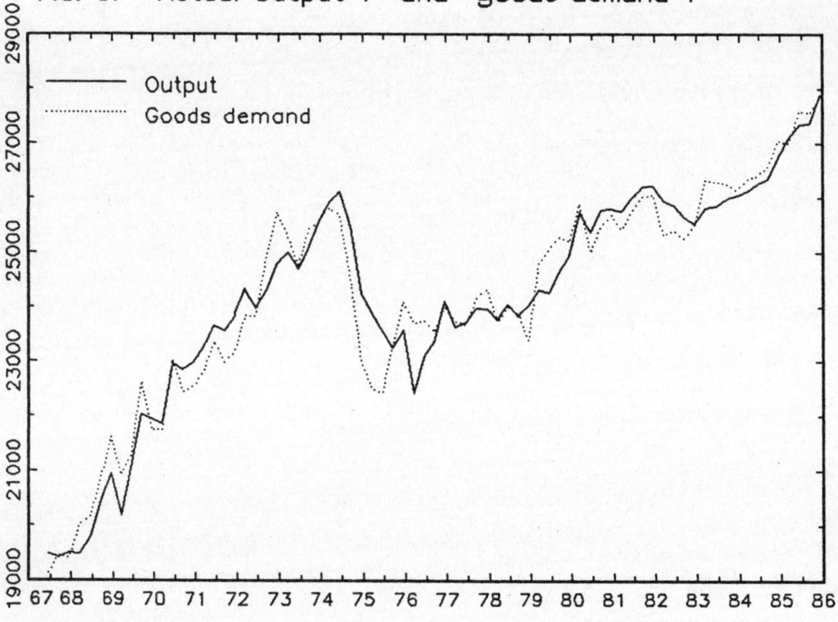

smaller than the standard deviation of ΔY^d (by a factor of about 0.8). It is quite obvious how differing k-values would modify fig. 6: For small values of k (smaller than 3000), buffer changes become numerically unimportant so that movements in Y^d almost coincide with those in Y; large values of k (greater than 9000) on the other hand produce fluctuations in Y^d that seem unrealistically large.

As noted in section 6.3, a single-equation technique is appropriate for estimating the demand equation (37) provided that u_1 in [19°.1'] is independent from the other error terms of the model. In the following, we do a preliminary analysis of the demand equation under this assumption. Calculating Y^d via (63) by setting k = 6000 (values shown in fig. 6), we obtain:[8]

a_1	a_2	a_3	a_4	a_5	a_6	λ_G	
.695	-132.	.0201	88.3	486.	-.0933	.712	(64)
(.111)	(61.5)	(.280)	(34.3)	(108.)	(.0549)	(.0852)	

$\bar{R}^2 = 0.968$ SER = 0.0556 SSR = 0.232 DW = 1.95

The parameter estimates look reasonable by and large. Parameter a_1, the 'marginal propensity to consume out of GDP' (including government spending and residential construction), assumes a plausible value of about 0.7. The estimate for a_3, measuring the contribution of investment to demand for domestic output, seems too low, even considering the large import share in investment demand, but a plausible value for a_3 certainly lies within the wide confidence interval. Parameters a_2, a_4 and a_5 are best interpreted at the sample means of the associated variables (refer to footnote 5, p. 106): If the real interest rate increases by 1% point, Y^d falls by about 0.5%

8. In the framework of the complete buffer model, which will be estimated over the period 1967.2 to 1985.4 by ML, the demand equation appears with one-quarter lag. To ensure comparability, we estimate it here over the period 1967.1 to 1985.3.

(a_2);[9] a 1%-increase in Y^F (foreign GDP) entails a 0.32%-rise in Y^d (a_4); an acceleration in the growth of Y^F by 1% implies a 1.7%-increase in Y^d (a_5). The elasticity of Y^d with respect to p/p^F, a_6, seems rather low. All these estimates are long-term impacts; according to λ_G, the short-run adjustment is however quite rapid.

We turn now to method (b). A grid search for k shows that the fit of the demand equation improves for higher k. For example, setting k to 9000 - a value that must already be considered large in the light of (a) - we obtain:

a_1	a_2	a_3	a_4	a_5	a_6	λ_G
.466	-239.	.0696	152.	788.	-.159	.602

$\bar{R}^2 = 0.972$ SER = 0.0529   SSR = 0.210   DW = 2.11

If we increase k further, the fit steadily improves and the parameter estimates keep on moving in the same direction as between k = 6000 and k = 9000. The best fit (minimal sum of squared residuals: SSR = 0.176) is eventually reached at k = 66000. This is of course a totally unrealistic value. It also produces highly implausible parameter estimates. Hence, we have to conclude that adjusting k on basis of the fitting criterion does not work out well. In the sequel we shall therefore rely on considerations (a), i.e. set k to a value that seems plausible on a priori grounds. The comforting thing with this procedure is that the choice of k, while strongly influencing the parameters of goods demand (as can be seen by comparing the outcomes for k = 6000 and k = 9000 above), leaves the parameter estimates of the remaining equations in the model largely unaffected; this can be seen when estimating goods demand for alternative values of k jointly with

9. Note that the real interest rate affects goods demand additionally via the impact of the user cost of capital on fixed business investment. This effect is not included in parameter a_2.

the other equations of the model my ML.[10] The disturbing point is that the grid search is not just inconclusive in the sense that the SSR would be flat along the k-axis; it rather suggests quite strongly an unrealistically large value of k: In a F-test, the constraints k = 6000 or k = 9000 for example are clearly rejected against the value of k that minimizes SSR (F-values of 20.4 and 12.2 vs. $F_{.99}$= 7.1). In other words, in the buffer model we are again forced to impose an data-wise "unlikely" constraint in order to obtain economically sensible demand parameters. This indicates that the specification of goods demand and/or transformation equation [19°.1'] need improvement, a task that must be left to future work though.

In the following, we estimate the complete buffer model jointly, conditional on the restriction k = 6000. It will turn out - an this is a clear advantage over Models 1 and 2 - that all parameter estimates assume plausible values.[11] The estimation results for Model 3 are listed in the summary table (p. 102). Note that the definition of the residuals $\hat{u}_1$ differs from Models 1 and 2 - as [19°.1'] replaces [19°.1] - so that the associated SER are not comparable across models. Also, likelihood comparisons with Models 1

10. This independence is not surprising: Goods demand and the remaining equations are only connected by a potential correlation of the error terms (no cross-equation restrictions, buffers predetermined disregarding stochastic terms); see also next footnote.
11. It is not clear whether this can be attributed to a more appropriate specification of the link between goods demand and output in the buffer model. It might as well be due to the fact that the determination of the buffer variable P_G in [19°.1'] is econometrically largely independent from the rest of the model, whereas in Models 1 and 2 the (differently defined) variable P_G is jointly endogenous and eq. [19°.1] involves several cross-equation restrictions (α_L, τ, κ_Y) so that troubles with the equation for goods demand interfere with the remaining equations.

and 2 are not strictly valid. To be sure, the likelihood functions take into account the mapping from the error terms to the observable endogenous variables (Y, L, P_G, P_L), but the variable P_G in Model 3 is not the same as in Model 1 and Model 2.[12] On a very cursory level, some weak evidence in favor of Model 3 can be read off the somewhat lower SER for the residuals $\hat{u}_2$, $\hat{u}_3$ and $\hat{u}_4$ as these are defined identically across models.[13] On the other hand, the DW-value for $\hat{u}_3$ (labor demand) indicates quite strong serial correlation, the more so as the test statistic is known to be biased towards 2 when lagged dependent variables are present. The main reason to give preference to Model 3 at this stage is the plausibility of all its parameter estimates once an economically reasonable constraint on k is imposed, whereas Models 1 and 2 produce either implausible parameters values for goods demand or a wrong sign for τ (positive spillover from rationed labor demand to output).

When interpreting Model 3, two points should be kept in mind. First, the transformation parameter κ in Model 3 refers to a differently defined variable P_G and thus cannot be compared across models. Second, the impact of the

---

12. In Models 1 and 2 P_G measures the proportion of firms reporting (profitable) capacities as "too small"; in Model 3, P_G measures the proportion of firms assessing inventories as "too small" or unfilled orders as "too large" (roughly speaking). The two variables are highly correlated but the latter has a smaller variance. This is likely to bias a likelihood comparison in favor of Model 3.
13. Moreover, as is clear from transformation equation [19°.1'], we may multiply SER ($\hat{u}_1$) by k = 6000 and relate it then to the sample mean of Y^d; this yields a "relative" SER of .0135, which is slightly smaller than the corresponding SER obtained for Models 1 and 2.
    Another way to compare the fit of the models would be to determine for each period the models' joint predicions for the observable endogenous variables and to compute the respective RMSE.

buffer variable $\dot{P}_G$ on firms' decision on output supply and labor demand is modelled according to the 'partial adjustment'-scheme (62.1) (p. 97); notice that the condition for labor hoarding ($\lambda_L < \lambda_Y$) is met by the estimates. A detailed discussion of Model 3 is left to the reader. Most parameter values are fairly similar to those obtained for Models 1 and 2, and one can easily assess differences by referring to the comments given there. Additional remarks will follow for Model 4 below, which differs from Model 3 only in that investment is endogenized and that the dynamic adjustment of output supply and labor demand is captured by the more flexible 'error correction'-mechanism (62.2).

As to the question whether it is admissible to estimate goods demand uncoupled from the rest of the model by single-equation nonlinear least squares, we may first note that the single-equation estimates reported in (64) differ only negligibly from the values obtained by the joint estimation of Model 3 (see summary table, p. 102). To address the issue more rigorously, we have to test for 'weak exogeneity' of goods demand with respect to the rest of the model, which hinges on the independence of u_1 from the other error terms. This condition can be tested as a constraint on Ω, the covariance matrix of (u_1, u_2, u_3, u_4). The associated loss in likelihood turns out to be insignificant ($-2\Delta\ln \mathcal{L} = 2.82$ vs. $\chi^2_{.95}(3) = 7.81$).[14] Separate estimation of goods demand can be considered admissible thus. We shall come back to this point when the extended Model 4 is discussed.

---

14. In a linear model one could perform a Lagrange Multiplier test based on the **score** with respect to the critical elements of Ω in the **constrained** model only [see e.g. Engle (1982)]. In a nonlinear model, however, comparing the constrained with the unconstrained model in a Likelihood Ratio test seems saver.

7.5 Model 4: Inclusion of the investment equation

In a final step, we want to endogenize investment demand. This is indicated, first, from an estimation point of view (joint decision of firms on investment, labor demand and output supply, contemporaneously correlated errors, cross-equation restrictions for parameters b_2 and β_2). Second, including the investment equation makes the model also more interesting with regard to simulation possibilities. Of course, both points apply to all the models discussed so far. However, as the version with buffer stocks (Model 3) is the most promising one, we confine ourselves to a refinement of that model.

One weak point of Model 3 is the rather strong autocorrelation of the residuals in the equation for labor demand (DW-statistic of 1.32). This suggests that the dynamics are not well represented by the simple 'partial adjustment'-scheme (62.1). Hoping to improve things in this respect, we replace the PA-scheme by the more flexible 'error correction'-specification (EC), affecting the dynamics of both labor demand and output supply; see (62.2), p. 98. This modification, along with the simultaneous estimation of investment demand, yields Model 4; estimation results for the 'unrestricted' version of this model are listed in the summary table on page 121, column 1.

The EC-formulation gives rise to a more satisfactory error process in labor demand (DW = 1.54). On the other hand, the autocorrelation of the output supply residuals slightly increases without becoming alarming though (DW = 1.51). The standard error (SER) of the buffer equation of 0.0558 translates into a relative standard error of goods demand of 1.34% at the sample mean of Y^d. The SER of the investment equation of 122.1 amounts to 3.6% at the sample mean of I, which is relatively large. The other SERs shown in the table are already expressed in relative terms: 1.55% for goods supply, 0.68% for labor demand, 0.78% for labor supply. As Model 4 contains investment as an additional endogenous variable, it cannot be compared with Model 3 in terms of likelihood values. It is interesting to note, however, that the cross-restrictions with the investment equation hardly affect the standard errors of the remaining equations as compared to Model 3.[15]

In the following, we test several **parameter restrictions** on a Likelihood Ratio (LR) criterion, positing Model 4 (column 1) as maintained hypothesis. The first two tests aim at a more parsimonious econometric parametrization of the model. In section 7.6 below, we shall consider some additional parameter restrictions that are motivated by economic a priori reasoning.

First we discuss the question whether it is admissible to estimate the equation for goods demand separated from the rest of the model, as was done in (64). **Weak exogeneity of goods demand** amounts to a constraint on Ω, the covariance matrix of (u_1, u_2, u_3, u_4, u_5). Let us first have a look at the unrestricted estimate of Ω obtained from the unconstrained maximization of the likelihood function. We report it in form of the easier to interpret correlation matrix:

$$\widehat{RHO} = \begin{bmatrix} 1. & .216 & .0647 & .0464 & .12 \\ & 1. & .616 & .0199 & .1219 \\ & & 1. & .0651 & .0292 \\ & & & 1. & -.1293 \\ & & & & 1. \end{bmatrix}$$

It turns out that u_2 and u_3 are strongly correlated (0.616), which is not surprising since goods supply (u_2) and labor demand (u_3) have been derived from a common theoretical basis. All other contemporaneous correlations, including those between u_1 and (u_2, u_3, u_4, u_5) (displayed in the first line

15. In fact, the SERs of Model 4 are slightly smaller than those of Model 3. This may be explained by the inclusion of two additional parameters in the 'error correction' formulation (γ_Y and γ_L).

of $\hat{RHO}$) are fairly weak, considering that the critical value for a significant correlation at the 5%-level is approximately $2/\sqrt{T} = 0.231$. To test for independence of u_1 from all other error terms we re-estimate Model 4 with Ω constrained comformably ($\omega_{12} = \omega_{13} = \omega_{14} = \omega_{15} = 0$). The associated loss in likelihood turns out to be insignificant ($-2\Delta\ln \pounds = 2.60$ vs. $\chi^2_{.95}(4) = 9.49$). Treating goods demand and the rest of the model as separate blocks can be considered admissible thus.

Next, we discuss the empirical **relevance of the EC-specification** of labor demand and output supply as compared to the simpler PA-scheme. As already noted, the former specializes to the latter if $\lambda_Y = \gamma_Y$ and $\lambda_L = \gamma_L$. Although the empirical estimates do not differ drastically (see column 1, p. 121), the joint constraint ($\lambda_Y = \gamma_Y$ and $\lambda_L = \gamma_L$) is clearly rejected on a LR-criterion ($-2\Delta\ln \pounds = 8.44$ vs. $\chi^2_{.95}(2) = 5.99$) and moreover entails stronger serial correlation of the error terms in labor demand. On the other hand, imposing only $\lambda_Y = \gamma_Y$ (PA) while estimating λ_L and γ_L freely (EC) produces almost no loss in likelihood ($-2\Delta\ln \pounds = 0.11$ vs. $\chi^2_{.95}(1) = 3.84$). This means that the EC-specification has a clear advantage over PA only in case of labor demand.

Imposing now both constraints ($\omega_{12} = \omega_{13} = \omega_{14} = \omega_{15} = 0$ and $\lambda_Y = \gamma_Y$) simultaneously, we obtain the estimation results shown in column 2 of the summary table (p. 121). The parameters of goods demand are of course identical to those reported in (64) and commented there. Most other parameter values are fairly similar across models so that the reader can refer to the earlier comments. However, as Model 4 (column 2) will form the basis of extensive simulation experiments, we give a brief interpretation of its equations nevertheless, including investment demand, which has been treated as exogenous so far. In addition, we shall perform several specification tests and discuss the structural stability of the estimated parameters.

7.6 Interpreting Model 4 - Testing a priori parameter restrictions

Transformation parameters (mismatch and spillovers):

According to the estimates obtained for $\alpha_L = \alpha_0 e^{\nu t}$, the SURE (structural unemployment rate at equilibrium, defined in (a), p. 51/52) rises in the estimation period from .91% in the late 1960s to 2.23% in the mid 1980s. This outcome of a **growing mismatch** on the Swiss labor market agrees well with the empirical findings for most other countries for which similar models have been estimated.[16] On the other hand, an increase in SURE to more than 2% in recent years contrasts with Switzerland's extremely low unemploy-

16. The following estimates are reported:
    Austria: Neudorfer, Pichelmann and Wagner (1988) estimate a SURE that increases from 1.3% in 1965 to 3% in 1968, falls back to 1.3% in the 70's and increases then until 1986 to 3.5%.
    Belgium: Sneessens and Drèze (1986) find SUREs of 3.4% in 1973 and 4.5% in 1982; Metha and Sneessens (1988) report an increase from 1.39% in 1955 to 2.92% in 1985; the cyclical specification of Lambert (1988) implies an average SURE of 1.4%.
    France: Gagey, Lambert and Ottenwaelter (1988) report an increase in SURE from a value close to zero in 1968 to 3.3% in 1986.
    Germany: Entorf, Franz, König and Smolny (1988) estimate a SURE that increases from 2.5% in 1960 to 6% in 1986; this estimate includes however labor hoarding which amounts to about 2% of the labor force on average since 1975.
    Netherlands: Driehuis (1988) finds a practically constant SURE of about 2.2% in the period 1962-86.
    USA: Burda (1988) estimates an increase in SURE from 3.8% in 1955 to 5.4% in 1986.

SUMMARY TABLE: Estimation Results (standard errors in parenthesis,
(continued) insignificance at 5%-level indicated by *)

Model 4

		(1)	(2)	(3)
mismatch spillovers	α_0	.0128 (.00311)	.0132 (.00309)	.0211 (.00617)
	ν / ν_1	ν .0120 (.00418)	ν .0120 (.00418)	ν_1 −.0227 (.00423)
	ν_2			.000464 (.000197)
	τ	.359* (.312)	.442* (.273)	.683 (.277)
	κ	.148 (.0185)	.151 (.0192)	.164 (.0207)
output demand	a_1	.741 (.126)	.695 (.105)	.695 (.105)
	a_2	−110.* (76.3)	−132. (58.3)	−132. (58.3)
	a_3	.0660* (.307)	.0201* (.267)	.0201* (.267)
	a_4	77.0 (37.1)	88.3 (32.5)	88.3 (32.5)
	a_5	511. (106.)	486. (101.)	486. (101.)
	a_6	−.0809* (.0579)	−.0933* (.0519)	−.0933* (.0519)
	λ_G	.674 (.0902)	.712 (.0808)	.712 (.0808)
output supply, labor demand, investment	b_1	.416 (.0374)	.420 (.0388)	.443 (.0427)
	b_2	.328 (.0633)	.316 (.0625)	.316 (.0594)
	β_2	.00212 (.00054)	.00194 (.00051)	.00215 (.00052)
	e_1	.170 (.0115)	.170 (.0107)	.170 (.0108)
	c_1	.0297 (.00811)	.0293 (.00840)	.0336 (.00905)
	e_2	.0759 (.0221)	.0737 (.0203)	.0735 (.0202)
	c_2	.650 (.108)	.652 (.114)	.507 (.112)
	e_3	−2.67 (.939)	−2.64 (.875)	−2.64 (.871)
	r	.568 (.170)	.553 (.171)	.670 (.190)
	β_3	.00654 (.00044)	.00648 (.00042)	.00656 (.00042)
	s	.0302 (.00296)	.0306 (.00295)	.0302 (.0 303)
	λ_I	.206 (.0746)	.215 (.0739)	.216 (.0731)
	λ_Y	.457* (.275)	.695 (.0952)	.714 (.0984)
	γ_Y	.742 (.107)	($\gamma_Y = \lambda_Y$)	($\gamma_Y = \lambda_Y$)
	λ_L	.365 (.0952)	.403 (.0783)	.376 (.0741)
	γ_L	.219 (.0575)	.213 (.0522)	.213 (.0556)
labor supply	d_2	−.00397 (.00159)	−.00386 (.00142)	−.00324 (.00127)
	d_3	.222* (.257)	.210* (.246)	.114* (.229)
	d_4	.150* (.107)	.154* (.106)	.181* (.106)
	d_5	.0992* (.0671)	.109* (.0607)	.117* (.0612)
ln £		−1115.14	−1116.50	−1114.08
$\hat{u}_1$		.0558 / 1.96	.0556 / 1.95	.0556 / 1.95
$\hat{u}_2$		.0155 / 1.51	.0154 / 1.63	.0158 / 1.62
$\hat{u}_3$		.0068 / 1.54	.0068 / 1.58	.0071 / 1.63
$\hat{u}_4$		.0078 / 1.79	.0079 / 1.77	.0077 / 1.77
$\hat{u}_5$		122.1 / 2.25	121.9 / 2.25	121.9 / 2.25

ment rates which hardly ever exceeded 1%. Although official Swiss unemployment statistics must be expected to be rather incomplete, we want to test the issue. Re-estimation of the model under the constraint $\nu = 0$ leads to a higher value of α_0, roughly corresponding to the mean value of α_L in the unconstrained version (all other parameters, which are not reported below, remain practically unaffected by the constraint on ν):

	ν	α_0	$-2\Delta\ln £$
unconstrained:	0.0120	0.0132	
ν fixed:	0	0.0204	7.67

We thus have $\alpha_L = \alpha_0 = 0.0204$ (instead of $\alpha_L = 0.0132\ e^{0.012 \cdot t}$), implying a SURE that remains constant at 1.4% in the estimation period. The restriction is however strongly rejected in a LR-test ($-2\Delta\ln £ = 7.67$ vs. $\chi^2_{.95}(1) = 3.84$). Hence, with respect to labor market mismatch, Switzerland does not seem to differ as strongly from other countries as one might expect in view of the very low Swiss unemployment figures.

Of course, the question arises whether the mismatch has indeed been growing steadily through time, as postulated in $\alpha_L = \alpha_0 e^{\nu t}$. One way to address this issue is to re-estimate the model over subperiods. For instance, removing the last 20 quarters from the sample so that the estimation period ends in 1980.4, we obtain $\nu = 0.00556$ and $\alpha_0 = 0.01646$, and the hypothesis $\nu = 0$ cannot be rejected at all. This suggests that the mismatch was nearly constant until 1980 and began to increase sharply thereafter. To allow for such a possibility, we specify the trend as $\alpha_L = \alpha_0 e^{\nu_1 t + \nu_2 t^2}$ and re-estimate the model. The results are displayed in column 3 of the summary tabel (p. 121). The estimates of α_0, ν_1 and ν_2 imply that SURE, starting in 1967.2 at 1.45%, first slightly decreases to a minimum of 1.1% in 1973 and then grows with an accelerating rate to reach a value of 3.4% at the end of the estimation period (1985.4). This specification on the one hand outperforms the version of column 2 on a LR-criterion. On the other hand, it implies an unrealistically steep increase in mismatch in the periods after 1985 (which will be used below to test post-sample stability of the parameters), with SURE becoming as large as 7.8% in 1989. Therefore, we prefer to stick to the version of column 2.[17]

The **'repressed inflation'-spillover** (from rationed labor demand to effective output supply), parametrized by α_L and τ, can be demonstrated by assuming an aggregate labor market equilibrium and letting then L^s decrease by 1% (α_L fixed at the sample mean); this produces declines in employment L and output Y of 0.56% and 0.25% respectively. The concavity of the short-run production function, reflected in the estimate $\tau = .442 < 1$, is responsible for the less-than-proportionate output effect.

In order to discuss the **Keynesian spillover effect**, consider equation [19°.1'], which maps goods demand Y^d onto P_G (proportion of firms with 'desired production' larger than 'profitable capacities'), and specifications (62.2) and (62.1), showing how output supply and labor demand dynamically respond to P_G. Assume now that firms had entered the previous period with zero 'aggregate buffer stocks', i.e. $BU_{t-1} = UO_{t-1} - IV_{t-1} = 0$, implying $P_{G_{t-1}} = 0.5$, and were experiencing during that period a demand Y^d_{t-1} which fell short of output Y_{t-1} by 1%, corresponding to 241.85 at the sample mean of Y. Firms will then move into the current period with buffer stocks of -241.85, implying a drop in P_G from 0.5 to 0.484. Substituting the estimate for κ, one may compute from (62.1) and (62.2) that output supply and labor

17. In future work, instead of experimenting with more complicated time trends, one should rather try to advance economic hypotheses explaining the development of labor market mismatch.

demand both fall by 0.49% in the long-run. The short-run reductions, according to the empirical values of λ_Y and λ_L, are 0.34% and 0.20% respectively. Hence, buffer stocks and labor hoarding dampen the short-run spillover from goods demand onto labor demand to a considerable degree. We shall shed more light on this point later by means of dynamic simulations.

Notional labor demand and output supply (vintage and scrapping eqs.):

In Model 4, parameters b_2 (elasticity of the capital coefficient on new equipment with respect to w/uc) and β_2 (technical progress in the vintage production function) are cross-restricted with the investment equation. This brings about only minor parameter changes compared to Model 3 (comp. tabels on p. 102 and 121). In Model 4 (column 2), the elasticity of substitution of the vintage production function, c_2, assumes a plausible value of 0.652. The elasticity of the capital coefficient with respect to w/uc, b_2, is estimated at 0.316, which is - as expected from theory - smaller than c_2. The rate of **technical progress** on new equipment, β_2, is estimated at 0.194% per quarter, which is lower than in Model 3 and seems now definitely too low. Note that the investment equation (to be discussed below) provides another estimate of technical progress in the form of parameter β_3 (technical progress interpreted as labor augmenting); the value of 0.648% per quarter looks more reasonable. As mentioned in footnote 15, p. 83, the ratios b_2/c_2 and β_2/β_3 should both correspond to β_1, the output elasticity with respect to labor in the vintage production function. This condition can be used as a plausibility check. The first ratio is .485, which is a fairly plausible value for β_1. The second ratio is .299. This appears too low and points again to an underestimation of β_2. Forcing β_2 to higher values, we obtain (only parameters that change notably are reported):

	β_2	b_2	e_2	e_3	λ_I	$-2\Delta\ln £$
unconstrained:	0.00194	-0.316	0.0737	-2.64	0.215	
β_2 fixed:	0.003	-0.423	0.0903	-3.38	0.166	3.93
	0.004	-0.546	0.119	-4.49	0.118	11.56

Imposing a higher rate of technical progress enhances the impact of relative factor costs on the capital coefficient and makes investment more dependent on 'pressure of demand' and 'profitability' in the long run while the short-term adjustment becomes weaker. The loss in likelihood associated with the constraint $\beta_2 = 0.03$ just exceeds the 5%-significance level but $\beta_2 = 0.004$ is clearly rejected by the data.

The **scrapping elasticity** r, measuring the impact of real wages on notional labor demand through scrapping of old equipment, assumes a reasonable value of 0.553. According to the value of s, the deterioration of labor productivity on existing equipment is 3.06% per quarter, implying scrapping factors F_t^L and F_t^Y of 0.983 and 0.959 if $(w/p)_t = (w/p)_{t-1}$. In other words, if the real wage remains constant and no new equipment is installed, notional labor demand and output supply fall by 1.7% and 4.1% per quarter respectively as a result of the efficiency loss on existing equipment.

Investment demand:

The investment equation (specification see section 5.3.3) includes, in multiplicative form, an excess demand term (parameters e_1 and e_2), a profitability term (e_3, β_3) and a term explaining variations in the capital coefficient (b_2, β_2). Parameters b_2 and β_2 (cross-restricted with notional goods supply) have already been discussed. The other parameters can be interpreted as follows. As point point of reference, we set $(w/p)_{t-1} = (w/p)_0$, $t = 0$, $(w/uc)_{t-1} = 1$ and $P_{G_{t-1}} = 0.5$. In such a situation we have $I_t^* = Y_{t-1}e_1 = Y_{t-1}\cdot 0.17$, implying an investment rate of about 17%. Let now **goods demand** Y^d

exceed actual output Y by 1% or 241.85 at the sample mean of Y. $\Phi^{-1}(P_G)$ according to [19°.1'] increases then from 0 to 0.0403 (with a one-quarter lag), and the value of e_2 implies that I^* rises by 1.7% (again with a one-quarter lag). The elasticity of I^* with respect Y^d is thus about 1.7, which seems reasonable. The **profitability** term remains unchanged over time (equal to 1) if w/p increases exactly with the rate of labor augmenting technical progress β_3, which is estimated at 0.656% per quarter. According to e_3, deviations of actual w/p from this trend affect investment demand with an elasticity of -2.64. Profitability thus exerts a strong influence on investment. All these impacts refer to the long run; the value obtained for λ_I says that about half of a certain long-term change is completed within 3 quarters.

In view of the rather substantial weight of lagged investment in the investment equation, one may wonder how well the equation performs in a dynamical simulation (using calculated values for lagged I). As fig. 7 shows, the accord between simulated and actual investment is pretty good. The lower pannel makes clear that the short-run fluctuations in investment are mainly caused by the excess demand term. Improved profitability may explain why investment demand - in contrast to the 1975 slump - remained fairly stable in the recession of 1982 and increased markedly thereafter when demand picked up as well. In 1985, when profitability and pressure of demand are about where they were at the beginning of the estimation period, investment is notably higher. This is partly due to a higher capital coefficient (the third term in the investment equation) and partly to an increased output level (note that the equation explains investment relative to the previous period's output).

FIG. 7: Investment equation

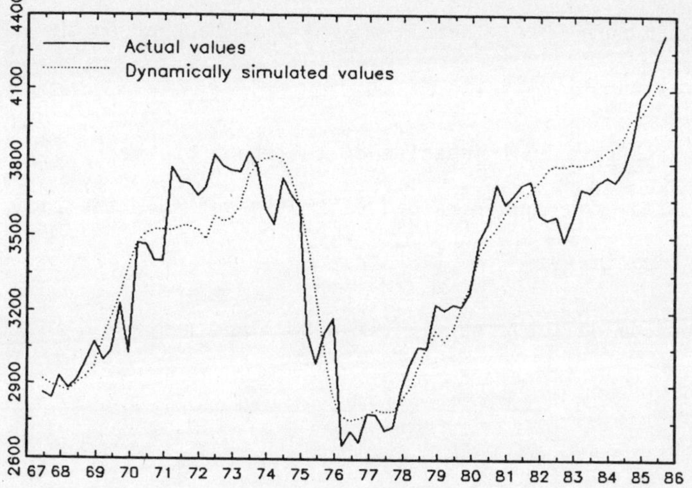

Determinants of investment

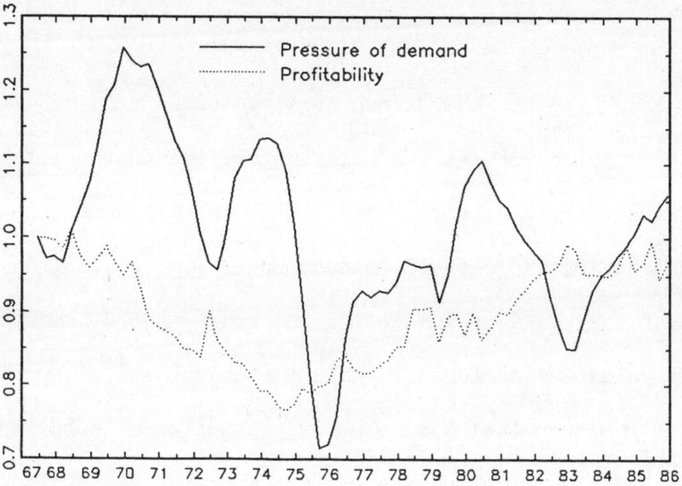

<u>Labor supply</u>:

The estimated parameter are economically quite reasonable but not well determined econometrically, i.e. subject to large standard errors. For an interpretation of the point estimates the reader is referred to the discussion of Model 1 for which very similar values were obtained (p. 105). In what follows we perform a sensitivity analysis for the labor supply parameters and add some more general remarks with respect to the elasticity of intertemporal substitution.

In order to give an impression of the shape of the likelihood surface, we restate below the unconstrained estimates and show the location of several constrained maxima:[18]

Restrictions on labor supply parameters and reduction in likelihood

	d_2	d_3	d_4	d_5	$-2\Delta\ln \pounds$
Unconstrained:	-0.00386	0.210	0.154	0.109	
d_2 fixed:	→ -0.002	-0.113	0.176	0.0834	1.89
	→ 0.0	-0.645	0.188	0.0192	3.70
d_4 fixed:	-0.00370	0.0577	→ 0.3	0.106	1.75
	-0.00352	-0.0521	→ 0.4	0.113	4.85

- First, we check whether the strong negative time trend (d_2 = -0.00386), implying a reduction of labor supply in relation to the potential labor force by 0.386% per quarter, captures a negative income effect which might as well be attributed to the permanent net real wage wr* (d_3). As shown in the table, fixing d_2 at values of -0.002 and 0 indeed leads to smaller and even negative estimates for d_3, while the adjustment of wr* to wr (d_5) becomes notably slower (which enables wr* to act as a 'substitute' for the time trend) and the elasticity of intertemporal substitution (d_4) slightly increases. The likelihood surface is in fact quite flat along this 'ridge' and even the restriction d_2 = 0 cannot be rejected at the 5%-level.
- Second, we explore the likelihood function in direction of a higher elasticity of intertemporal substitution. Forcing d_4 from the low estimate of 0.154 (which does not significantly differ from zero) to 0.3 and 0.4

18. Parameters of other equations are not reported as they respond only little to the restrictions imposed on the labor supply parameters.

causes opposite movements in d_3, the elasticity with respect to wr*. In fact, d_3 and d_4 always add up to a total 'income elasticity' of about 0.35. However, substitution elasticities of 0.4 or larger must be rejected on a LR-criterion.

These calculations show that the information in the data is not sufficient to determine the various theoretical influences on labor supply separately. In particular, we cannot distinguish beween the 'income effect' of real wages and long-term demographic trends. Moreover, it is not possible to obtain a precise estimate of the elasticity of intertemporal substitution, although the hypothesis of pronounced intertemporal substitution behavior is not supported by the data.

7.7 Intertemporal substitution in labor supply - Comparison with other studies

The extent of intertemporal substitution in labor supply is a crucial element of short-term labor market behavior and has important implications for macro modelling in general. New classical models stipulate that the observed fluctuations in employment continuously reflect optimizing intertemporal choices of both households and firms (continuous market clearing); involuntary unemployment is ruled out by assumption. In contrast, the disequilibrium model of this paper explicitly takes into account that households (and/or firms) may be rationed so that the observed variations in employment do not necessarily reflect changes in desired labor supply (labor demand). In new classical models, a high elasticity of intertemporal substitution is required in order to explain the observed fluctuations of employment in terms of optimizing labor supply behavior, taking further for granted that real wages move procyclically. In our framework, there is no such need since labor supply may be on the 'long side' of the market; but pronounced intertemporal substitution effects might of course limit the amount of involuntary unemployment in a recession. Given the importance of the issue, it seems worthwhile to compare our estimate of intertemporal substitution with the results of some other studies for Switzerland.

Our model indicates - at best - weak intertemporal substitution. This is not particularly surprising as even elaborate models in the new classical vein have in general not been able to establish significant intertemporal substitution elasticities empirically; compare, e.g., Altonji (1982, 1986), Mankiw, Rotemberg and Summers (1985). Interestingly, however, some recent Swiss studies have yielded - at least partially - more favorable results:

- Kugler and Schwendener (1988) estimate a dynamic life-cycle model of labor supply with micro data for men and women separately. As no panel data are at hand in Switzerland, the authors are forced to assume that the available cross-section of data for a single year conveys information as to the behavior of individuals over time. The estimated elasticity of intertemporal substitution for women is close to 1 and significant; for men, it is slightly negative and insignificant.
- Kugler (1988a) tests the intertemporal substitution hypothesis with quarterly time series for the U.S., the U.K., West Germany and Switzerland. The results obtained for the dynamic optimality conditions clearly reject the model. More favorable estimates are reported for the static optimality condition (substitution between current consumption and leisure), but only as far as consumption is concerned. With respect to labor supply, intertemporal substitution turns out insignificant.
- Using the same data sets but adopting alternative stochastic assumptions, suggested by the recent theory of cointegrated processes, and further imposing equal elasticities for consumption and leisure, Kugler (1988b)

finds an elasticity of intertemporal substitution of about 0.75. Results for the three other countries are similar.

The evidence of these studies is mixed. Still, if one likes the idea of intertemporal substitution, one may read off some indication of such effects that go beyond our estimate. Of course, the approaches differ in several ways so that one should not expect identical results in the first place. In particular, as mentioned before, our labor supply equation is not forced to cope with fluctuations in employment that potentially are largely demand-determined. Loosely stated, in a disequilibrium model there is less cyclical variation to be explained by labor supply because labor demand may do the job (typically in a recession). From this perspective, it is easy to understand why models that impose continuous market clearing may produce larger elasticities of intertemporal substitution. However, even if one believes in intertemporal substitution elasticities as high as 1, it is not possible to reconcile the observed fluctuations in employment, which have been quite strong in Switzerland, with optimizing labor supply behavior. The reason is simply that the relative fluctuations in employment exceed those in real wages by far - so that substitution elasticities much larger than 1 would be required to explain the observed employment variations from the supply side or the labor market.

Another type of reaction to labor market conditions may arise from the so-called **discouraged worker effect:** In the presence of transaction costs, workers may be dissuaded from actively looking for jobs if they assess the probability of being rationed as high. This can be viewed as an optimal intertemporal decision in response to **quantity signals** (as opposed to price signals). It can also be interpreted as a spillover effect that remains within the labor market. This type of behavior gives rise to two different definitions of labor supply. Discouraged workers do not enter the labor force and presumably do not show up in unemployment statistics. Nevertheless, they must be regarded as involuntarily unemployed in the sense that they would accept a job at the prevailing wage.[19] Eaton and Quandt (1983) have developed an econometric disequilibrium model along these lines for the U.S. The parameter estimates support the hypothesis that a high likelihood of unemployment reduces effective labor supply. In view of the combination of pronounced employment fluctuations, low official unemployment rates and rather sluggish real wage adjustments, it might be worthwhile to explore the hypothesis for Switzerland in future research.

---

19. There is an obvious connection to the different concepts of effective trade offers that have been proposed in the fix-price literature: In Clower (1965) or Benassy (1977) agents, when formulating the effective trade offers in a certain market, take into account only the quantity constraints they face in other markets; in Drèze (1975) the agents' effective trade offers reflect all quantity constraints simulaneously.

8. TESTING PARAMETER STABILITY

This section addresses the question whether the estimated parameters can be regarded as structurally stable. One may be sceptical about this point in particular with respect to the spillover coefficients (κ and τ), the elasticity of intertemporal substitution in labor supply (d_4) and the various dynamic adjustment speeds (λ_Y, λ_L, γ_L, λ_I, λ_G and d_5) as all these parameters are likely to depend on the state of expectations of firms and households and thus may be expected to vary over time. But structural instability may be suspected for other parameters as well, due for instance to a changed composition of aggregates or the emergence of new technologies. In the following, we try to shed some light on this issue in two ways. First, we simply re-estimate the model over the shortened period 1967.2 to 1980.4 (removing the last cycle 1981.1 to 1985.4 from the original sample) in order to see which parameters are subject to the most significant shifts. Second, we perform a more formal post-sample stability test, confronting the model's forecasts with truly 'new' data for the period 1986.1 to 1989.4 (data that have not been used in the 'search process' leading to Model 4).

Re-estimation of the model over the period 1967.2 to 1980.4 yields parameters that in their majority prove fairly stable compared to those obtained for the entire sample. From the 30 parameters shown in column 2 of the summary table only 7 change by more that 33%. These are:

	1967.2-1985.4	1967.2-1980.4	relative change
ν	0.0120	0.00556	-54%
a_3	0.0201	0.0385	+92%
a_6	-0.0933	-0.132	+42%
β_2	0.00194	0.00305	+57%
d_3	0.210	0.00626	-97%
d_4	0.154	0.265	+72%
d_5	0.108	0.357	+228%

The fact that the labor supply parameters d_3, d_4 (elasticities with respect to wr* and wr) and d_5 (adjustment of wr* to wr) differ strongly across the two samples is of course not surprising in view of the above sensitivity analysis (p. 128). The same applies to the goods demand parameters a_3 and a_6, which also are subject to relatively large standard errors. The observed variability in these parameters as such must not be interpreted as evidence of changed behavior but rather points to the fact that the information in the data is not sufficient to get precise estimates. More indicative of structural instability are large shifts in parameters for which the estimated **standard** errors are relatively small, as is the case for ν (increase in mismatch) and β_2 (technical progress on new equipment).[1] Expressed in terms of the respective standard errors (taken from column 2 of the summary table), the following parameters change most:

	1967.2-1985.4	1967.2-1980.4	change in SE-units
α_0	0.0132	0.0165	+1.07
ν	0.0120	0.00556	-1.54
b_1	0.420	0.496	+1.96
β_2	0.00194	0.00305	+2.18
s	0.0306	0.0397	+3.08
λ_Y	0.695	0.854	+1.67
β_3	0.00648	0.00693	+1.07
d_4	0.154	0.265	+1.05
d_5	0.109	0.357	+4.09

All other parameters vary by less than 1 SE. Interestingly, neither the spillover coefficients κ and τ nor the dynamic adjustment parameters (with the exception of λ_Y) are subject to notable shifts between the two samples. On the other hand, several parameters that influence the long-term behavior of the model (since they measure the impact of trended variables or since

1. As to ν, compare the discussion on pp. 120/122.

they get accumulated over time through the investment/scrapping process) change quite strongly; besides ν and β_2 these are: b_1 (capital productivity on new vintages), s (deterioration of productivity on existing equipment) and β_3 (rate of labor augmenting technical progress).

To discuss now the issue of parameter stability more rigorously, we perform a **post-sample stability test** for the complete model with data that have not been used as yet. Based on the parameter values listed in column 2 of the summary table, we forecast the model's endogenous variables for the post-sample period 1986.1 to 1989.4 and compare the outcome with actual developments. The forecast errors for periods t = T+1 through t = T+k are denoted by $\hat{u}_t' = (\hat{u}_{1t}, \hat{u}_{2t}, \hat{u}_{3t}, \hat{u}_{4t}, \hat{u}_{5t})$, and the estimated covariance matrix of errors (arising from the ML-estimation of Model 4) is denoted by $\hat{\Omega}$. Under the null hypothesis of stable parameters the statistic

$$G = \sum_{t=T+1}^{T+k} \hat{u}_t' \hat{\Omega}^{-1} \hat{u}_t$$

is asymptotically χ^2-distributed with q·k = 80 degrees of freedom (q = 5, k = 16). Performing these calculations, it turns out that the hypothesis of parameter stability is clearly rejected (G = 424.3 vs. $\chi^2_{.95}(80) = 101.9$).

In order to locate the reason for this unfavorable test result, we must have a closer look at the individual forecast errors. Whereas the equations for output demand, labor supply and investment perform pretty well, those for output supply and labor demand strongly overestimate the actual course of the associated dependent variable during the whole post-sample period. It is instructive to know in this respect that the Swiss economy has witnessed an outstanding investment boom in the second half of the 1980's whereas the growth of output and employment has exceeded long-term trend values only by a comparatively small margin. This implies that both capital productivity and labor intensity of investment must have notably fallen in the forecast period. In the framework of our vintage equations

$$Y^{\Delta} = b_1 I \left[\frac{w}{uc}\right]^{-b_2} e^{\beta_2 t} \quad \text{and} \quad L^{\Delta} = c_1 I \left[\frac{w}{uc}\right]^{-c_2},$$

such a development can only be explained by a higher factor cost ratio w/uc. Empirically, however, w/uc has increased only very little after 1985. As the reductions in capital productivity (Y^{Δ}/I) and labor intensity (L^{Δ}/I) cannot be traced back to higher values of w/uc, they have to be accomodated in the above vintage equations by downward shifts in the parameters b_1 and c_1.

In fact, if we let b_1 and c_1 adjust in the post-sample period on a fitting criterion, they decrease by 21% and 14% respectively. The same direction of parameter change is observed if we compare the estimates for the periods 1967.2-1980.4 and 1967.2-1985.4 (b_1 = 0.496 vs. 0.420, c_1 = 0.0326 vs. 0.0296). Hence, there seems to be a long-term tendency towards more capital intensive production technologies even if relative factor costs are constant. This is not implausible and may be due to changing micro level production functions or to a growing weight of capital intensive industries in the economy. Allowing for such downward shifts in b_1 and c_1 (21% and 14%) improves the outcome of the forecast simulation considerably: The test statistic G assumes a value of 87.1, corresponding to a marginal significance level of the $\chi^2(78)$-distribution of more than 20%. Thus, with the exception of b_1 and c_1, the hypothesis that the estimated parameters are stable passes the test quite easily. Of course, this testing procedure is rather crude and must be expected to have low power, the more so as the post-sample adjustments in b_1 and c_1 - although not implausible - have a touch of a rescue operation. Therefore, what the test may show is merely that the assumption of stable parameters is not completely out of place.

9. SIMULATIONS

In this section we simulate values for the endogenous variables of Model 4 under several conditions.[1] Frist, we perform a static simulation in order to examine the fit of the model (section 9.1). The latent demand and supply variables implied by this simulation are then used to characterize the development of the Swiss economy in terms of regimes and spillovers (section 9.2). Next, we shall discuss the performance of the Swiss labor market, comparing the unemployment rates derived from the model with official figures (section 9.3). In section 9.4, we evaluate the model as to its tracking performance in a dynamic simulation. Finally, we let certain exogenous variables assume alternative values and figure out short-term and long-term dynamic multipliers (section 9.5).

9.1 Fit of the model (static simulation)

To examine the fit of Model 4, we solve the model for the observable endogenous variables Y, L, P_G, P_L and I, using actual values for all exogenous and lagged endogenous variables and setting the error terms to zero.[2] The outcome of this static simulation is confronted with actual values in fig. 8 (P_G is transformed into the buffer variable $\Phi^{-1}(P_G) = \frac{1}{k}$ BU). As measures of fit we compute unadjusted R^2's, obtaining:

	Y	L	P_G	P_L	I
R^2	0.971	0.967	0.950	0.888	0.916

1. The model is summarized in section 6.2, p. 88, the empirical parameter values are listed in column 2 of the summary table on p. 121.
2. Due to the nonlinearity of the model with respect to the error terms, this procedure does not yield conditional expectations for Y, L, P_L and P_G. In order to compute conditional expectations, one would have to perform a stochastic simulation (repeated generation of normal deviates with the same variance as estimated for the various equations).

FIG. 8: Static model simulation - Output Y (ln)

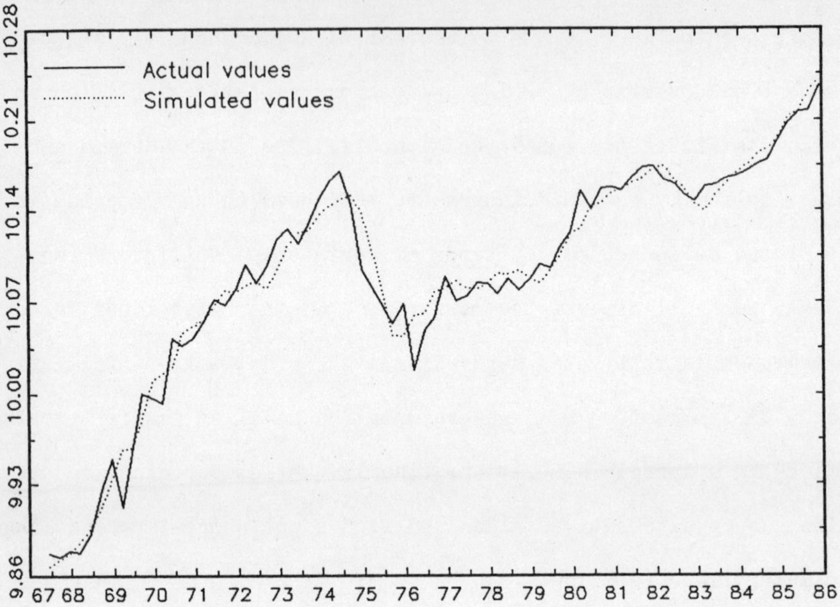

- Employment L (ln)

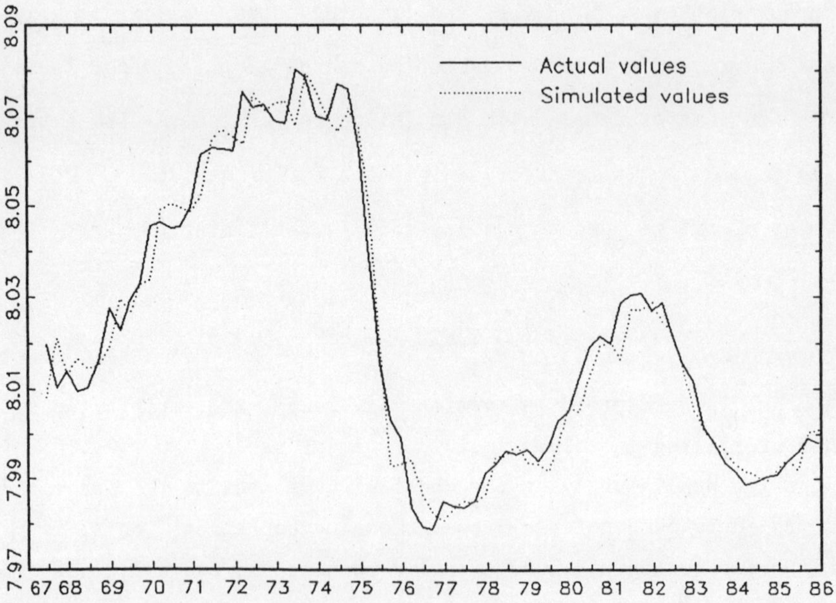

- Buffer stocks BU/k

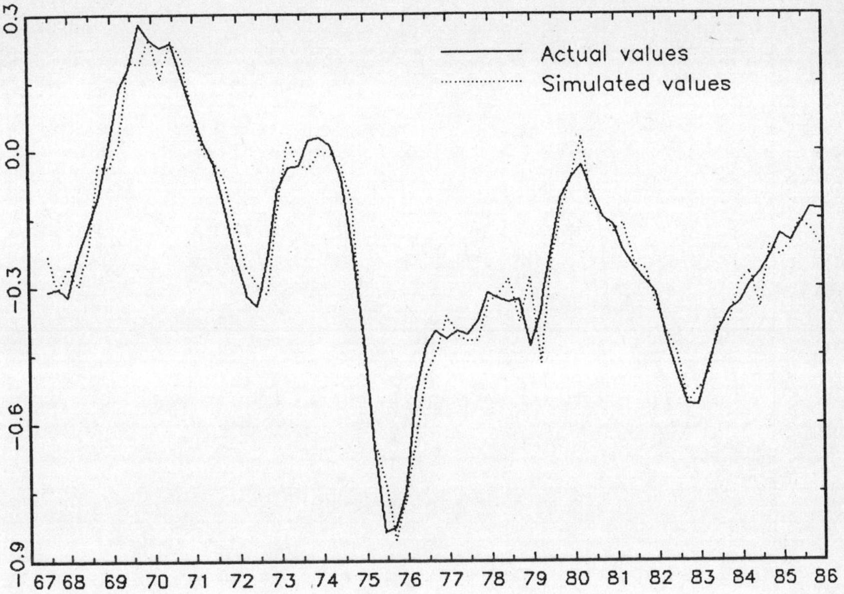

- Proportion of labor constrained firms P_L

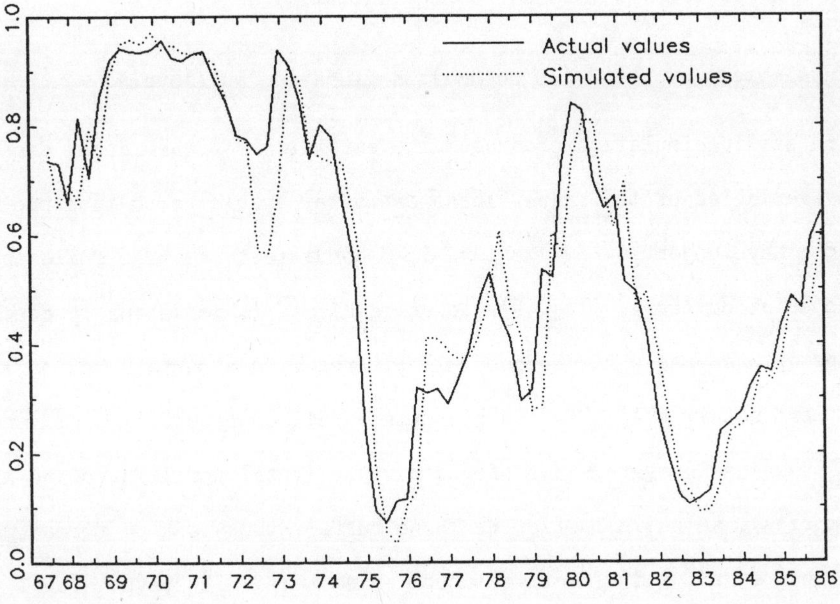

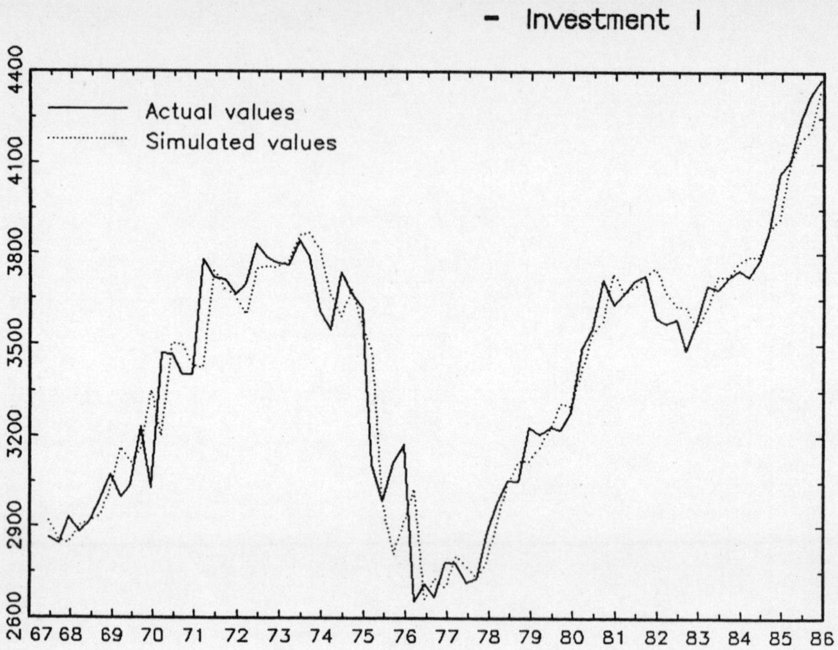

The fit turns out to be acceptable; one should however not overevaluate this result since any model with lagged values of endogenous variables can be expected to perform well in a static simulation.

9.2 Development of the Swiss economy: Regimes and spillovers

The static simulation produces also estimates for the latent demand and supply variables of the model. These estimates enable us to interpret the economic development in Switzerland in a consistent way. The following main characteristics emerge (fig. 9). Goods demand Y^d (which strongly depends on developments in the world economy) fluctuates with a certain lead around more inert actual output Y. The accumulated differences between Y^d and Y entail changes in aggregate buffer stocks BU (total unfilled orders minus inventories), as shown in fig. 8. These buffers work back on firms' planned output supply Y^{sp} and effective labor demand L^d: If Y^d stays below Y for a

FIG. 9: Latent endogenous variables
(derived from static simulation)

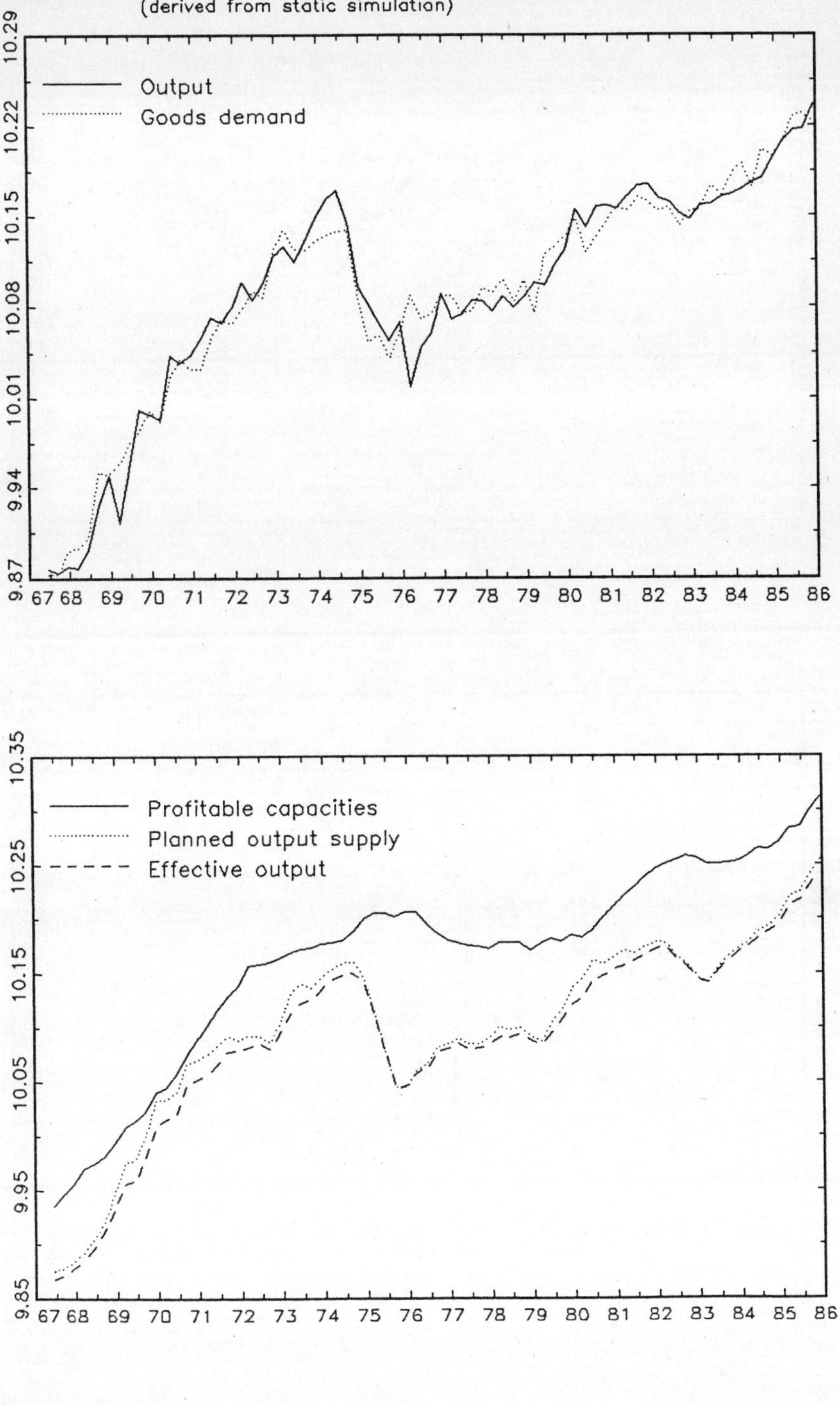

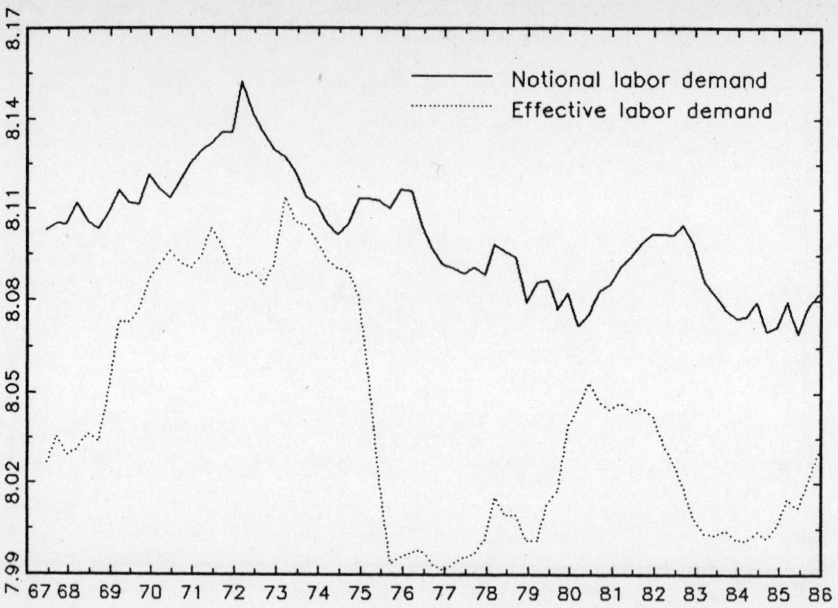
Notional labor demand
Effective labor demand
8.17
8.14
8.11
8.08
8.05
8.02
7.99
67 68 69 70 71 72 73 74 75 76 77 78 79 80 81 82 83 84 85 86

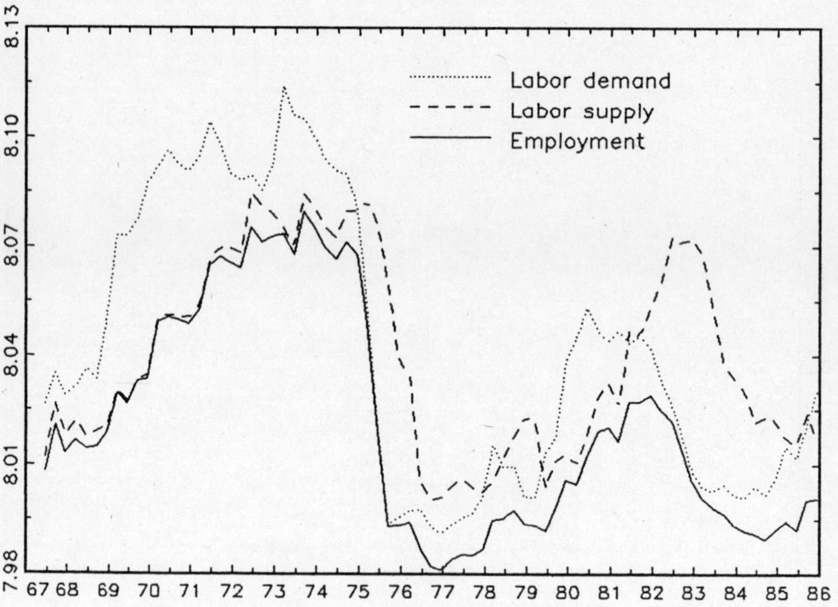
Labor demand
Labor supply
Employment
8.13
8.10
8.07
8.04
8.01
7.98
67 68 69 70 71 72 73 74 75 76 77 78 79 80 81 82 83 84 85 86

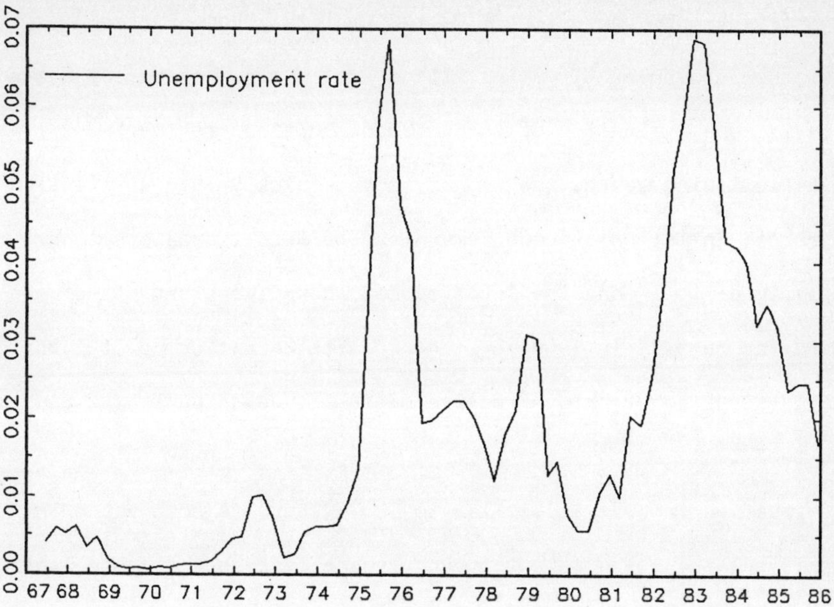

prolonged period, buffers BU fall, entailing a reduction of Y^{sp} and L^d in relation to notional output supply $\tilde{Y}^s$ and notional labor demand $\tilde{L}^d$ respectively (Keynesian spillover); if Y^d is larger than Y, buffers BU increase, leading to a recovery of Y^{sp} and L^d towards the notional levels. In boom periods, effective output Y is typically below planned output supply Y^{sp}. This is the spillover effect arising from a rationing of labor demand L^d by labor supply L^s (repressed inflation regime). Compared to the Keynesian spillover, which becomes as large as 12.5% in the recession of 1975, the 'repressed inflation' spillover is relatively weak with a maximum of 2.4% in the period 1969/70.

In **chronological** order, the development of the Swiss economy can be described as follows (see again fig. 8 and 9):

- The simulation starts from the trough of the minor 1967 recession: The goods market is characterized by low buffers (low unfilled orders, high inventories), pushing output Y below 'profitable capacities' $\tilde{Y}^s$. Nonetheless, the labor market remains with a small amount of excess demand. Hence there is some indication of an 'underconsumption' regime.[3]

- In the following years, the economy moves quickly into a situation of 'repressed inflation': Goods demand and buffers increase, planned output supply tends to $\tilde{Y}^s$ and the labor market shows large amounts of excess demand (up to 5.3% in 1969/70). The associated rationing of labor demand entails a spillover onto effective output Y, reducing Y by 2.4% in relation to $\tilde{Y}^s$.
- The situation in 1972 is similar to 1967: There is some weakening of goods demand, but the slack is not strong enough to push aggregate labor demand below labor supply.
- The period 1973/74 is again dominated by 'repressed inflation', involving a negative spillover from rationed labor demand into the goods market.
- The fast decline in goods demand in the second half of 1974 leads - somewhat delayed by buffer stocks - to a drastic drop in output and a reduction in effective labor demand (Keynesian spillover), entailing a complete reversal of the rationing situation in the labor market: Employment becomes almost entirely demand-determined and excess supply of labor reaches a peak value of almost 7% in 1975. The economy is now in a state of 'Keynesian unemployment'. Note however that there is a flattening of profitable capacities and a pronounced downward trend in notional labor demand already since 1972, long before Keynesian spillovers come into play. To understand these developments, one should know that the early 1970s were characterized by fast growing wages followed by a sudden restrictive reorientation of monetary policy and a sharp increase in the

---

3. Recall that the aggregate economy is always characterized by a mixture of regimes.

Swiss franc's foreign exchange rate. These factors gave rise to a profitability squeeze as well as a surge in real wages and relative labor costs, which in turn accelerated scrapping, hampered investment and reduced the labor intensity of new equipment. In view of these developments, it would be rather misleading to describe the 1975 recession as a purely Keynesian event, i.e. as being exclusively due to 'insufficient demand'.

- In the following years we observe a partial recovery of goods demand and output, a slight downward adjustment of profitable capacities towards the reduced level of activity and a renewed slack of goods demand in 1978/79; this period is characterized by a mixed rationing situation, the labor market being close to an aggregate equilibrium.
- In 1979/80 the economy moves again into a situation which is dominated by 'repressed inflation': Goods demand increases and exceeds actual output, the latter being subject to negative spillovers resulting from rationed labor demand, buffer stocks rise (without reaching the peak level of 1969/70) and the gap between planned output supply and profitable capacities narrows.
- In the period 1982/83 we observe a downturn of goods demand and - with some buffer-related delay - a reduction in output (not as severe as in 1975). Effective labor demand falls (Keynesian spillover), moving to the short side of the labor market, so that employment becomes largely demand-determined. The economy is again dominated by 'Keynesian unemployment'. Notice that the 1982/83 recession, unlike the 1975 slump, was not preceded by a deterioration in profitability. Quite to the contrary, profitability (in terms of relative prices) was improving between 1980 and 1983 (compare fig. 7). The flattening of profitable capacities and the fall of notional labor demand set in only later, as a response to the lower level of activity (captured by the excess demand term in the investment equation).

Hence, looking at the underlying forces, one discovers a remarkable difference between the recessions of 1975 and 1982, although both eventually showed up as 'Keynesian unemployment', i.e. as a situation with underutilized capacities and excess supply in the labor market. The combination of slackening world demand with 'classical' factors (deteriorating profitability and competitiveness) may explain, among other factors, why the 1975 recession was notably stronger in Switzerland than in the world economy in general.

- From 1983 on, there is a sustained upward trend in goods demand and output, buffers increase (restoration of low unfilled orders, reduction of excessive inventories), profitable capacities grow as a result of the pronounced investment boom and the labor market moves towards an aggregate equilibrium. At the end of the simulation period, the various regimes are strongly mixed.

9.3 The Swiss labor market - A miracle?

The unemployment rates generated by the model (see last panel of fig. 9) qualify official Swiss unemployment statistics as very incomplete. Cyclical peak values of nearly 7% in the recessions of 1975 and 1982/83 contrast with official unemployment rates that hardly ever exceeded 1%. This discrepancy can be traced **back** partly (a and b) to statistical measurement problems, partly - and presumably more importantly - to the 'discouraged worker' phenomenon (c):

(a) Swiss unemployment statistics are based on the number of persons **registered** at the **employment offices.** Registration with the labor office is a requirement for collecting unemployment benefits. Until 1977 - and thus during the 1975 recession - coverage by unemployment insurance was extremely low in Switzerland. For persons not insured, the incentive to register as unemployed was probably weak: The possibility to get information about job offers had to be balanced against the annoyances of complying with the strict practices at the labor offices and the social stigma of being officially recorded as unemployed. In 1977, unemployment insurance became however mandatory for all employees. From that time on - and thus during the 1982 slack - one may assume that a majority of active job seekers got registered.

(b) Unemployment statistics count only the number of **full-time** unemployed. The employment variable L in our model, on the other hand, measures '**total hours worked**'. Therefore, the use of short-time work during recessions, which is quite extensive in Switzerland, shows up in our model but is not reflected in official unemployment figures. In the trough of 1982, for example, short-time work amounted to about one half of full-time unemployment in terms of total hours lost.[4]

(c) The estimate of unemployment produced by our model is based on a specification of labor supply that does not include a **discouraged worker effect**. It thus reflects the amount of labor households would like to supply if jobs were available at the going wage. The associated unemployment measure fits the definition of '**involuntary unemployment**'. However, there may be people who are involuntarily unemployed in this sense but have temporarily withdrawn from the labor force because they regard the chances of finding a job as low. Such flexible behavior seems to be quite widespread in Switzerland, especially among married women and people in the retirement age, keeping official unemployment figures low.

---

4. For more details about the measurement of unemployment in Switzerland, the system of unemployment insurance and other institutional facts of the Swiss labor market compare OECD (1985).

From this we may conclude that our model gives a more accurate account of involuntary unemployment than official unemployment statistics. Still, even when assessed on basis of our estimates, the situation in Switzerland looks quite idyllic compared to most other European countries. In particular, at the end of the estimation period the model implies approximately an aggregate labor market equilibrium with $L^d = L^s$ (see fig. 9), so that the associated unemployment rate of about 2% just reflects **structural mismatch** (SURE). At earlier intersection points of L^d and L^s, the difference to actual employment L is smaller, illustrating that the structural imbalances on the labor market have increased over time. This certainly constitutes a policy problem, but it is located at the microeconomic level and not rooted in a macroeconomic imbalance between demand and supply.[5] In terms of macroeconomic aggregates, the recovery in recent years has brought about a situation that looks almost ideal. Therefore, in contrast to most other European countries, there is no need to create new jobs across-the-board in Switzerland. How can we explain this favorable record of the Swiss economy?

To begin with, it must be emphasized that it is not an especially successful stabilization policy that can be credited with the employment miracle in Switzerland. Quite to the contrary, output and employment have

---

5. The model's mismatch parameters and the implied measure for "structural unemployment at equilibrium", SURE, are to be interpreted in a wide sense. They capture all types of microeconomic inefficiencies that are likely to push aggregate employment below both aggregate supply and demand (i.e. cause a simultaneous occurence of unemployment and vacancies). These include sectoral, regional and skill mismatch as well as seasonal fluctuations and search activities. After the recession of 1982/83, there was some minor sectoral and regional concentration of unemployment in Switzerland, whereas in recent years one observes an increasing shortage of high-skilled labor; compare Gaillard (1988).

actually been more volatile than in most other countries. Furthermore, taking a longer-term perspective, one must note that employment in Switzerland is still below the pre-1975 level. Hence, the fact of low Swiss unemployment resides neither in a smaller cyclical variability nor in a more favorable long-term development of labor demand. It is rather due to quick adjustments on the supply side of the labor market. In addition to the above-mentioned cyclical behavior of female labor supply, there is a notable flexibility introduced by **foreign workers,** in particular those with only temporary (i.e. seasonal or annual) work permits.[6] Due to a high "turnover" among these foreigners, Swiss authorities can reduce total labor supply by limiting the number of new permits issued. Such a policy was pursued extensively in the 1975 recession and, to a lesser extent, in the 1982 slack. This explains why the collapse of labor demand in the mid-1970s, which entailed a rather long-lasting reduction in total employment, resulted only in a short-lived peak in unemployment followed by a quick normalization: In the second half of 1976, the unemployment rate was already back to 2% (our estimate) without any notable improvement in labor demand (see again fig. 9). There is no doubt, on the other hand, that the reduction in the foreign

6. **Share of foreign workers in the labor force** (in percent):

	1960	1970	1980
Total share:	19.5	26.3	23.5
By type of permit:			
Permanent	2.7	5.9	12.4
Annual	10.0	13.1	4.2
Seasonal	5.3	5.0	3.6
Frontier*	1.5	2.4	3.3

* Frontier workers do not take residence in Switzerland but commute from neighbouring countries.

Source: OECD (1985)

population has aggravated the recession via Keynesian multiplier effects.

Since the mid-1970s the share of foreigners with only temporary work permits has been more or less continuously falling. This tendency has already limited the possibility of using foreign labor as a cyclical buffer in the 1982/83 recession on a large scale - and will further reduce it in future. Nevertheless, the share of foreigners with only temporary work permits is still large enough to preserve a certain short-run flexibility in labor supply at the margin, at least in less-qualified job categories.[7]

9.4 Dynamic tracking performance

Next, we want to evaluate the model by means of a dynamic simulation, thus entering - in contrast to the static simulation of section 9.1 - calculated values for the lagged endogenous variables. Checking for dynamic tracking performance is usually regarded as a powerful method of model evaluation. However, Hendry and Richard (1982) have raised some convincing objections against this practice. Although they primarily call in question the usefulness of dynamic simulations as a means of model selection, which is not our purpose here, the following two points seem noteworthy.

First, we must realize that is is quite normal for the errors of a dynamic simulation to be autocorrelated and heteroscedastic. More precisely: The error variances typically increase over time (tending to a maximum though provided that the model is dynamically stable). This is the case even if the model's error terms are well-behaved (e.g. are i.i.d.). The reason is simply

---

7. The presence of foreign workers may also explain why the mismatch is somewhat lower in Switzerland than in most other countries (compare the studies mentioned in footnote 16, p. 120): To some extent, foreign labor can be adjusted not only globally but also with respect to skill structure and seasonal patterns to the changing needs of Swiss firms.

that errors are partly carried over from period to period, the more so if characteristic roots are close to unity. This implies in particular that stocks are usually simulated badly even when changes in stocks are well determined. In our model, for example, the buffer stock equation [19º.1'], with (37) substituted for goods demand, would be subject to a random walk simulation error if Y_{t-1} was exogenous. To be sure, the complete model involves a feedback from buffers to output, which - hopefully - will ensure stability of the model and stationarity of the error process. Nevertheless, in a dynamic simulation we have to expect a considerable 'accumulation' of errors with respect to the variables BU and P_G. Similar considerations apply to the adding-up of vintages in the equations for notional output supply and notional labor demand (41)[8] as well as to the several partial adjustment and error correction mechanisms in the model.

Second, in order for a dynamic simulation to reflect the appropriateness of a model as a description of the data generating process, the variables which are technically treated as exogenous must in fact be 'strongly exogenous'. The calculated dynamic tracks, on the other hand, usually show a better fit if a large part of the model's endogenous data variance is attributed to 'outside' variables, regardless of whether or not these are in fact strongly exogenous. In our case, it may be legitimate, from an estimation point of view, to treat wages and prices as 'weakly exogenous'; 'strong exogeneity' of these variables can hardly be asserted though. Treating them in the simulation as if they were strongly exogenous has a favorable effect on the model's tracking performance, even though a model with endogenous

8. Scrapping functions F^Y and F^L that in general assume values somewhat smaller than 1 will prevent the associated simulation errors from becoming random walks.

prices and wages would characterize the data generating process in a more appropriate way.

Conditioning a dynamic simulation on variables that cannot in fact be regarded as strongly exogenous is admittedly problematical (and becomes even more disturbing in policy experiments). Nevertheless, we think that a careful investigation of the dynamic paths can be a useful tool for exploring the dynamic structure of our model. The static simulation reported in section 9.1 may at best provide weak support for a model that includes many lagged endogenous variables, the more so as these are strongly autocorrelated. Performing a dynamic simulation constitutes a much tougher test. In particular, it is interesting to see whether the model still reproduces the main cyclical movements in the endogenous variables with reasonable accuracy if the information contained in the actual values of the lagged endogenous variables is discarded. In view of the first point above, we should however not be troubled too much if the simulated paths deviate for some prolonged periods of time from actual ones. On the other hand, dynamic tracks that diverge progressively from actual developments would suggest that the estimated model is dynamically unstable.[9]

As shown in fig. 10, the main cyclical movements in output, buffer stocks and investment are reproduced reasonably well by the dynamic simulation. In particular, there are no progressive deviations that would indicate dynamic instability. This is also true for the other observable endogenous variables, employment and the proportion of labor constrained firms (not displayed in the figure). In some periods, deviations are fairly large however. For example, the drastic fall in output in 1975 is underestimated and

9. The issue of dynamic stability will be investigated more thoroughly in section 9.5 by simulating various shocks.

the recession of 1982 shows up in the simulation only in form of a stagnation. As to the tracking of buffer stocks, we should first recall that we were forced to impose a brute force constraint on scaling factor k in order to obtain sensible parameter estimates for goods demand. It is comforting now to see that this equation, together with the supply part of the model, reproduces actual buffer stocks quite well. As far as 'turning points' are concerned, tracking performance is nearly perfect. A notable divergence occurs in the last couple of years of the sample period when actual buffer stocks increase (since $Y^d > Y$) whereas the simulated path decreases (implying $Y^d < Y$). This divergence can be explained in connection with the overestimation of output in the same period: As the third panel of fig. 10 reveals, investment is strongly over-estimated in the 1982 recession and the following years; this entails a larger than actual increase in production capacities that pushes output from the supply side beyond actual values (the aggregate demand effect of investment is weak) and leads to the counterfactual decline in the simulated buffer variable.

In order to figure out to what extent the investment equation is responsible for the discrepancies between simulated and actual paths, we perform a simulation in which investment is treated as exogenous. We thus condition the vintage equations (49.2) and (49.3) on actual investment instead of relying on the modelled impact from current pressure of demand and profitability onto the creation of new production capacities (which is central for the model's long-term behavior). The last two panels of fig. 10 show that the accord between simulated and actual values becomes indeed much better. Of course, in view of the opening remarks to this section, this should not be taken as evidence against the full model with endogenous investment.

FIG. 10: Dynamic tracking performance - Output ln[Y]

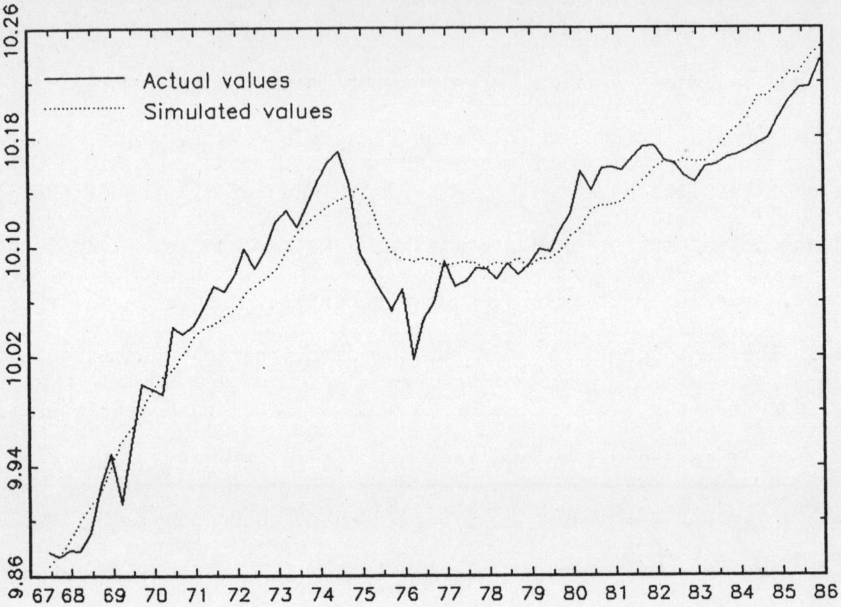

- Buffer stocks BU/k

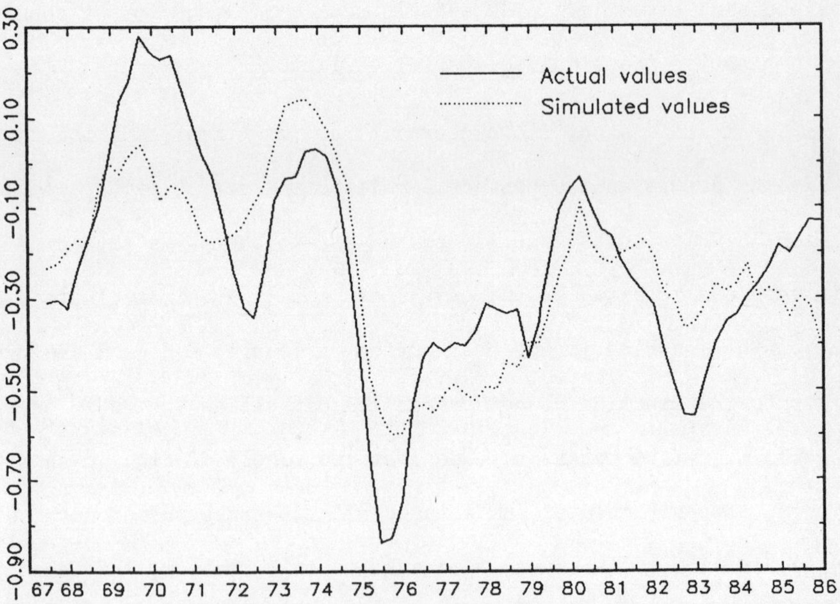

- Investment I

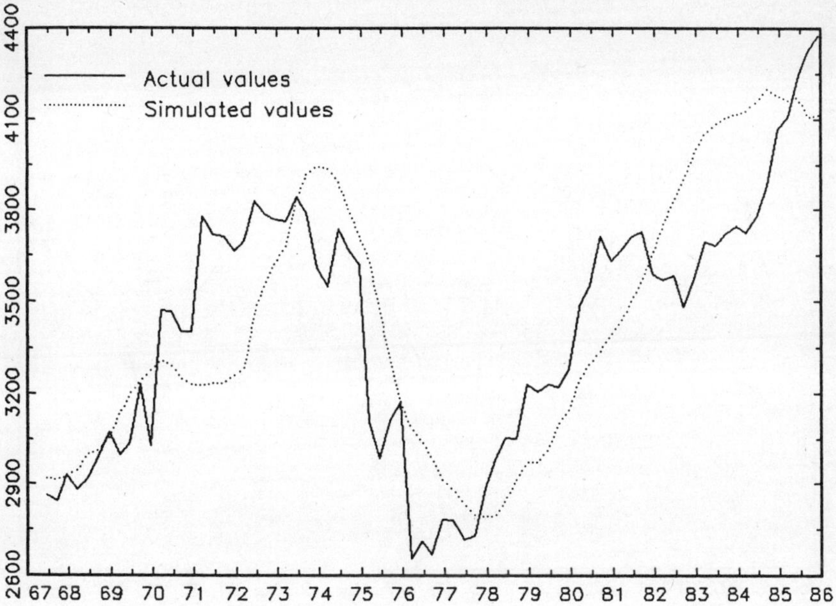

- Output ln(Y) (Investment treated as exogenous)

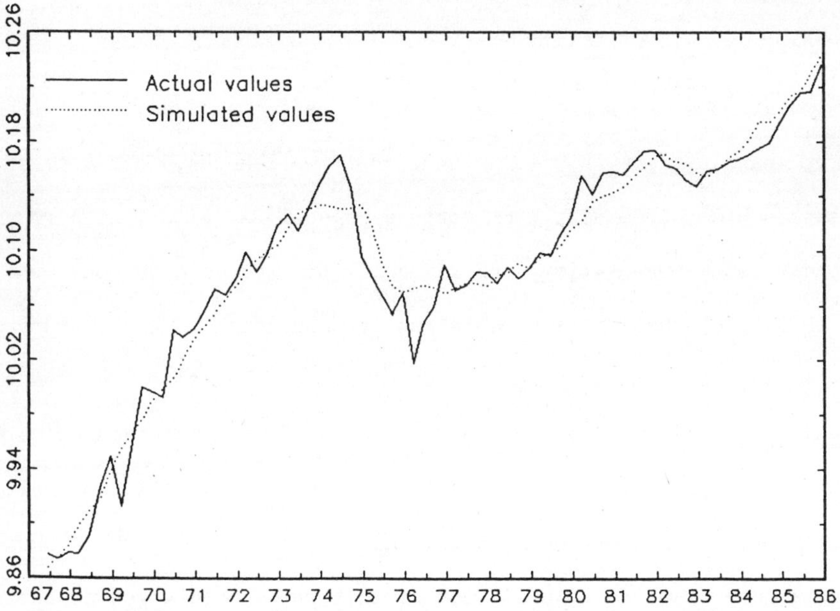

- Buffer stocks BU/k (Investment treated as exogenous)

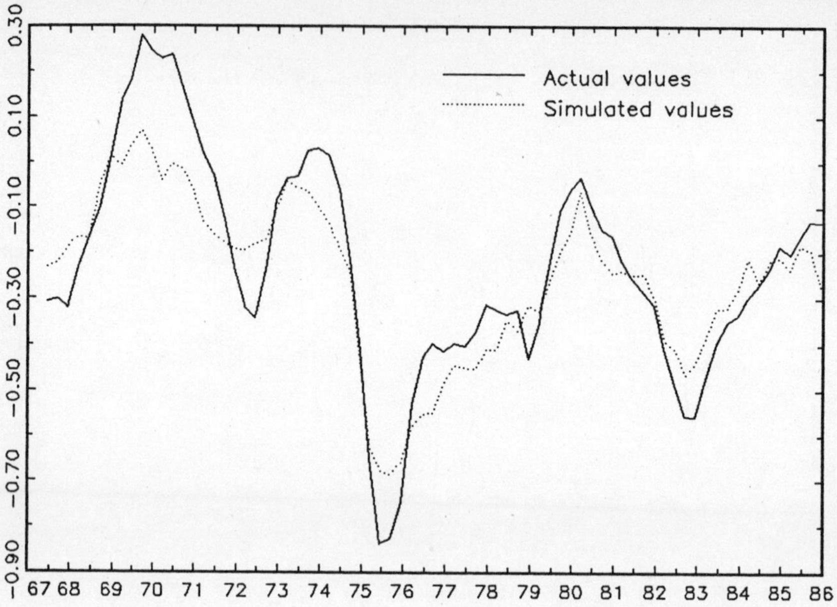

9.5 Simulating short-run and long-run effects of autonomous changes, assessing dynamic stability

We simulate now the short-run and long-run effects of several autonomous changes by means of dynamic simulations. As is well-known, this type of exercise is subject to a couple of serious objections: **First,** with regard to conditional **n-step forecasting,** the variables treated as exogenous in a dynamic simulation must in fact be 'strongly exogenous' [Engle, Hendry and Richard (1983)]. In our case, the set of exogenous variables includes prices and wages. While one may justify 'weak exogeneity' of prices and wages in the estimation of a disequilibrium model by invoking the notion of only interperiod price and wage adjustments, the assumption of strong exogeneity seems quite unrealistic; it would require that prices and wages do not depend at all on the extent of excess demand in the respective markets (neither current nor lagged).[10] **Second,** as an instrument of **policy analysis,** dynamic simulations are moreover vulnerable to the Lucas-critique, saying that ad hoc adjustment parameters (i.e. parameters that are not "deeply rooted in taste and technology") are likely to change if the "policy rule" changes [Lucas (1976)].

As far as the second point is concerned, it is interesting to recall from section 8 that the assumption of structural parameter stability seems more doubtful with respect to certain technology parameters, in particular b_1 and c_1, than with respect to the dynamic adjustment speeds, which prove fairly stable across the different sample periods.[11] Therefore, from the two problems mentioned above, the first one (questionable strong exogeneity) appears to be more critical in case of our model. To be sure, in the short run (over a few quarters), the assumption that wages and prices do not deviate from the reference course when demand is stimulated (for example) may be roughly admissible. But to assess the desirability of a certain policy, long-term consequences, which often turn out less favorable than the immediate impacts, should be taken into account as well. The limitations of the following simulation experiments are thus obvious. Nevertheless, we regard them as useful because they help to explore the dynamic characteristics of the estimated model. Moreover, they will provide some valuable insights into the functioning of the Swiss economy. One must however be careful not to draw too far-reaching policy conclusions. For instance, the

---

10. Strong exogeneity of several other variables may be questioned as well (compare the list of exogenous variables on p. 90).
11. Although the periods 1981.1 to 1985.4 (excluded from the orignal sample in order to re-estimate the model) and 1986.1 to 1989.4 (used to perform a post-sample stability test) are not associated with clear-cut changes in the policy rule, they nevertheless differ considerably with respect to general business conditions and concrete policy measures.

possible outcome of a simulation experiment that employment would strongly respond to an aggregate demand stimulus is an important piece of information as to the state of the economy in a given period; but the question whether such a policy should in fact be pursued - and how it could be implemented in due time - is much more complex and has to be addressed in a framework that goes beyond the model of this paper.

9.5.1 Short-term impact of a demand shock (Keynesian demand stimulation)

According to eq. (37), autonomous changes in goods demand can arise from different sources:

- From changes in fiscal policy, to be associated with shifts in parameters a_0 and a_1;
- from changes in monetary policy, affecting the long-term real interest rate i^r, investment I (via the user cost of capital) and the foreign price level expressed in domestic currency p^F (via the exchange rate);
- from variations in foreign activity represented by Y^F (weighted GDP of Switzerland's main trading partners).

In the following we do not deal with these factors individually but simply raise goods demand in each period by 2% and compute the resulting effect on output and employment one period later.[12]

The outcome of this simulation, displayed in fig. 11, points to a well-known feature of disequilibrium models: The efficacy of a Keynesian demand stimulation varies with the prevailing regime. The maximum short-run impact of the demand stimulation is attained in the trough of the 1975 recession: A

12. Output and employment respond only with a one-quarter delay. Capacities (notional output supply and notional labor demand) are still unaffected after one quarter.

FIG. 11: Simulation of an autonomous 2% demand shock - Short-run effect on output and employment (ln)

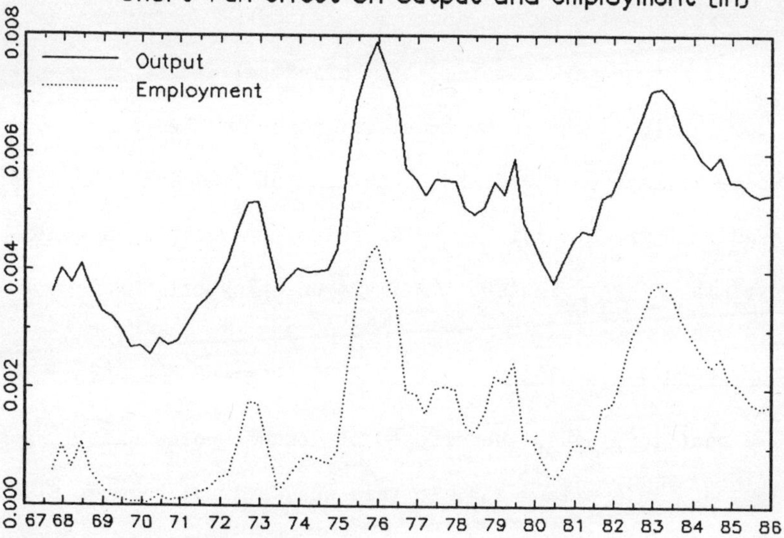

2%-demand shock would have raised output by 0.8% and employment by 0.4%. This was a situation with prevalent 'Keynesian unemployment', i.e., the majority of firms was neither capacity-constrained nor labor-constrained. By contrast, in 1970 the same demand shock would have entailed only a 0.3%-increase in output, and employment would have remained practically unaffected. This period was dominated by the 'repressed inflation' regime with most firms producing at full capacity and/or constrained by labor supply.

Another theoretical implication of our model is that Keynesian demand stimulation is also largely ineffective (only inflationary) if unemployment is predominantly 'classical', that is, in a situation in which profitable capacities are fully utilized but insufficient to absorb the available labor supply. Has this type of unemployment played any notable role in the Swiss economy? The point may be clarified, for example, by comparing fig. 11 with the last panel of fig. 9: All periods in which unemployment reached (minor or major) peaks are at the same time periods in which higher goods demand would have had significant employment effects. Situations of a predominant 'classical unemployment' regime cannot be identified during the estimation period. This is not to say, however, that classical causes of unemployment have been completely absent in Switzerland (refer to the remarks on pp. 145/146, where we have compared the recessions of 1975 and 1982). It also does not mean that traditional Keynesian policy prescriptions would have been appropriate in every instance to fight unemployment.

9.5.2 Reference simulation for examining long-run effects

Next, we want to discuss the effects of demand shocks and alternative wage developments in the long run. To this end, we must however first work out a suitable reference simulation. As just shown, the response of the endogenous variables to exogenous shocks depends on the prevailing regime-mix, which can be expressed in terms of the rationing proportions P_G and P_L for the goods and labor market respectively. This result was obtained above specifically for the short-run impact of a demand shock. It is however clear that a similar dependence obtains for long-run effects of demand shocks and other exogenous changes as well. Thus, if we were to use as reference simulation the dynamic tracks of section 9.4 (computed for the actual values of the exogenous variables), the associated changes in the rationing situation would interfere with the long-run effects that we want to simulate. To prevent such a confusion, we must first set the model on a steady growth path on which the regime proportions P_G and P_L remain constant. We can determine then the long-run effects of exogenous changes as deviations from this reference path.

Producing a steady growth path involves some experimentation with the exogenous variables of the model (see list of variables on p. 90): We hold p, i^r, p^F, POP and RFS constant near the respective sample means, fix the mismatch parameter α_L at its mean value as well, and let w, uc, wr and Y^F increase with rates chosen such that the variables L (L^s, L^d), P_L and P_G remain constant over time while Y (Y^d, Y^{sp}) and I grow steadily.[13]

9.5.3 Checking for dynamic stability

A first indication of dynamic stability of the model has already been offered by the dynamic simulation in section 9.4. Here we discuss the issue more rigorously. It is evident from the structure of the model that dynamic stability hinges primarily on the buffer equation [19°.1'] and the relative strength of the impact of the variable P_G (measuring firms' assessment of buffer stocks)

(a) on **actual output** Y - in [19°.2], dynamically modified as (62.2);

(b) on **profitable capacities** $\tilde{Y}^s$ - via investment (49.1) and the vintage equation (49.3) (capacity effect of investment);

(c) on **goods demand** Y^d - in connection with (a) via the 'income term' a_1Y_{t-1} and the term a_3I_t in (37) (demand effect of investment).

The strength of (a) varies - as noted above - with the value of the variable P_G itself and further depends on the rationing situation in the labor market reflected in P_L. Consider for instance a positive shock to goods demand. The response of output Y will be weak if P_G is close to 1 (most firms producing at full capacity) and/or if P_L is close to 1 (most firms being constrained by labor supply). In such situations one may be sceptical about dynamic stability of the model, especially with respect to buffer stocks: Output Y can increase only at the rate by which new capacities are added (impact b), which must be viewed as a rather slow long-term process. It is even more

---

13. On the resulting reference path, output Y and investment I increase with rates of 0.4% per quarter while the proportions P_L and P_G as well as employment L are constant at values of 0.49, 0.37 and 3000 respectively.

questionable whether Y can keep up with rising Y^d if a majority of firms is labor constrained, since in this case Y can increase only to the extent that the newly created capacities increase average labor productivity. Note however that the 'Keynesian multiplier' effect on goods demand (c) gets weaker as well when Y becomes supply constrained.

To test now for dynamic stability of the model in such a limiting situation, we start from the reference simulation outlined in section 9.5.2 and impose a **strong permanent demand shift.** We raise goods demand during the whole simulation by a constant amount, corresponding to 7% of reference value of goods demand in the first period. As can be seen from fig. 12, employment moves quickly to the upper bound defined by labor supply, i.e. practically all firms are labor constrained. [14] The other panels of fig. 12 display the resulting deviations of output Y, buffer stocks $BU = k\Phi^{-1}(P_G)$ and investment I from the reference paths. BU increases sharply for several periods, but there is a turning point in the 11th quarter, implying that Y has catched up by then with increased Y^d. Thus, even in a situation in which all firms are labor constrained, the capacity effect of investment (brought about by higher labor productivity) proves to be sufficient to prevent a progressive departure of buffer stocks from the reference path. Investment and output show similar but somewhat delayed cyclical patterns. The oscillations can be traced back to the investment equation, implying some "overshooting" of capacities relative to goods demand. The length of a full cycle is about 40 quarters, which seems rather long. While buffer stocks in the long run return to a level which is only slightly above the reference path, the demand shift has strong permanent effects on investment and output.

---

14. In the reference simulation we let wr increase at a rate that just compensates for the negative time trend in the labor supply equation; labor supply is thus constant over time.

FIG. 12: Simulation of a strong permanent demand shift of 7% [Reference simulation: steady growth path]

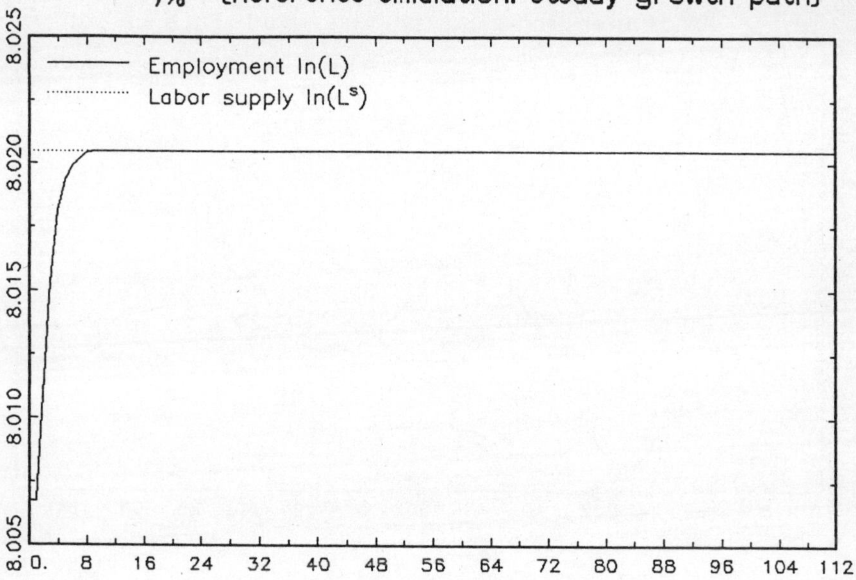

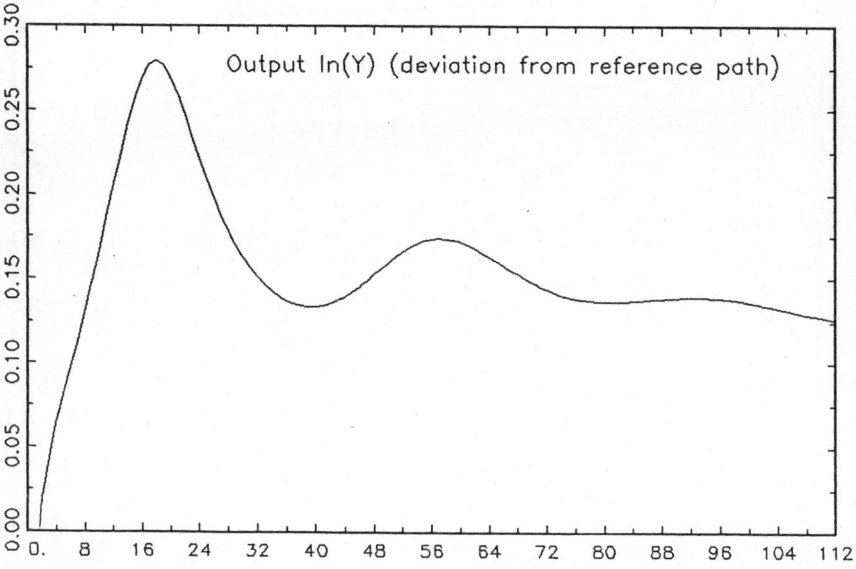

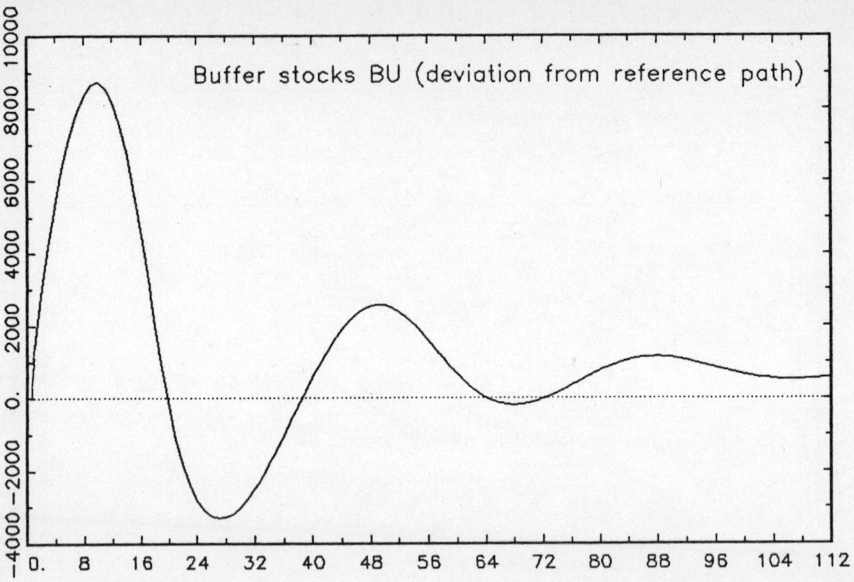
Buffer stocks BU (deviation from reference path)
-4000 -2000 0. 2000 4000 6000 8000 10000
0. 8 16 24 32 40 48 56 64 72 80 88 96 104 112

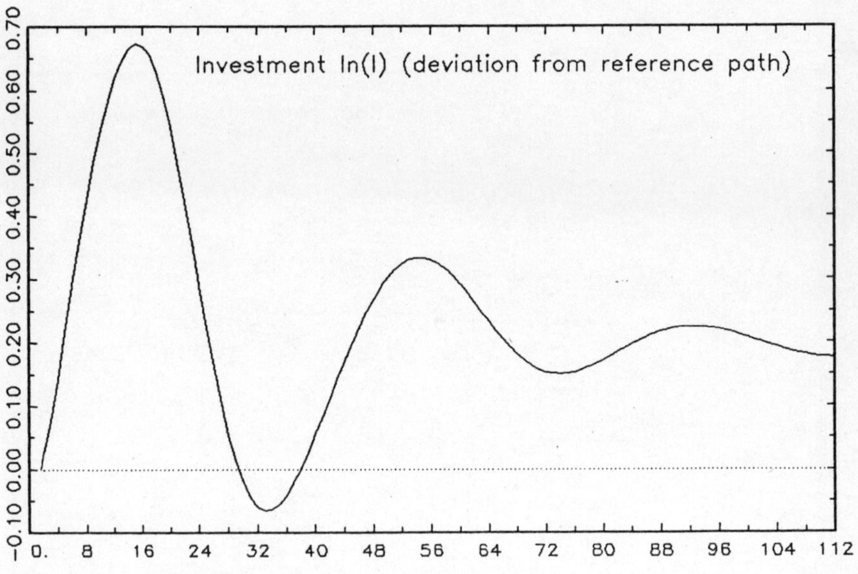
Investment ln(I) (deviation from reference path)
-0.10 0.00 0.10 0.20 0.30 0.40 0.50 0.60 0.70
0. 8 16 24 32 40 48 56 64 72 80 88 96 104 112

9.5.4 Long-run effects of permanent and single-period demand shocks

The purpose of the preceding simulation was to check for dynamic stability in an extreme situation. In reality, autonomous changes in goods demand (brought about e.g. by fiscal policy) are of smaller magnitude and will not move the economy into a one-sided rationing situation. In the following, we simulate the effects of a moderate autonomous increase in goods demand, first in form of a permanent shift and then as a single-period shock.

To discuss the impact of a **permanent demand shift,** we displace the equation for goods demand over the entire simulation period by a constant positive amount, corresponding to 1.75% of the reference value of goods demand in the first period. In contrast to the preceding simulation, employment does not become completely supply constrained but exhibits a cyclical pattern as well (see fig. 13). The other dynamic paths are not

FIG. 13: Simulation of a permanent demand shift of 1.75% (Reference simulation: steady growth path)

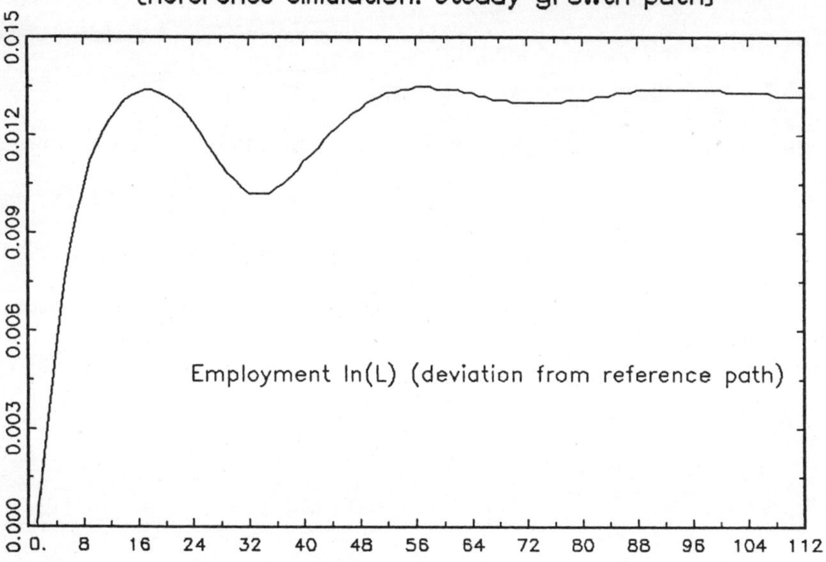

presented graphically since they look quite similar to those reported in fig. 12 for the strong demand shift. Of course, the amplitudes are much smaller. In the long run, output rises by about 3% and employment by about 1.3% compared to the reference path. Regarding policy conclusions, recall that wages, prices and interest rates are all held fixed at the values of the reference simulation. This clearly limits the relevance of this simulation experiment for assessing the effectiveness and the desirability of a 'Keynesian' demand stimulation.

To simulate a **single-period demand shock,** goods demand is raised by 1.75% only in the first quarter. In subseqent periods, the demand equation is left unchanged compared to the reference simulation. The resulting paths again illustrate the model's dynamics. We present only plots for output Y and capacities $\tilde{Y}^s$ (fig. 14). The output response is relatively weak with a peak value of 0.75%, but positive deviations from the reference course extend over many periods. This reflects the production smoothing role of buffer stocks as well as secondary effects on goods demand (37) arising from the income and investment terms (Keynesian multiplier). The reaction of $\tilde{Y}^s$ (profitable capacities) is somewhat smaller and subject to an additional delay. In the long run, all endogenous variables return to their reference paths. Again, while the general pattern of the responses looks reasonable, a cycle length of about 9 years is not entirely plausible. The oscillations originate from the investment equation (overshooting of capacities). This can be shown by imposing the same single-period demand shock while suppressing the response of investment (i.e. keeping I on the reference path); the last panel of fig. 14 displays the resulting output path.

FIG. 14: Simulation of a one-time demand shock of 1.75% in first period [Deviations from reference path]

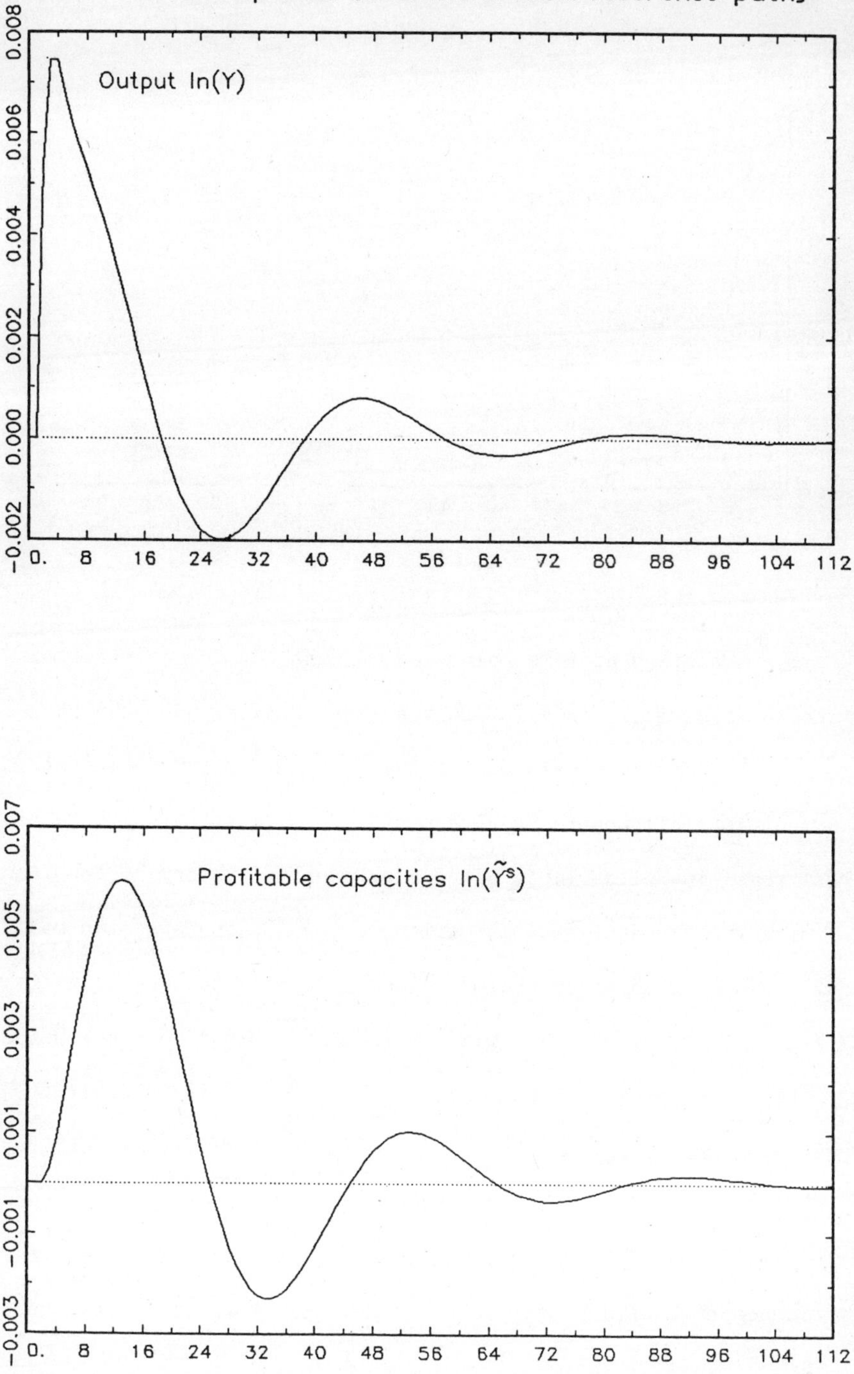

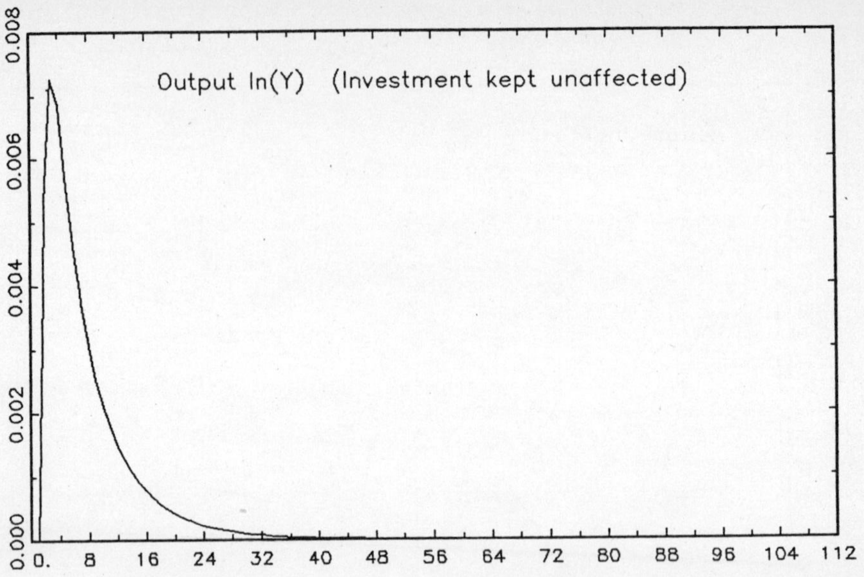

It is interesting at this point to confront our demand shock experiments with another empirical study for Switzerland, dealing with the variability of employment vis-à-vis business fluctuations. Etter (1985) investigates to what extent **implicit contracts** have contributed to stability of employment and real wages in Switzerland. Of course, contract theory differs im many ways from Keynesian analysis. In particular, while in Keynesian models nominal rigidities in wages and/or prices give rise to large quantity adjustments, contract theory implies relative stability of real wages and employment.[15] To check the empirical relevance of implicit contracts, Etter (roughly speaking) first estimates elasticities of employment and real wages with respect to output for a number of industries. He then regresses these elasticities across industries on indicators which are assumed to reflect the incidence of implicit contracts. It actually turns out that industries

15. Refer to the introduction, in particular footnote 10, p. 10.

for which implicit contracts seem more likely show in general a lower variability of employment, real wages and labor income. Of course, an existence of implicit contracts in such a 'relative' sense does not invalidate Keynesian macro models (as stated by the author himself), nor does it contradict our specific finding that demand shocks exert weak short-run and stronger long-run effects on employment.[16] Etter's analysis is not carried out in a general equilibrium framework (i.e. it does not account for the multiplier effects arising from the fact that income variations in one industry affect demand in other industries). Moreover, according to his estimates, the elasticities of employment with respect to output are considerably larger than those of real wages. The former range from 0.36 to 1.95, the latter from 0.0 to 0.68. This result is of course not 'anti-Keynesian' at all.

9.5.5 Simulation of a permanent wage (and price) reduction

It follows from our analysis in section 9.3 (and can be supported by business surveys and everyday observations) that the Swiss labor market in recent years has suffered from a considerable (skill) mismatch problem. In terms of macroeconomic aggregates, the economy seems however to be in good balance. Hence, there is certainly no need of creating jobs on a large scale in Switzerland at present. Neither the above demand shock experiments nor the following simulation of a wage restraint are thus meant to be relevant to economic problems of the present day. The purpose is rather to explore the dynamics of the model and to draw some general conclusions about the functioning of the Swiss economy.

---

16. According to our simulations, a permanent demand shift of 1.75% produces a long-term employment effect of about 1.3%. A one-quarter demand shock of 1.75% entails an employment effect that rises to a peak of 0.25% by the sixth quarter and decays thereafter.

To determine the effects of a **permanent wage reduction,** we assume that the nominal wage falls back in relation to the reference path stepwise by 0.5% in each of the first 4 quarters of the simulation period and remains then constantly 2% below the reference path. Recall that wages show up in the model at different places: As real wages w/p in the scrapping functions and the profitability term of the investment equation; as factor price ratio w/uc in the vintage equations and the investment equation; as net real wage wr (net wage deflated by CPI) in the labor supply equation. All these variables are affected by the alternative wage course. Hence the simulation reflects the joint impact of the following mechanisms: Scrapping of old equipment is reduced due to the slower real wage increase (this effect is at work only during the first 4 quarters); the installation of new equipment is enhanced through the impact of improved profitability on investment; new vintages becomes more labor intensive due to the altered factor price ratio; labor supply decreases as a result of the lower net real wage. Fig. 15 displays the implications of this scenario for the labor market. Labor demand rises, labor supply falls and employment remains virtually unchanged. Thus a wage reduction can not be viewed as an effective means of **employment** policy; it however reduces **unemployment** by depressing labor supply: the unemployment rate, which is constant in the reference simulation at about 1.5%, is reduced to 0.9% by the 8th quarter and tends to a value of about 0.8% in the long run.

The outcome of the wage experiment depends of course strongly on the initial **regime-mix** in the economy. The reference path of our long-term simulations is chosen such that P_L, the proportion of labor constrained firms, is 0.49, and P_G, the proportion of firms producing at full capacity,

FIG. 15: Simulation of a permanent 2% wage reduction, [Deviations from reference path]

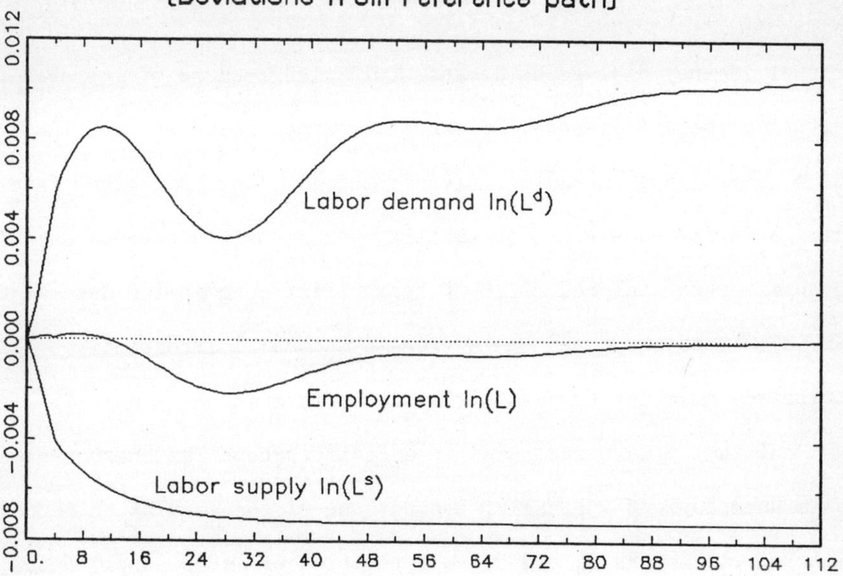

is 0.37. Hence, employment can increase only in about 50% of the firms. Further, unemployment is rather 'Keynesian' than 'classical' in character, implying that the 'sales constraint' becomes quickly more binding if capacities are expanded. Obviously, the situation on the reference path is more favorable to a Keynesian policy than to a classical wage restraint. It can be shown that under conditions of predominant 'classical unemployment' the same wage reduction yields positive employment effects. But, as noted above, the classical regime has never dominated in Switzerland. In fact, the conditions underlying the simulation reported in fig. 15 are chosen such as to reflect the long-term average regime-mix in the Swiss economy. However, choosing a higher initial level of unemployment (actually attained in recessions) one may, even under Keynesian conditions, obtain some weak positive employment effect of a wage reduction, arising from the increased labor intensity of investment.

The following additional points should be kept in mind with respect to the above wage experiment. First, firms are assumed not to pass lower wages onto prices; if they did, goods demand would rise because of improved international price competitiveness. On the other hand, remember that the model involves a (numerically weak) positive impact of lower real wages onto aggregate goods demand - via profitability and firms' investment demand - but neglects a potential reduction of households' consumption demand: Consumption is assumed to depend on 'aggregate income' Y irrespective of how it is distributed. Allowing for a distribution effect in the model, it might well turn out that a wage restraint is a counterproductive measure under 'Keynesian unemployment'. Finally, the outcome of the simulation depends critically on parameters d_3 and d_4 (elasticities of labor supply with respect to the permanent and the actual net real wage), which are estimated with large standard errors. In the following, we discuss this latter point and consider then a scenario in which firms are assumed to pass lower wages partly onto prices.

In the model used for simulation, parameters d_3 and d_4 add up to a fairly large total long-term wage elasticity of 0.364 (see column 2 of the summary table on p. 121). This is of course the reason for the drop in labor supply in the preceding simulation. However, the estimates for the individual labor supply parameters are not well determined econometrically. In fact, as may be seen from the sensitivity analysis on p. 128, one may find points on the likelihood surface inside a 95%-confidence contour for which the sum of d_3 and d_4 is zero or even negative. Hence, it may quite well be that labor supply is insensitive to wages in the long run. In order to figure out the consequences of such a possibility, we replace the **labor supply** equation in the model by a **constant** and simulate the same 2% wage reduction as above. As expected, there is now a positive response of employment (see fig. 16); the maximum effect is however only about 0.35%. In contrast to employment, output returns to the reference path in the long run. This reflects an intrinsic property of the model: As a consequence of the buffer feedback, output must coincide with goods demand over long periods of time so that buffer stocks remain stationary. The long-term rise in employment brought about by lower wages is thus exclusively due to the increased labor intensity of new investment vintages.

FIG. 16: Simulation of a permanent 2% wage reduction, labor supply hold const. (dev. from ref. path)

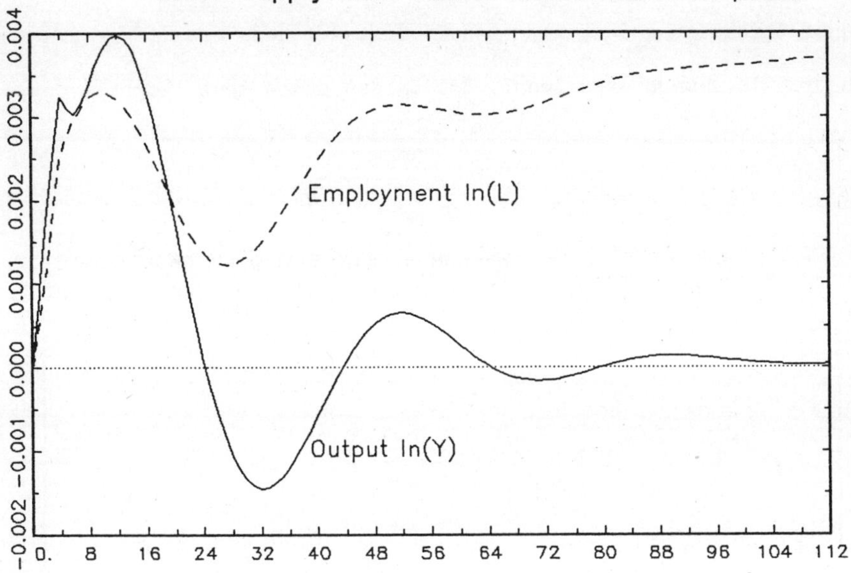

In a final simulation we want to examine the case of a **wage reduction that is passed by firms partly onto prices,** using again the model with constant labor supply. We reduce nominal wages by 4% (stepwise over the first 4 quarters as above) and simultaneously let prices fall by 2% in relation to the reference path. It is assumed that all "domestic" prices

- i.e. p, p_c (used in the definition of uc) and the consumer price index (used to compute wr) - are reduced by 2%, implying that w/p, w/uc and wr all fall by 2% (4% minus 2%), exactly as in the preceding simulation. Only p^F, the foreign price level, is held constant, so that the ratio p/p^F decreases by 2%, representing improved **international price competitiveness** of domestic firms. As a result, goods demand (more precisely: demand for domestically produced output) increases. Other channels by which prices might influence goods demand (Pigou-effect, impact of reduced money demand on interest rates) are not taken into account by the model. Note that the estimated price elasticity of demand is rather small (a_6 = -0.093). Therefore, the outcome of this simulation, reported in fig. 17, does not differ drastically from the previous wage experiment. Employment and output increase now in the

FIG. 17: Simulation of a permanent wage and price reduction of 4% and 2% resp., labor supply const. [dev. from ref. path]

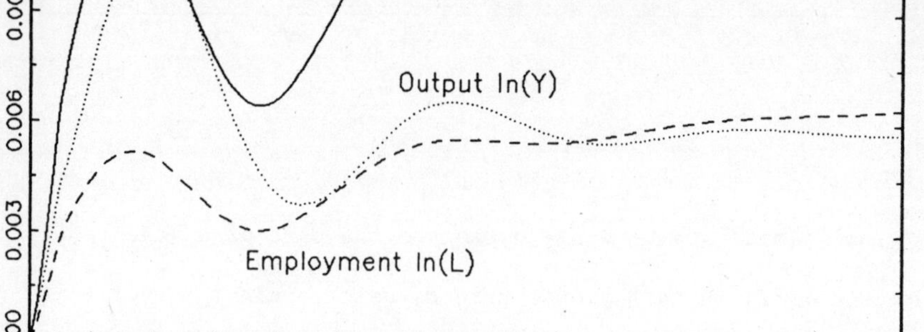

long-run by about 0.6%. This rise exceeds the direct price effect ($0.093 \cdot 2\%$ $= 0.186\%$), which illustrates the Keynesian multiplier mechanism originating from the terms a_1Y_{t-1} and a_3I_t in the equation for goods demand.

Somewhat stronger effects on employment and output can be generated by simulating the same wage-price scenario on basis of a model that sets the (implausibly low) price elasticity a_6 to a larger absolute value still accepted by the data. On the other hand, we have to recall that the associated shift in the income distribution is likely to have an adverse effect on consumption demand, which is neglected in the model. On balance then, our analysis suggests that a wage reduction, even in the "ideal" combination of lower real wages (improving profitability) and lower prices (improving price competitiveness), has relatively weak effects on output and employment.

Of course, one may call in question a policy interpretation of the above simulation exercise from the very base. In particular, wages are not in fact an exogenous instrument of economic policy. Rather, wages and prices should be treated as endogenous variables. In such a framework, an alternative wage policy would have to be represented in form a parameter change in the wage equation. Furthermore, our model - focusing on the 'production sector' of the economy and squeezing the whole 'demand side' into just one single equation - does certainly not provide the most appropriate framework for assessing the effect of prices and wages on aggregate demand. Maybe in a more detailed modelling approach (distinguishing between several components of aggregate demand) on could establish larger empirical price elasticities. If this was the case, there might be more appeal to the 'classical' idea that improving price competitiveness by lowering wages has favorable effects on output and employment in a small open economy.

10. SUMMARY AND CONCLUSIONS

The aim of this study was to analyse the development of the Swiss economy on basis of a macro disequilibrium model, focusing on the interdependence of the markets for goods and labor and spillovers between these markets transmitted by firms' decisions in the production sphere. The main features of the **theoretical specification** are as follows:

- The macroeconomic markets for goods and labor are regarded as heterogeneous aggregates, consisting of a multitude of **micro markets** on which demand/supply ratios differ. The distribution of these ratios in the population of firms is described by statistical density functions. By aggregation, the "sharp corners" of the firm level minimum-conditions are converted into continuous nonlinear macro relationships, mapping aggregate demand and supply onto aggregate transactions (observed output and employment). In this framework, the different regimes - discrete states for individual firms - and the associated spillover effects always co-exist at the macro level, in varying proportions though, depending on the course of the aggregate demands and supplies. This modelling approach nicely captures a characteristic property of business surveys, namely that the overall business cycle is superimposed in the cross-section of firms by numerous "local" or "market-specific" factors. Hence, incorporation of **business survey** data as regime-classification information, measuring the proportions of firms in the different regimes, is straightforward.
- The specifications in the production sector of the model - i.e. firms' decisions on investment, output supply and labor demand - are derived on basis of a **vintage-approach.** Thus, the development of the production apparatus is explained in terms of scrapping of old capacities and the

creation of new ones, involving demand expectations, profitability and relative factor costs as determinants.

- The model allows for a production smoothing role of **buffer stocks.** The basic notion is that firms let differences between current demand and predetermined output be absorbed within the period (quarter) by inventories or unfilled orders; when deciding on next period's output and employment, they attempt to gradually reduce deviations of these buffer stocks from target levels. As compared to usual disequilibrium models that neglect the existence of buffer stocks, this specification gives rise to a modification of the short-term link between current demand and output, but does not invalidate the concept of spillovers between goods and labor markets in a fundamental way.

The model developed along these lines integrates (a) traditional Keynesian elements of demand-side analysis with (b) supply-side considerations (profitability, relative prices) and at the same time allows for (c) micro-level imbalances between supply and demand. The resulting econometric structure is inherently nonlinear, reflecting that the dependence of output and employment on demand-side and supply-side factors varies systematically in the cycle with the aggregate mix of regimes. Estimation of the model is with quarterly data from 1967.2 to 1985.4, while data for the period 1986.1 to 1989.4 are used to perform a post-sample test of parameter stability. The **empirical results** can be summarized as follows:

- The model indicates a growing structural mismatch on the labor market (micro-level dispersion of demand/supply ratios): Structural unemployment, defined as unemployment in a situation where aggregate demand equals aggregate supply, increases from about 1% in 1967 to about 2% in 1985. As far as the cyclical development of the aggregate labor market is concerned, two broad subperiods may be distinguished: In the late 1960s and the first half of the 1970s, the model generates varying amounts of excess demand, reaching a maximum of sightly more that 5% in 1969/70. The picture changes with the recession of 1975; from that time on the model indicates mainly situations of excess supply (peak values of nearly 7% in the recessions of 1975 and 1982/83), interrupted in 1980 by a short interval with some excess demand. In recent years, the labor markets moves towards an aggregate equilibrium (see fig. 9, pp. 142-144).

- The short-run variations in employment are primarily due to fluctuations in labor demand. Labor supply tends in general in the same direction, but its movements are less pronounced and delayed, absorbing thus the swings in labor demand only partly. This gives rise to unemployment in recessions and rationing of labor demand in boom periods.

- The cyclical fluctuations in labor demand are mainly traced back to the Keynesian spillover effect, arising from 'insufficient demand' on the goods market (effective labor demand). Notional labor demand and the associated concept of 'profitable capacities' show much less cyclical variability. The Keynesian spillover is especially strong in the recessions of 1975 and 1982/83, thus identifying both spells of unemployment as predominantly 'Keynesian'. However, notional labor demand shows a marked downward trend from 1972 through 1980 as well. In the first three years of this period - which were characterized by fast growing wages, a sudden shift to a restrictive monetary policy and an increase in the Swiss franc's foreign exchange rate - this reduction was caused to a notable degree by a surge in relative labor costs and a profitability squeeze. After 1975, when profitability was improving, the fall in notional labor demand mainly reflects the gradual downward adjustment of production capacities to the lower level of economic activity, captured in the investment equation by the 'pressure of demand'-term (fig. 7, p. 127).

- In boom periods like 1969/70, 1973, 1980 and 1985, effective output falls short of planned output supply, reflecting that firms are not able to fully realize labor demand (see again fig. 9). This 'repressed inflation'-spillover amounts to a maximum output reduction of about 2.5% in 1969/70. The effect is thus relatively small as compared to the above-mentioned Keynesian spillover on labor demand, which reached a maximum of 12.5% in the recession of 1975.
- Driving force behind the fluctuations in goods demand are of course cyclical developments in the world economy. These movements set in motion an internal multiplier-accelerator process that itself exhibits cyclical properties, associated with a certain "overshooting" of production capacities (compare the various shock experiments reported in figures 12 to 17). While the impact of demand fluctuations on output is dampened in the very short run by buffer stocks, the more persistent movements in goods demand entail adjustments of output of comparable size.

By modelling the demand-side of the economy along with the supply-side and by allowing for structural imbalances at the micro level, the approach of this paper provides - at least potentially - a comprehensive empirical basis for **policy analysis.** As a most interesting feature, the model implies that the efficiency of traditional policy instruments hinges on the **regime-mix** in the aggregate economy. The Keynesian multiplier effect, for example, is low if 'classical unemployment' or 'repressed inflation' are predominant; it is large however if the majority of firms is neither capacity-constrained nor labor-constrained. Such a situation of 'Keynesian unemployment' actually prevailed in the recessions of 1975 and 1982/83, suggesting that a stimulation of aggregate goods demand would have been most effective in fighting unemployment (fig. 11, p. 159).

However, one should be careful not to jump too quickly from the regime indication of the model to the **schematic policy prescriptions** of textbook disequilibrium models. Two points must be kept in mind. First, it is quite easy in retrospective to identify for a certain period, say, predominance of 'Keynesian unemployment' and to conclude that increased demand would have had positive employment effects; but it is another thing to accurately analyse current economic trends in due time and to implement a concrete, well-timed countercyclical policy. Second, it must be stressed that the distinction between the different regimes and spillovers in our model primarily aims at a correct specification of the econometric relationships. But a momentary rationing situation that shows up in the model for instance as 'Keynesian unemployment' can be due to **underlying forces** that are more 'classical' than 'Keynesian' in character, so that a traditional Keynesian policy would be inapt. A prominent case are adverse supply shocks like a sharp rise in prices of imported inputs (e.g. oil) or an excessive wage increase. Such shocks will at first impair profitability and move the economy in direction of 'classical unemployment'. But once firms begin to adjust output prices, thereby partly restoring profitability while at the same time depressing sales, there may well result a tendency towards the 'Keynesian' regime, that is, a situation in which goods demand appears as 'insufficient'.

Whereas in case of demand shocks, there exists, in principal, an ideal countercyclical policy which avoids both unemployment and inflation, **supply shocks** pose a much more difficult problem: Policy is confronted then with the question of whether or not to 'accomodate' the cost increase by an expansionary policy. In the related unemployment-inflation tradeoff there is no easy choice of policy measures. The appropriate policy response has to be defined by carefully comparing the social costs of alternative dynamic adjustment paths. Only looking at the momentary regime-mix is certainly not sufficient. Another difficulty for economic policy may arise from the fact that macroeconomic contractions go often hand in hand with intensified structural problems. For example, in the period since 1973 the appreciation of the formerly undervalued Swiss franc has put many firms supplying mass products on international markets under heavy pressure, rendering part of their production capacities obsolete. This factor is properly reflected in our model by a deterioration of profitability and a downturn in notional labor demand. But in the trough of the 1975 recession, when the labor market showed widespread unemployment, the goods market was in excess supply as well, thus indicating a situation of 'Keynesian unemployment'. However, given the Swiss economy's strong dependence on exports and considering the long-term need to restructure production activities, it seems doubtful whether an extensive demand stimulation would have been an adequate policy response. Still, a more resolute shift to an expansionary policy would certainly have mitigated the downturn. The same may be said with respect to the (weaker) recession of 1982/83, the more so as it was less intertwined with a profitability squeeze and structural problems. In fact, monetary policy was cautiously relaxed and there were some moderate programs of fiscal stimulation in this period. The decision not to do more, i.e. to keep economic policy centered on the target of long-term price stability, was considerably helped by the fact that in both recessions, despite the steep declines in employment, official unemployment rates remained extremely low due to a remarkable flexibility on the supply side of the labor market (foreign and female workers).

These few remarks may illustrate that "real world" policy discussions always involve a broad array of issues, ranging from the timely perception and correct interpretation of recent trends and disequilibria through the concrete problems of implementation of policy measures to the consideration of possible side-effects. By comparison, the model of this paper is inevitably of limited scope. Nevertheless, in conjunction with other analytic instruments, it can play a significant role in policy evaluation, providing useful information about the existence and causes of disequilibria, the specific spillover effects at work at the various stages of the cycle and the magnitude of micro-level mismatch. A significant (though corrigible) flaw of the model is the exogeneity of prices and wages. Endogenizing these variables must be a prior topic in future research.[1]

Switzerland's most urgent economic problem of the day, indicated by the model as well as everyday observations, is the growing structural mismatch on the labor market. In recent years, it has increasingly taken the form of a shortage of high-skilled labor [Gaillard (1988)]. The problem is likely to be a persistent one: The ongoing restructuring of production will entail further shifts in labor demand towards better qualified jobs. On the supply side of the labor market, on the other hand, reactions are subject to long lags. Increasing wage differentials may be expected to stimulate participation in higher education. But this effect is largely limited to new entrants into the labor force, whose number will be relatively low for demographic reasons. Special training programs for prime-age workers, offered both

---

1. Several models for other countries have already accomplished this task; compare in particular the work mentioned in footnote 16, p. 120.

within private firms and by public institutions, are required to reduce the skill mismatch. Another possibility recently discussed is to reorientate foreign labor policy by restricting the number of less skilled workers in favor of better skilled immigrants. In this respect, one should however consider that the employment prospects of high skilled workers are better in other countries as well, while the alternative for many of the less skilled foreign workers is unemployment in their home countries.

Notwithstanding the limited scope of our analysis, some tentative **comparison between Switzerland and other countries** are possible at this stage. The persistence of high unemployment in Western Europe is no doubt one of the most distressing economic problems of the present days. For a number of economies, empirical disequilibrium models similar in spirit to the one constructed in this paper attribute this unsatisfactory state of affairs to a mixture of negative demand shocks, increased structural mismatch, excessive relative labor costs, a deterioration of profitability and insufficient capital formation. Although the recovery of demand in recent years has brought back capacity utilization to peak levels, overall unemployment has remained high in most countries. Given this situation, there is little room for fighting unemployment by a short-run stimulation of aggregate demand: Insufficient production capacities and structural imbalances on the labor market would strongly limit the employment effect of such a policy while renewed inflationary pressures would be unavoidable. Thus, the task for economic policy is a very complex one; a "two-handed" approach, working on the demand side and the supply side simultaneously, is required.[2] By comparison, the situation in Switzerland looks quite favorable. To be sure, the model of this paper indicates that the labor market

2. Compare the policy proposal outlined in Drèze (1987).

mismatch has increased as well, and the cyclical peak values of involuntary unemployment implied by the model are notably larger than the official unemployment figures. But there is definitely no capital shortage in the sense that profitable capacities and associated notional labor demand would be too small to absorb the available labor supply. Rather, in contrast to most other European countries, the economic recovery has brought about a situation that seems almost ideal in terms of macroeconomic aggregates. How can we explain this favorable record of the Swiss economy?

It may be tempting to attribute low Swiss unemployment - inspired by 'new classical' views - to predictable government policies centered on price stability with little discretionary intervention, free trade policies, reasonable unions, decentralized wage negotiations responding quickly to signs of deteriorating business conditions, reflecting the consensus that maintaining international competitiveness is a decisive element of long-term prosperity, etc. All these factors are no doubt characteristic of Switzerland and may have had favorable employment effects. However, what really needs explanation in comparison with other countries is neither an outstanding cyclical stability nor a better long-term course of output and employment. It is rather the fact that the cyclical fluctuations have not resulted in higher unemployment. To explain this, we have to look at the supply side of the labor market: Labor supply is highly responsive to disequilibria in the labor market. This elasticity is due to a flexible labor supply behavior of women and - even more important - to the presence of a large number of **foreign workers.** The fact that many of them had only temporary work permits has enabled Switzerland in the past two recessions to put the burden of falling labor demand on foreigners, on a very large scale in 1975 and to a lesser extent in 1982/83, equilibrating thus the labor market in relatively short time from the supply side. The cyclical flexibility of labor supply has two main implications. First, Swiss authorities could politically afford to keep economic policy rather tightly centered on the objective of price stability. Second, after both recessions the Swiss economy could start from a situation with a notably reduced labor supply; to some extent labor supply was even adapted in terms of skill structure and occupations to the changed composition of demand. However, the share of foreign workers with only temporary work permits has considerably decreased since the mid-1970s and will continue to fall. This trend will limit the possibility of using foreign labor as a cyclical buffer in coming recessions. Stabilization policy might thus well be confronted with more difficult choices in future.

REFERENCES

Altonji, J.G., 1982, The Intertemporal Substitution Model of Labour Market fluctuations: An empirical Analysis, Review of Economic Studies 49, 783-824.

Altonji, J.G., 1986, Intertemporal Substitution in Labour Supply: Evidence from Micro Data, Journal of Political Economy 94, S177-S215.

Amemiya, T., 1981, Qualitative Response Models: A Survey, Journal of Economic Literature 19, 1483-1536.

Ando, A.K., F. Modigliani, R. Rasche and S.J. Turnovsky, 1974, On the Role of Expectations and Technological Change in an Investment Function, International Economic Review 15, 384-414.0

Artus, P., G. Laroque and G. Michel, 1984, Estimation of a Quarterly Macroeconomic Model with Quantity Rationing, Econometrica 52, 1387-1415.

Artus, P., and P.A. Muet, 1984, Investment, Output and Labor Constraints, and Financial Constraints: The Estimation of a Model With Several Regimes, Recherches Economiques de Louvain 50 (1-2), 25-44.

Azariadis C., and J.E. Stiglitz, 1983, Implicit Contracts and Fixed-Price Equilibria, Quarterly Journal of Economics 98 (supplement), 1-22.

Ball L., N.G. Mankiw and D. Romer, 1988, The New Keynesian Economics and the Output-Inflation Trade-off, Brookings Papers on Economic Activity 1, 1-65.

Barro, R. and H. Grossman, 1971, A General Disequilibrium Model of Income and Employment, American Economic Review 61, 82-93.

Barro, R. and H. Grossman, 1976, Money, Employment and Inflation (Cambridge University Press, Cambridge).

Bean, C.R., and A. Gavosto, 1988, Outsiders, Capacity Shortages and Unemployment in the U.K., Paper presented at the Conference on European Unemployment, Chelwood Gate, Sussex England, May 22-25 (Centre for Labour Economics, London School of Economics, London).

Benassy, J.P., 1977, On Quantity Signals and the Foundation of Effective Demand Theory, Scandinavian Journal of Economics 79, 147-168.

Benassy, J.P., 1982, The Economics of Market Disequilibrium (Academic Press, New York).

Benassy, J.P., 1986, Macroeconomics: An Introduction to the Non-Walrasian Approach (Academic Press, Orlando).

Blanchard, O.J., 1987, Aggregate and Individual Price Adjustment, Brookings Papers on Economic Activity 18 (1), 57-109.

Blinder, A.S., 1980, Inventories in the Keynesian Macro Model, Kyklos 33, 585-614.

Blinder, A.S., 1981, Inventories and the Structure of Macro Models, American Economic Review 71, 11-16.

Blinder, A.S., 1982, Inventories and Sticky Prices: More on the Microfoundations of Macroeconomics, American Economic Review 72, 334-348.

Blinder, A.S. 1986, Can the Production Smoothing Model of Inventory Behavior be saved?, Quarterly Journal of Economics, CI, 431-453.

Blinder A.S., 1987, Keynes, Lucas, and Scientific Progress, American Economic Review 77 (Papers and Proceedings), 130-136.

Burda, M.C., 1988, Is Mismatch Really the Problem? - Some Estimates of an Aggregate Disequilibrium Model with US Data, Paper presented at the Conference on European Unemployment, Chelwood Gate, Sussex England, May 22-25 (INSEAD, Fontainebleau, France).

Büttler, H.-J., G. Frei and B. Schips, 1986, Estimation of Disequilibrium Models (Springer, Berlin).

Clower, R.W., 1965, The Keynesian Counterrevolution: A Theoretical Appraisal. in: F.H. Hahn and F. Brechling (eds.), The Theory of Interest Rates (Macmillan, London).

Christiano, L.J., and M. Eichenbaum, 1987, Temporal Aggregation and Structural Inference in Macroeconomics, in: K. Brunner and A.H. Meltzer (eds.), Carnegie Rochester Conference on Public Policy: Bubbles and Other Essays, 26, 63-130.

Drazen, A., 1980, Recent Developments in Macroeconomic Disequilibrium Theory, Econometrica 48, 283-306.

Drèze, J.H., 1975, Existence of an Exchange Equilibrium under Price Rigidities, International Economic Review 16, 301-320.

Drèze, J.H., 1979, Demand Estimation, Risk Aversion and Sticky Prices, Economic Letters 4, 1-6.

Drèze, J.H., 1987, Underemployment Equilibria, Presidential Address to the 1986 EEA-Congess in Vienna, European Economic Review 31, 9-34.

Drèze, J.H., Ch. Bean, J.P. Lambert, R. Layard and H.R. Sneessens, 1990, Europe's Unemployment Problem (forthcoming MIT Press).

Drèze, J.H. and Ch. Bean, 1990, European Unemployment: Lessons from a Multicountry Econometric Study, Scandinavian Journal of Economics 92, 135-165.

Driehuis W., 1988, An Application of Disequilibrium Analysis to the Netherlands Economy, Paper presented at the Conference on European Unemployment, Chelwood Gate, Sussex England, May 22-25 (University of Amsterdam, Amsterdam).

Eaton J., and R.E. Quandt, 1983, A Model of Rationing and Labour Supply: Theory and Estimation, Economica 50, 221-233.

Engle, R.F., 1982, A General Approach to Lagrange Multiplier Model Diagnostics, Journal of Econometrics 20, 83-104.

Engle, R.F., D.F. Hendry and J.-F. Richard, 1983, Exogeneity, Econometrica 51, 277-304.

Entorf, H., W. Franz, H. König and W. Smolny, 1988, The Development of German Employment and Unemployment: Estimation and Simulation of a Disequilibrium Macro Model, Paper presented at the Conference on European Unemployment, Chelwood Gate, Sussex England, May 22-25.

Etter, C., 1985, Löhne und Beschäftigung im Konjunkturverlauf (Haupt, Bern).

Etter, R., M. Nerlove and D. Willson, 1989, Swiss Inventory Investment Behaviour - A Recursive Simultaneous Equations Model, KOF-Arbeitspapier 25 (Konjunkturforschungsstelle ETH, Zürich).

Fitoussi, J.-P., 1983, Modern Macroeconomic Theory (Basil Blackwell, Oxford).

Fluri, R. and E. Spörndli, 1981, Micro-Analysis of Swiss Business Test Variables by Bivariate Methods and by Multivariate Log-Linear Probability Models, Paper presented at the 15th CIRET Conference, Athens.

Frick A., H. Hollenstein, R. Loertscher und P. Stalder, 1983, Die Ausrichtung der empirischen Konjunkturforschung im Lichte der Kontroverse zwischen traditionell-keynesianischen, neuen keynesianischen und neuen klassischen Makromodellen, KOF-Arbeitspapier 7 (Konjunkturforschungstelle ETH, Zürich).

Friedman, M, 1968, The Role of Monetary Policy, American Economic Review 58, 1-17.

Gagey, F., J.P. Lambert and B. Ottenwaelter, 1988, A Disequilibrium Estimation of the French Labour Market Using Business Survey Information, Paper presented at the Conference on European Unemployment, Chelwood Gate, Sussex England, May 22-25.

Ghali, M.A., 1987, Seasonality, Aggregation, and the Testing of the Production Smoothing Hypothesis, American Economic Review 77, 464-469.

Gaillard, S., 1988, Arbeitskräftemangel und Lohnstruktur, Konjunktur - Monatsbericht 9, 7-15 (Konjunkturforschungsstelle ETH, Zürich).

Goldfeld, S.M. and R.E. Quandt, 1972, Nonlinear Methods in Econometrics (North-Holland, Amsterdam).

Goldfeld, S.M. and R.E. Quandt, 1979, Estimation in Multimarket Disequilibrium Models, Economics Letters 41, 341-347.

Gordon, R.J., 1981, Output Fluctuations and Gradual Price Adjustment, Journal of Economic Literature 19, 493-530.

Gordon, R.J., 1985, Understanding Inflation in the 1980s, Brookings Papers on Economic Activity 8 (1), 253-77.

Gordon, R.J., 1988, Postwar Developments in Business Cycle Theory: An Unabashedly New-Keynesian Perspective, Keynote Lecture presented at the 18th CIRET Conference, Zurich.

Gordon, R.J., 1990, What Is New-Keynesian Economics?, Journal of Economic Literature 28, 1115-1171.

Gourieroux, C., J.J. Laffont and A. Monfort, 1980, Disequilibrium Econometrics in Simultaneous Equation Systems, Econometrica 48, 75-96.

Gourieroux, C., J.J. Laffont and A. Monfort, 1984, Econométrie des Modèles d'Equilibre avec Rationnement: Une Mise à Jour, Annales de l'INSEE 55/56, 5-38.

Gourieroux, C. and G. Laroque, 1985, The Aggregation of Commodities in Quantity Rationing Models, International Economic Review 26, 681-700.

Grandmont, J.M., 1977, Temporary General Equilibrium Theory, Econometrica 45, 535-72.

Green, J. and J.J. Laffont, 1981, Disequilibrium Dynamics with Inventories and Anticipatory Price-Setting, European Economic Review 16, 199-221.

Hahn, F.H., 1978, On Non-Walrasian Equilibria, Review of Economic Studies 45, 1-17.

Houthakker, H.S., 1955, The Pareto Distribution and the Cobb-Douglas Production Function in Activity Analysis, Review of Economic Studies 23, 27-31.

Hendry, D.F. and J.F. Richard, 1982, On the Formulation of Empirical Models in Dynamic Econometrics, Journal of Econometrics 20, 3-33.

Hey, J.D., 1891, Economics in Disequilibrium, (Camelot Press, Southampton).

Hollenstein H. und R. Loertscher, 1982b, Das schweizerische Arbeitsangebot - Analysen zum WIF-Vier-Sektoren-Modell, WIF-Arbeitspapier 32 (Institut für Wirtschaftsforschung ETH, Zürich).

Ito, T., 1980, Methods of Estimation for Multi-Market Disequilibrium Models, Econometrica 48, 97-126.

Kooiman, P. and T. Kloek, 1979, Aggregation of Micro Markets in Disequilibrium, Working Paper (Econometric Institute, Rotterdam).

Kooiman, P., 1984, Smoothing the Aggregate Fix-Price Model and the Use of Business Survey Data, The Economic Journal 94, 899-913.

Kooiman, P. and T. Kloek, 1985, An Empirical Two Market Disequilibrium Model for Dutch Manufacturing, European Economic Review 29, 323-354.

Kooiman, P., 1986, Estimating Average Excess Supply on Goods and Labor Markets from a Cross-Section of Business Survey Reports, Paper presented at the ESEM-Conference, Budapest.

Kugler P., and P. Schwendener, 1988, Arbeitsangebot, Grenzsteuerbelastung und der permanente Lohnsatz: Emprische Ergebnisse für die Schweiz, Schweiz. Zeitschrift für Volkswirtschaft und Statistik 3, 243-257.

Kugler P., 1988a, Intertemporal Substitution and Random Changes in Preferences: Time Series Evidence for Four Countries, Empirical Economics 13, 17-34.

Kugler P., 1988b, Intertemporal Substitution, Taste Shocks and Cointegration, Economic Letters 26, 235-39.

Lambert, J.P., 1984, Disequilibrium Macro Models Based on Business Survey Data, Theory and Estimation for the Belgian Manufactoring Sector, Mimeo. (CORE, Louvain-la-Neuve).

Lambert, J.P., 1988, Disequilibrium Macro Models, Theory and Estimation of Rationing Models Using Business Survey Data (Cambridge University Press, Cambridge).

Lambert, J.P., M. Lubrano and H.S. Sneessens, 1984, Emploi et Chômage en France de 1955 à 1982: Une Modèle Macroéconomique Annuel avec Rationnement, Annales de l'INSEE 55/56, 39-76.

Lambert, J.P. and B. Mulkay, 1986, Investment in a Disequilibrium Context, or Does Profitability Really Matter?, CORE Discussion Paper 8703 (Université Catholique de Louvain, Louvain-la-Neuve).

Laroque, G., 1988, Comparative Estimates of a Macroeconomic Disequilibrium Model: France, Germany, the U.K. and the U.S.A., Document de Travail 8806 (INSEE, Paris).

Laroque, G. and B. Salanié, 1989, Estimation of Multi-Market Fix-Price Models: An Application of Pseudo Maximum Likelihood Methods, Econometrica 57, 831-860.

Leijonhufvud, A., 1968, On Keynesian Economics and the Economics of Keynes (Oxford University Press, Oxford).

Leijonhufvud, A., 1973, Effective Demand Failures, Swedish Journal of Economics 75, 27-48.

Lucas, R.E., 1976, Econometric Policy Evaluation: A Critique, in: K. Brunner and E. Meltzer, eds., The Phillips Curve and Labor Markets, Carnegie-Rochester Series on Public Policy, supplementary series to the Journal of Monetary Economics, vol. 1, 19-46.

Lucas, R.E. and T.J. Sargent, 1978, After Keynesian Macroeconomics, in: Federal Reserve Bank of Boston, After the Phillips Curve: Persistence of High Inflation and High Unemployment, 49-72.

Maccini, L.J. and R.J. Rossana, 1981, Investment in Finished Goods Inventories: An Analysis of Adjustment Speeds, American Economic Review, Proceedings, 17-22.

Maddala, G.S, 1983, Limited-dependent and Qualitative Variables in Econometrics (Cambridge University Press, Cambridge).

Malinvaud, E., 1977, The Theory of Unemployment Reconsidered (Basil Blackwell, Oxford).

Malinvaud, E., 1980, Profitability and Unemployment (Cambridge University Press, Cambrige).

Malinvaud, E., 1981, Econometrics Faced with the Needs of Macroeconomic Policy, Econometrica 49, 1363-1375.

Malinvaud, E., 1982, Wages and Unemployment, Economic Journal 92, 1-12.

Malinvaud, E., 1982, An Econometric Model for Macro Disequilibrium Analysis, in: M. Hazewinkel and A.H.G. Rinnooy Kan (eds.), Current Developments in the Interface: Economics, Econometrics, Mathmematics, (Reidel Publishing Comp., Dordrecht).

Malinvaud, E., 1987, Capital productive, incertitudes et profitabilité, Annales d'économie et statistique 5, 1-36.

Mankiw, N.G., J.J. Rotemberg and L.H. Summers, 1985, Intertemporal Substitution in Macroeconomics, Quarterly Journal of Economics 100, 225-251.

Martin, C. and R. Portes, 1987, Effective Demands and Spillovers, Birbeck College Discussion Paper (University of London, London).

Metha, F. and H.R. Sneessens, A Discussion of Belgian Unemployment Based on an Aggregate Disequilibrium Model: An Update, Paper presented at the Conference on European Unemployment, Chelwood Gate, Sussex England, May 22-25.

Miron, J.A. and S.P. Zeldes, 1988, Seasonality, Cost Shocks, and the Production Smoothing Model of Inventories, Econometrica 53, 1251-1279.

Muellbauer, J., 1978, Macrotheory vs. Macroeconometrics: The Treatment of Disequilibrium in Macromodels, Birbeck Discussion Paper 59 (Birbeck College, London).

Muellbauer, J. and R. Portes, 1978, Macroeconomic Models with Quantity Rationing, Economic Journal 88, 788-821.

Neudorfer, P., K. Pichelmann and M. Wagner, Unfavourable Shifts of Rationing Equilibria, Austrian Unemployment 1965-1986, Paper presented at the Conference on European Unemployment, Chelwood Gate, Sussex England, May 22-25 (Institute for Economic and Social Research, Vienna).

Nickell, S., 1978, The Investment Decisions of Firms (Cambridge University Press, Cambridge).

OECD, 1985, Switzerland, Economic Survey, (OECD, Paris)

Portes, R., 1977, Effective Demand and Spillovers in Empirical Two-market Disequilibrium Models, Harvard Institute of Economic Research Discussion Paper 595 (Harvard University, Cambridge).

Portes, R., R.E. Quandt, S. Yeo, 1985, Testing the "All Excess Demand" Hypothesis, Financial Research Center Memorandum 59 (Princeton University, Princeton).

Quandt, R.E., 1982, Econometric Disequilibrium Models, Econometric Reviews 1, 1-63.

Quandt, R.E., 1983, Computational Problems and Methods, in: Z. Griliches and M.D. Intriligator, Handbook of Econometrics 1 (North Holland, Amsterdam).

Quandt, R.E. and H.S. Rosen, 1985, Unemployment, Disequilibrium, and the Short Run Phillips Curve: An Econometric Approach, Financial Research Center Memorandum 61 (Princeton University, Princeton).

Quandt, R.E., 1986, Estimation in Disequilibrium Models with Aggregation, Financial Research Center Memorandum 68 (Princeton University, Princeton).

Quandt, R.E., 1988, The Econometrics of Disequilibrium (Basil Blackwell, Oxford).

Rahiala, M. and T. Terasvirta, 1988, Formation of Firms Production Decisions in Finnish Manufacturing Industries, Journal of Applied Econonmetrics 3, 125-127.

Ramser, H.J., 1981, Stand und Entwicklungsperspektiven der Konjunkturtheorie, Volkswirtschafliche Beiträge 158 (Universität Konstanz, Konstanz).

Ramser, H.J., 1987, Beschäftigung und Konjunktur, Studies in Contemporary Economics (Springer, Berlin-Heidelberg).

Rosen, S., 1985, Implicit Contracts, Journal of Economic Literature 23, 1144-1175.

Rothschild, K.W., 1981, Einführung in die Ungleichgewichtstheorie (Springer, Berlin-Heidelberg).

Salzgeber, R. 1989, Microeconomic Behaviour of Firms - An Empirical Study for Switzerland, Paper presented at the 19th CIRET Conference, Osaka, Japan, KOF-Arbeitspapier 24 (Konjunkturforschungsstelle ETH, Zürich).

Sato, K., 1975, Production Function and Aggregation (North-Holland, Amsterdam).

Schelbert, H., 1983, Neue Makroökonomik: Gegensätze und Gemeinsames, in: G. Bombach et al. (eds.), Makroökonomik heute: Gemeinsamkeiten und Gegensätze (Mohr, Tübingen).

Schelbert, H., 1985, Arbeitsmarktforschung in der Schweiz, Schweizerische Zeitschrift für Volkswirtschaft und Statistik, Heft 3, 285-303.

Schultze, C., 1986, Other Times, Other Places: Macroeconomic Lessons from the U.S. and European History (Brookings Institution, Washington).

Seitz, H., 1988, Still More on the Speed of Adjustment in Inventory Models: A Lesson in Aggregation, Mimeo. (University of Mannheim, Mannheim).

Sneessens, H.R., 1981, Theory and Estimation of Quantity Rationing Models, (Springer, New York).

Sneessens, H.R., 1983, A Macroeconomic Rationing Model of the Belgian Economy, European Economic Review 20, 193-215.

Sneessens, H.R., 1985, Two Alternative Stochastic Specifications and Estimation Methods for Quantity Rationing Models, European Economic Review 29, 111-136.

Sneessens, H.R. and J.H. Drèze, 1986, A Discussion of Belgian Unemployment, Combining Traditional Concepts and Disequilibrium Economics, Economica 53, 89-119.

Sneessens, H.R., 1987, Investment and the Inflation-Unemployment Tradeoff in a Macroeconomic Rationing Model with Monopolistic Competition, European Economic Review 31, 781-815.

Stalder, P. 1983, Die traditionell-ökonometrischen Keynesianischen Konjunkturmodelle in der Kritik der Neuen Klassischen und Neuen Keynesianischen Makroökonomie, KOF-Arbeitspapier 4 (Konjunkturforschungsstelle ETH, Zürich).

Stalder, P., 1985a, Schätzung eines kleinen Ungleichgewichtsmodells für den schweizerischen Arbeitsmarkt, KOF-Arbeitspapier 13 (Konjunkturforschungsstelle ETH, Zürich).

Stalder, P., 1985b, Schätzung eines Ungleichgewichtsmodells des schweizerischen Arbeitsmarktes mit Unterscheidung zwischen klassischer und keynesianischer Arbeitsnachfrage, KOF-Arbeitsspapier 16 (Konjunkturforschungsstelle ETH, Zürich).

Stalder, P., 1989a, A Disequilibrium Model with Smooth Regime Transitions and a Keynesian Spillover for Switzerland's Labor Market, European Economic Review 33, 863-893.

Stalder, P., 1989b, Excess Demand and Capacity Utilization - An Empirical Analysis Based on Swisss Business Survey Data, Applied Economics 21, 1383-1395.

Stalder, P., 1990, Die Reaktion von Unternehmungen auf Nachfrage- und Kostenschocks - Eine Untersuchung mit KOF-Konjunkturtestdaten, KOF-Arbeitspapier 28 (Konjunkturforschungsstelle ETH, Zürich).

Sweezy, P., 1939, Demand under Conditions of Oligopoly, Journal of Political Economy.

Tobin, J., 1980, Asset Accumulation and Economic Activity (Basil Blackwell, Oxford).

Vol. 261: Th. R. Gulledge, Jr., N.K. Womer, The Economics of Made-to-Order Production. VI, 134 pages. 1986.

Vol. 262: H.U. Buhl, A Neo-Classical Theory of Distribution and Wealth. V, 146 pages. 1986.

Vol. 263: M. Schäfer, Resource Extraction and Market Structure. XI, 154 pages. 1986.

Vol. 264: Models of Economic Dynamics. Proceedings, 1983. Edited by H.F. Sonnenschein. VII, 212 pages. 1986.

Vol. 265: Dynamic Games and Applications in Economics. Edited by T. Başar. IX, 288 pages. 1986.

Vol. 266: Multi-Stage Production Planning and Inventory Control. Edited by S. Axsäter, Ch. Schneeweiss and E. Silver. V, 264 pages. 1986.

Vol. 267: R. Bemelmans, The Capacity Aspect of Inventories. IX, 165 pages. 1986.

Vol. 268: V. Firchau, Information Evaluation in Capital Markets. VII, 103 pages. 1986.

Vol. 269: A. Borglin, H. Keiding, Optimality in Infinite Horizon Economies. VI, 180 pages. 1986.

Vol. 270: Technological Change, Employment and Spatial Dynamics. Proceedings 1985. Edited by P. Nijkamp. VII, 466 pages. 1986.

Vol. 271: C. Hildreth, The Cowles Commission in Chicago, 1939–1955. V, 176 pages. 1986.

Vol. 272: G. Clemenz, Credit Markets with Asymmetric Information. VIII, 212 pages. 1986.

Vol. 273: Large-Scale Modelling and Interactive Decision Analysis. Proceedings, 1985. Edited by G. Fandel, M. Grauer, A. Kurzhanski and A.P. Wierzbicki. VII, 363 pages. 1986.

Vol. 274: W.K. Klein Haneveld, Duality in Stochastic Linear and Dynamic Programming. VII, 295 pages. 1986.

Vol. 275: Competition, Instability, and Nonlinear Cycles. Proceedings, 1985. Edited by W. Semmler. XII, 340 pages. 1986.

Vol. 276: M.R. Baye, D.A. Black, Consumer Behavior, Cost of Living Measures, and the Income Tax. VII, 119 pages. 1986.

Vol. 277: Studies in Austrian Capital Theory, Investment and Time. Edited by M. Faber. VI, 317 pages. 1986.

Vol. 278: W.E. Diewert, The Measurement of the Economic Benefits of Infrastructure Services. V, 202 pages. 1986.

Vol. 279: H.-J. Büttler, G. Frei and B. Schips, Estimation of Disequilibrium Models. VI, 114 pages. 1986.

Vol. 280: H.T. Lau, Combinatorial Heuristic Algorithms with FORTRAN. VII, 126 pages. 1986.

Vol. 281: Ch.-L. Hwang, M.-J. Lin, Group Decision Making under Multiple Criteria. XI, 400 pages. 1987.

Vol. 282: K. Schittkowski, More Test Examples for Nonlinear Programming Codes. V, 261 pages. 1987.

Vol. 283: G. Gabisch, H.-W. Lorenz, Business Cycle Theory. VII, 229 pages. 1987.

Vol. 284: H. Lütkepohl, Forecasting Aggregated Vector ARMA Processes. X, 323 pages. 1987.

Vol. 285: Toward Interactive and Intelligent Decision Support Systems. Volume 1. Proceedings, 1986. Edited by Y. Sawaragi, K. Inoue and H. Nakayama. XII, 445 pages. 1987.

Vol. 286: Toward Interactive and Intelligent Decision Support Systems. Volume 2. Proceedings, 1986. Edited by Y. Sawaragi, K. Inoue and H. Nakayama. XII, 450 pages. 1987.

Vol. 287: Dynamical Systems. Proceedings, 1985. Edited by A.B. Kurzhanski and K. Sigmund. VI, 215 pages. 1987.

Vol. 288: G.D. Rudebusch, The Estimation of Macroeconomic Disequilibrium Models with Regime Classification Information. VII, 128 pages. 1987.

Vol. 289: B.R. Meijboom, Planning in Decentralized Firms. X, 168 pages. 1987.

Vol. 290: D.A. Carlson, A. Haurie, Infinite Horizon Optimal Control. XI, 254 pages. 1987.

Vol. 291: N. Takahashi, Design of Adaptive Organizations. VI, 140 pages. 1987.

Vol. 292: I. Tchijov, L. Tomaszewicz (Eds.), Input-Output Modeling. Proceedings, 1985. VI, 195 pages. 1987.

Vol. 293: D. Batten, J. Casti, B. Johansson (Eds.), Economic Evolution and Structural Adjustment. Proceedings, 1985. VI, 382 pages. 1987.

Vol. 294: J. Jahn, W. Krabs (Eds.), Recent Advances and Historical Development of Vector Optimization. VII, 405 pages. 1987.

Vol. 295: H. Meister, The Purification Problem for Constrained Games with Incomplete Information. X, 127 pages. 1987.

Vol. 296: A. Börsch-Supan, Econometric Analysis of Discrete Choice. VIII, 211 pages. 1987.

Vol. 297: V. Fedorov, H. Läuter (Eds.), Model-Oriented Data Analysis. Proceedings, 1987. VI, 239 pages. 1988.

Vol. 298: S.H. Chew, Q. Zheng, Integral Global Optimization. VII, 179 pages. 1988.

Vol. 299: K. Marti, Descent Directions and Efficient Solutions in Discretely Distributed Stochastic Programs. XIV, 178 pages. 1988.

Vol. 300: U. Derigs, Programming in Networks and Graphs. XI, 315 pages. 1988.

Vol. 301: J. Kacprzyk, M. Roubens (Eds.), Non-Conventional Preference Relations in Decision Making. VII, 155 pages. 1988.

Vol. 302: H.A. Eiselt, G. Pederzoli (Eds.), Advances in Optimization and Control. Proceedings, 1986. VIII, 372 pages. 1988.

Vol. 303: F.X. Diebold, Empirical Modeling of Exchange Rate Dynamics. VII, 143 pages. 1988.

Vol. 304: A. Kurzhanski, K. Neumann, D. Pallaschke (Eds.), Optimization, Parallel Processing and Applications. Proceedings, 1987. VI, 292 pages. 1988.

Vol. 305: G.-J.C.Th. van Schijndel, Dynamic Firm and Investor Behaviour under Progressive Personal Taxation. X, 215 pages. 1988.

Vol. 306: Ch. Klein, A Static Microeconomic Model of Pure Competition. VIII, 139 pages. 1988.

Vol. 307: T.K. Dijkstra (Ed.), On Model Uncertainty and its Statistical Implications. VII, 138 pages. 1988.

Vol. 308: J.R. Daduna, A. Wren (Eds.), Computer-Aided Transit Scheduling. VIII, 339 pages. 1988.

Vol. 309: G. Ricci, K. Velupillai (Eds.), Growth Cycles and Multisectoral Economics: the Goodwin Tradition. III, 126 pages. 1988.

Vol. 310: J. Kacprzyk, M. Fedrizzi (Eds.), Combining Fuzzy Imprecision with Probabilistic Uncertainty in Decision Making. IX, 399 pages. 1988.

Vol. 311: R. Färe, Fundamentals of Production Theory. IX, 163 pages. 1988.

Vol. 312: J. Krishnakumar, Estimation of Simultaneous Equation Models with Error Components Structure. X, 357 pages. 1988.

Vol. 313: W. Jammernegg, Sequential Binary Investment Decisions. VI, 156 pages. 1988.

Vol. 314: R. Tietz, W. Albers, R. Selten (Eds.), Bounded Rational Behavior in Experimental Games and Markets. VI, 368 pages. 1988.

Vol. 315: I. Orishimo, G.J.D. Hewings, P. Nijkamp (Eds.), Information Technology: Social and Spatial Perspectives. Proceedings, 1986. VI, 268 pages. 1988.

Vol. 316: R.L. Basmann, D.J. Slottje, K. Hayes, J.D. Johnson, D.J. Molina, The Generalized Fechner-Thurstone Direct Utility Function and Some of its Uses. VIII, 159 pages. 1988.

Vol. 317: L. Bianco, A. La Bella (Eds.), Freight Transport Planning and Logistics. Proceedings, 1987. X, 568 pages. 1988.